Xpress Redi Set Go Recipes
Anyone Can Learn

Brought To You By: TAK Technology LLC.

XPRESS REDI SET GO RECIPES ANYONE CAN LEARN

TAK Technology, LLC
179 South Main Street
Gardner, MA 01440 U.S.A

All rights reserved. No part of this book may be reproduced or transmitted in any form by any means, electronic, or mechanical, including photocopying, recording, or by any information storage and retrieval system, without written permission from the author, except for the inclusion of brief quotations in review.

Copyright © 2010 By TAK Technology LLC.

ISBN - 978-0-9826947-3-2

Note: This book contains the opinions and ideas of its author. It is intended to provide helpful and informative material on the subject matter covered. It is sold with the understanding that the author and publisher are not engaged in rendering professional services in the book. If the reader requires personal assistance or advice, a competent professional should be consulted.

The author and publisher specifically disclaim any responsibility for any liability, loss, or risk, personal or otherwise, which is incurred as a consequence, directly or indirectly, of the use and application of any of the contents of this book.

Welcome to Xpress Redi Set Go Recipes Anyone Can Learn!

Here you will find over 500 Recipes for the Xpress Redi Set Go. I have tried a lot of these recipes and they were delicious. So thumb through, find a recipe that interests you and give it a whirl. ENJOY!!

~Remember recipes that use the divided pan can also be used with your GT Xpress 101!!~

A Few Xpress Redi Set Go Tips

- Always clean after each use to prevent build up of cooking residue.

- Do not immerse your Redi Set Go in water or any other liquid and do not place in a dishwasher.

- Your insertable pan and the spatula are dishwasher safe – make sure to allow the pans to cool completely before removing from unit.

- After use and before cleaning or storing, remove plug and allow unit to cool completely.

- Wipe the inside and the edges of the unit with a damp, soft cloth, or sponge. (Small amount of dishwashing detergent can be used as needed.)

- Only use cleaning pads marked safe for non stick surfaces.

- Don not use harsh or abrasive cleaners or scouring pads on the non stick or the exterior surfaces as they may cause damage.

- Dry with a soft cloth.

- There is a handy cord wrap on the bottom of the unit for compact and neat cord storage.

- The unit is designed to close and stand on the hinged surface for compact storage.

- To clean the exterior simply wipe with a damped cloth and polish dry with a dry soft cloth. Do not use steel wool, scouring pads or abrasive cleaners as these will scratch the surface.

- Before using for the first wipe the interior and exterior surfaces of the unit with a soft damp cloth to remove any dust that may have accumulated during packaging then dry completely.

- When using Redi Set Go for the first time you may notice a fine smoke haze being emitted from the unit. This is normal, it is due to the initial heating of the internal components.

- We recommend a onetime seasoning of the non stick surface of the cooking unit before using to ensure the non stick release performance of the finish: After cleaning and drying, switch on the unit for the first time, let it preheat and brush the top and bottom of the cooking surface lightly with cooking oil or butter. Rub lightly and wipe away any excess with an absorbent paper towel or dry cloth. Close cover and switch off the unit. It is good to do this with the insertable pans as well.

Copyright © 2010 By TAK Technology LLC. All Rights Reserved

- When the green light illuminates, it indicates the unit is preheated. Unless otherwise indicated in the recipe, allow the unit to preheat.

- Never use the unit with the cover in the open position.

- If food will rise during the cooking, fill the base or insertable pans almost to the top to allow space for rising during cooking.

A note about Personal Pizzas
There are many items that can be kept on hand to use for pizza crust and the toppings are endless. When selecting pre-made items look for those with an approximate 6 inch diameter.

Crusts
Almost instant pizza dough
Boboli Crusts
Pita bread
Corn and flour tortillas
Tortilla bread
French bread or rolls
Refrigerated dough's like pizza, biscuit, crescent rolls and more
English muffins
Bagels

Sauces
Pizza sauce
Spaghetti sauce
Alfredo sauce
Salad dressings
Cream cheese

Toppings
Possibilities for toppings are endless. Because this is your personal pizza, you can choose all the ingredients.
Cooked meats
Cold cuts
Cheese
Cooked vegetables
Olives
Thinly sliced raw vegetables
Tomatoes
Fresh herbs
Pineapple
Pepperoni
And anything you think tastes good.

Table of Contents

Appetizers

Russian Cheese Stuffed Purses	1
Toasted Nuts and Cranberries	1
Spicy Roasted Pumpkin Seeds	1
Stuffed Soupwich	1
Hot Lobster Dip	2
Bean Dip	2
Pastelito de Guayaba	2
Huevos Ranchero	3
Diner Style Eggs a'la King	3
Easy Frittatas	3
Cheese Sticks	3
Philly Stuffed Mushrooms	4
Tapas-Mini Pepper Empanadas	4
Puff Pastry Shells with Cheesy Bacon Filling	4
Chorizo Quesadillas	5
"Hot Pockets"	5
Grilled Blue Cheese Apple Sandwich	5

Beef

Crescent Beef Bites	7
Steak au Poivre	7
Stuffed Italian Shells	7
Quick Sesame Steak	8
Chili Enchiladas	8
Hawaiian Beef Burgers	8
Po Boy Sandwich	8
Empanadas	9
XRSG Steak	9
Argentine Filet Mignon with Chimichurri Sauce	9
Bite Size Burgers	10
Reuben Wrap	10
Mock Steak Diane	10
Mexican Stuffed Peppers	11
Italian Beef Rolls	11
Beef Stew & Biscuit Bake	11
Chili Taco Bowls	12
Hot Roast Beef on a Roll	12
Quick Beef Stew	12

Toasted Bowls	12
Steak and Peppers over Rice	13
Hot Pastrami Wrap	13
Grilled Meatloaf Sandwich	13
Salisbury Steak	13
Sloppy Joes On Cornbread	14
Burritos a'la Leftovers	14
Grilled Stuffed Burritos	14
Asparagus & Beef Rollups	14
Asparagus & Savory Beef Rollups	15
Stuffed Beef Rolls	15
Indian Ground Beef	15
Easy to Make Frittatas	15
Spaghetti Roll A Go-go	16
Beef Wellington's Pockets	16
Liver & Onions	16
Mexican Burritos	17
RSG Steak & Cheese	17
Steak Pizzaialo Roll Up	17

Bread, Miffins amd Pastries

Cheesy Garlic Biscuits	19
Homemade Dough	19
Brown Sugar Muffins	19
Drizzle Frosting	19
Croissant Bread Pudding	20
Chocolate Chip Muffins	20
Double Corn and Bacon Bread	20
Crusty Dinner Rolls	20
Pesto Crescent Rolls	21
Strawberry Chocolate Kiss Crescents	21
Spicy Hush Puppy Sticks	21
Refrigerator Bran Muffins	22
British Scones	22
Beer Muffins	22
Muffin Mix	22
Pepper Jack Corn Cakes	23
Parmesan Dinner Muffins	23
Parmesan Bagel Bake	23
Easy Garlic Refrigerator Crescent Rolls	23
Hiker's Danish	24
Pepperoni Biscuits	24
Low Sugar Low Fat Banana Muffins	24

Herb Cheese Biscuits	25
Sour Cream Muffins	25
Pumpkin Muffins	25
Lite Biscuits and Gravy	25
Refrigerator Sweet Muffins	26
Garlic Spread	26
Kristin's Cornbread	26
Cranberry Walnut Muffins	27
Almond Bread	27
Bacon Cheese Muffins	27
Hawaiian Cornbread	27
Mexican Cornbread	28
Cheese and Spinach Muffins	28
Glazed Strawberry Filled	28
Cherry Banana Loaf	28
Calico Bell Pepper Muffins	29
Carrot Muffins with Cream Cheese Icing	29
Onion Poppy Seed Rolls	29
Apple Express Muffinwich	30
Pumpkin Apple Muffins	30
Cheese Stuffed Garlic Breadsticks	30
Foccacia Breads	30
Baby Elephant Ears	31
Banana Walnut Bread	31
Mini Parmesan Bites	31

Breakfast

Heavenly Ricotta Pancakes	33
Yesterday's Donuts Today's French Toast	33
Strawberry Stuffed French Toast	33
Fruit and Almond Coffee Cakes	34
Granola French Toast	34
Cinnamon Rolls	34
English Muffin French Toast	35
Fruit Syrup	35
Fluffy Pancakes with Fruity Syrup	35
Artichoke Omelet	35
Apple Sausage Pancake	36
Mini Breakfast Casserole	36
Zucchini Frittata	36
Mac and Cheese Omelet	36
Biscuits and Gravy	37
Bagel French Toast	37

Apple Bacon Brunchers	37
Southwestern Hash Browns	37
Hash and Egg	38
Egg Cups	38
Western Omelet	38
Easy Fruit Danish	38
Biscuit, Diced Ham and Eggs	39
Fried Eggs	39
Mincemeat Pies	39
Holiday French Toast	39
Noodle Kugel (Hanukkah)	40
Purim-Blintz Bake	40
Scotch Eggs	40
Strawberry Banana Pancakes	41
Natural French Toast Sticks	41
Salami and Eggs	41
Hot Cereal	41
Oatmeal Raisin Pancakes	42
Southwest Breakfast Bake	42
Steak and Egg Omelet	42
Low-fat Portabella Mushroom And Onion Omelet	42
Sausage & Cheese Strada	43
Quiche Lorraine	43
Breakfast Pigs in a Blanket	43
French Toast and Ham Wrap	44
Biscuit Breakfast Bake	44
Sloppy Joe and Egg Breakfast Pie	44
Breakfast Burritos To Go	45
Quickie Breakfast	45
Polenta, Sausage, Spinach and Cheese Snacks	45
Mixed Berry Corn Pancakes	46
Breakfast Hash	46
Poached Eggs	46
Egg Cheese and Canadian Bacon Bake	46
Veggie and Cheese Omelet	47
Meat Lovers Omelet	47
Low-Carb "Eggs Benedict"	47
Breakfast Bagel Nosh	48
Caviar Omelet	48
Tortillas & Eggs	48
Romantic Brunch Sweet Sandwiches	49
Ham and Egg Breakfast Sandwich	49
Veggi & Cheese Omelet	49

Steak & Potato Omelet	49
Eggs & Tortillas	50
Cinnamon Pancakes	50
Breakfast Potato Moons	50
Egg Tata tots	50
Denver Omelet	51
French Tomato Omelet	51
Picante Omelet	51
Eggs Benedict	51
Sausage & Cheese Strata	52
Puffy German Pancake	52

Deserts

Individual Pie or Quiche Crust	53
Cherry Cola Cake	53
Boston Cream Donuts	53
Filo Wrapped Apple Pie	54
Individual Cheesecakes	54
Mini Crumb Cake	54
Pears in Chocolate Sauce	55
Raspberry Chantilly filled White Cake	55
Peach Flan	55
Bananas Foster	55
Cherry Turnovers	56
Impossible Pecan Pie	56
Strawberry Kiwi Cheesecake	56
Impossible Cranberry Pie	57
Caramel Apple Dessert	57
Easter Cake	57
Peach Melba	57
Cinnamon Twists	58
Grilled Strawberry & Chocolate Sandwiches	58
Dessert Bruschetta	58
Rocky Road Squares	59
Luau Pineapple Sundae	59
Peach, Plum and Kiwi Compote	59
Hot Cini Minis	59
Any Time Cookies	60
Piña Colada Muffins	60
Root Beer Float Cake	60
Apple Spice Snack Cake with Caramel Sauce	61
Mini Cinnamon Twists	61
Pecan Ribbon Coffeecake	61

Fruit Filled No Roll Crepes	62
Caramel Nut Roll Cake	62
Almond Joy Cake	62
Frosted Apricot Cake	62
Black Forest Cake	63
Ruby Scones	63
Banana Split Cake	63
Pineapple Outside-in Cake	63
Wapple Pie	64
Raspberry Shortcake	64
Mocha Frappuccino Cake	64
Black Cherry Pie Turnovers	65
Mushroom Clouds	65
Braised Pears with Pomegranate Juice	65
"Almost Instant" Coconut Custard Pies	66
Pineapple Outside-in Cake	66
Ice Cream Cakewich	66
Cake for 2	66
Savory Brunch Cakes	67
Chocolate Cake for 4	67
Angel Food Cake	67
Lemon Cherry Pies	68
Heath Bar Cheesecake Tarts	68
Oatmeal Cookie Pies	68
Mini Cannoli Layer Cakes	69
Chocolate Biscotti Dessert Strata	69
Apple Tartlets	69
Fresh Peach Shortcake	70
Low-Fat Snack Cake	70
Brownie Overload	70
Lo-Cal Cherry Angel Food Pudding	71
Low Fat Mini Brownies	71
Mini Pumpkin Muffins	71
Giant Cookie	71
Chocolate Cheese Dream Roll	72
Quick and Simple Phyllo Pies	72
Banana Marshmallow Delight	72
Pumpkin Fluff Pockets	73
Pie Batter	73

Pizza

Pepperoni Calzone	75
Pizza Parlor Stromboli	75

Stuffed Spaghetti Pies	75
Pepperoni Pizza Wrap	76
Hawaiian French Bread Pizza	76
Meatball Pockets	76
Italian Chicken Pizza Bake	77
Just About Instant Pizza Dough	77
Meatballs Parmigianino Crescent Style	77
Mexican Pizza Rollups	78
Torta Rustica Pockets	78
Dough Batter	78
Hawaiian Pizza	78
Deep Dish Sicilian Pizza	79
Stromboli	79
Greek Pizza Wedges	79
Pizza Burritos	79
Calzones	80
Pizza Pita	80
Veggie Pizza	80
Pizza Burger Pies	80
Traditional Pizza Pies	81
Veggi White Pizza Pies	81
White Pizza	81
White Asparagus and Tomato Pizza	81
Mexican Stacked Pizza	82
Pepperoni and Provolone Roll Ups	82
Pepperoni Hot Pocket	82

Pork

Pork and Potato Croquettes	83
Sausage Corn Muffins	83
Lite Cheese and Sausage Biscuits	83
Hot Dog Wraps	83
Hot Ham Rocks	84
Three Alarm Chili Dog Bake	84
Spicy Barbecued "Fried" Boneless Pork Chop	84
Pot Stickers	84
Pork Egg Rolls	85
Biscuits Stuffed with Ham and Cheese	85
Ham and Cheese Pockets	85
Chicago Style Brat Wrap	86
Monster Grilled Sandwich	86
Mini Pork and Potato Loafs	86
Broccoli Ham Roll Ups	87

Steamed Dumplings	87
Marinated Pork Tenderloin	87
Sloppy Dogs	87
Boneless Oriental Pork Chops	88
Oktoberfest Bratwurst	88
Italian Porketta Wrap	88
Kielbasa & Kraut	88
Brats In Beer	89
Oriental Sesame Pork Buns	89
Ham and Swiss Frittata	89
Monte Cristo sandwich	89
French Poodles (Parisian-style hot dogs)	90
Stuffed Dogs and Taters	90
Hot Dog Macaroni	90
Hot Dog and Mashed Potato Bake	90
Cajun Style Pork Tenderloin with Citrus BBQ Sauce	91
Rich Girl Sandwich	91
Vienna Sausage and Bean Dip	91
Chili Dog Burrito's	91
White Beans and Ham	92
Glazed Ham Steak	92
Sweet and Sour Spam	92
Italian Stuffed Pork Roast	92
Ham Salad Poppers	93
Oriental Pork Cutlets	93
Quick Thai Brown Curry Pork	93
Pork Roll & Cheese Croissant	94
Orange Glazed Smoked Pork Chops	94
Ham & Cheese Panini	94
Corn Dogs	94
Spring Lamb Salad	95
Lamb Burger Loaves With Yogurt Sauce	95
Franks & Beans Burrito	95
American Panini	96
Cheatin' Boston Baked Beans	96
Ham and Scallop Potatoes	96
Honey Mustard Smoked Pork Chops	96
Polenta Panini's	97
Blue Cheese and Bacon Frittata	97
Whole Wheat HamamHam Pitawich	97
Mini Pigs in a Blanket	97
Sausage Tortellini Bake	98
Pork Tenderloin Stuffed with Dried Fruit and Herb Stuffing	98

Ham & Cheese Mini Frittatas	98
Pork Tenderloin w/ Sweet Potatoes	99
Ham & Cheese Dijon	99

Poultry

Italian Chicken Rolls	101
Crispy Potato Chicken	101
Chicken Pot Pie to Go	101
Chicken Croquettes	102
Barbecued Chicken and Corn Pockets	102
Coca-Cola Chicken	102
Crunchy Coated Chicken	102
Egg Foo Yung	103
Egg Foo Yung Sauce	103
Crab Stuffed Chicken	103
Chicken Moutarde	103
Spinach Stuffed Lemon Herb Chicken	104
Florentine Chicken Pinwheels	104
Blue Cheese Chicken	104
Asian Honey Chicken Tidbits	104
Low Fat Baked Chicken Chimis	105
Chicken Yassa (Kwanzaa)	105
Japanese Chicken Breasts	105
Chicken Tetrazzini	106
Easy Chicken Chow Mei Fun	106
Mexican Tequila Chicken	106
Chicken Pot Pie	107
Squash Stuffed Chicken Breasts	107
Doritos Chicken Fingers	107
Chicken Purses	108
California Chicken Cutlet Sandwiches	108
Healthy Rolled Chicken Scaloppini and Tomatoes	108
Low-carb Chicken Breast Stuffed with Vegetables Alfredo	109
Chicken Cordon Bleu	109
Stuffed Chicken Breasts	109
Aegean Chicken Cutlets	110
Turkey Rollatini	110
Quicky Chicken Parm	111
Buffalo Chicken Wrap	111
African Chicken Stew	111
BBQ Chicken Wraps	112
Chicken Vodka Hero Sandwich	112
Salsa Stuffed Chicken Breast	112

Pan-Blackened Chicken Caesar Salad	113
Chicken Chili	113
Chicken Fajitas	113
Chicken & Dumplings	114
Brochette Chicken	114
Sweet and Tasty Onion Chicken	114
Island Spice Sesame Chicken	115
Mandarin Chicken Salad	115
Chicken Lo Mein	115
Chicken Rolls with Cranberry Filling	116
Chicken with Corn and Tomato Salsa	116
Polynesian Chicken and Rice	116
Quick Chicken Tostadas	117
Bavarian Chicken	117
Greek Chicken Salad	117
Skewerless Satays	118
Roasted Red Pepper Turkey Ham & Cheese Wrap	118
Peanut Chicken	118
Almost Thanksgiving Turkey Loaves	118
Cream Cheese Turkey Rolls	119
Stuffed Turkey Tenderloin	119
Barbecued Turkey Bacon Cheeseburger	119
Grilled Turkey Bacon Ranch Rollup	120
Elegant Rosemary Turkey	120
Turkey Chimichangas	120
Cuban Spiced Turkey	121
Turkey Meatballs	121
Swedish Turkey Meatballs	121
Low Fat Fried Chicken	121
Thanksgiving Anytime Turkey Roll	122
Authentic Turkey Cuban Sandwich	122
Mini Turkey Meat Loaves	122
Turkey Corn Dogs	123
Chicken Melt	123
Chicken Pot Stickers	123
Marinated Teriyaki Chicken	124

Seafood

"Fried" Salmon and Vegetable Rice	125
Honey Mustard Salmon En Croute	125
Corn and Salmon Cakes	125
Salmon Puffs	126
Tartar Sauce	126

Steamed Clams	126
Mini Salmon Loaves	126
Salmon Omelet	127
Coconut Crusted Perch	127
Caribbean Jerk Seared Tuna	127
Maple and Mustard Salmon	128
Shrimp Quiche	128
Coconut Fish	128
Scrambled Eggs and Salmon	129
Hot Shrimp Big Easy Po' Boy	129
Simple Thai Curry Basil Shrimp	129
Clam Pies	130
Clam Chowder Soupwich	130
Cajun Style Swordfish	130
Mussel Fritters	131
Crabby Louie Pastry Cups	131
Creamed Cod Fish	131
Crab Quesadillas	132
Fishermen's Wharf Tacos	132
Crab Dip	132
Open Face Tuna Melt	133
Fish & Yogurt	133
Bacon Wrapped Stuffed Shrimp	133
Broccoli Fish Burger With Garlic Mayonnaise	134
Tuna Burgers	134
Poached Fish with Pineapple Salsa	134
Scallops Puttanesca	135
Warm Fish and Spinach Salad	135
Codfish Cakes	135
Pan- Blackened Swordfish W/ Sun-Dried Tomato Mayonnaise	135
Low Carb Tuna Melts	136
Orange Scallops	136
Tuna Puffs	136
Open-Face Crab Melt	137
Seafood Stuffed Salmon	137
Sherried Mussels	137
Grilled Shrimp and Asparagus Pizza	138
Flounder Stuffed with Broccoli and Cheese	138
Swordfish with Marinated Tomatoes	138
Crab Stuffed Mushrooms	139
Teriyaki Salmon with Wasabi Mayonnaise	139
Crab Cakes	139
Shrimp Stuffed Salmon Paddies	140

Open Face Tuna Crostini Sandwiches	140
Elegant Salmon and Zucchini Bake	140
Low-Carb Mussels Marinara	141
Fiji Island Sea Bass	141
Oriental Sea Bass	141
Poached Dill and Cucumber Salmon	142
Filet of Sole Veronique	142
Almond Tilapia	142
Steamed Oyster Dim Sum	143
Clams Casino	143
Mexican Catfish	143

Vegetables & Side dishes

Spinach and Potato Croquettes	145
Veggie Pockets	145
Couscous for One	145
Stuffed Peppers	146
Hot & Spicy Olives	146
Arroz con Gandules (Rice and Pigeon peas)	146
Warm German Potato Salad	147
Spanish Rice	147
Beet and Goat cheese Tapas	147
Tuscan Stromboli	148
Samosa	148
Loaded Mashed Potato Cakes	148
Mac & Cheese Boats	149
Italian Pepper and Egg Sandwich	149
Stilton & Bacon Bits	149
Warm Zucchini Salad	149
Fiddlehead Ferns & Linguine	150
Baby Spinach Frittata	150
Grilled Summer Vegetable Pita	150
Peas with Bacon and Dill	151
Cauliflower "Fritters"	151
Mushroom Pockets	151
Potato Wedges	152
Cheesy Bacon Potato Skins	152
Garlic Green Beans	152
Stuffing Rice	152
Paprika Potatoes	153
"Grilled" Veggies	153
EZ Spanish Rice	153
Portabella Mushroom Burgers	153

Spinach Pickups	154
Rice and Veggie Cakes	154
Eggplant Cheese Bake	154
Cheese- Onion Potato Casserole	155
Cheesy "Mashed Potato" Bake	155
Bacon & Swiss Stuffed Baby Bella Mushrooms	155
Potato Rice Pancakes	156
Fried Rice	156
Tofu Hash	156
Ranch Veggie French Bread Pizza	156
Carrot Dumplings	157
Rutabaga Casserole	157
Spanish Rice Omelet	157
Greek Pitawich	157
Hominy Bake	158
White Asparagus & Tomato Pie	158
Meatless Meatloaf	158
Savory Chickpea Patties	159
Polenta with Creamy Tomato Sauce and Cheese	159
Twice-Baked Cheesy Potatoes	159
Veggie Filled Puff Pastry Bundles	160
Sun Dried Tomato Goat Cheese Roasted Pepper Roll	160
Veggie Pitawich	160
Melted Cheese and Tomato Sandwiches	161
Hot Tomato Stacked Sandwiches	161
Crispy Baked Potatoes	161
Xpress Rice	161
Spinach Salad with Hot Bacon Dressing	162
Sweet Carrot Sandwich	162
Broccoli Dream Pocket	162
Exotic Succotash Boat's	163
Eggplant Vegetable Boats	163
Zucchini Boats	163
Broccoli and Cheddar Tarts	164
Twice Baked Potato	164
Sweet Potato Puffs	164
"Fried" Rice with Vegetables	164
Bean and Veggie Wraps	165
Spicy Orange Broccoli	165
Thyme Lime Potato Wedges	165
Greek Spanakopita	166
Spinach Soufflé	166
Curscous Vegetable Medley	166

Take-Out Dim Sum	167
Fresh Tomato Tart	167
Vegetarian Spring Rolls	167
Irish Bubble and Squeak Loaves	168
Broccoli Nut Wraps	168
Grilled Hot Chili Sandwiches	168
Spanish Rice	169
Leftover Tater Cakes	169
Broccoli Fritters	169

Appetizers

Russian Cheese Stuffed Purses

Ingredients
- 4 2oz frozen dough balls
- 2 ounces chopped Muenster cheese
- ¼ cup shredded cheddar cheese
- ¼ teaspoon garlic powder
- 2 chopped scallions
- 4 slices chopped cooked bacon
- Cooking spray

Servings~ 👥
Cooking Time~ Nine Minutes
Pan to Use: Divided or Base

Cooking Steps
A. Pre-heat and spray areas with non-stick cooking spray. Roll dough pieces into 5 inch circles. Combine remaining ingredients. Place 2 tablespoons mixture into center of each dough circle. Gather up and pinch together to make purses.
B. Place two purses in each area. Cook 7 minutes. Turnover and cook 2 more minutes.

Toasted Nuts and Cranberries

Ingredients
- 1 cup mixed cocktail nuts. (Preferably unsalted)
- 1 tablespoon sesame oil
- 1 tablespoon garlic powder
- ½ teaspoon Worcestershire sauce
- ½ teaspoon cayenne pepper
- ¼ cup dried cranberries
- 1 teaspoon brown sugar

Servings~ 👥
Cooking Time~ Six Minutes
Pan to Use: Divided, Mini or Base

Cooking Steps
A. Pre-heat for about 3 minutes and mix all ingredients.
B. Pour equal amounts of nut mixture into each area. Cook for 6 minutes and mix halfway through to promote even toasting.

Spicy Roasted Pumpkin Seeds

Ingredients
- 1 cup raw pumpkin seeds
- 2 tablespoons melted butter
- 1 tablespoon Tabasco sauce
- 1 tablespoon Cajun spice mix
- 1 teaspoon garlic salt

Servings~ 👥
Cooking Time~ Fifteen Minutes
Pan to Use: Divided, Mini or Base

Cooking Steps
A. Pre-heat and spray with cooking spray.
B. Mix all ingredients and divide mixture between cooking areas. Close cover and cook 15 minutes.

Stuffed Soupwich

Ingredients
- 1 can (18.8 ounces) prepared chicken or corn chowder
- 2 ½ cups chicken flavored dry stuffing mix
- 3 ounces shredded cheddar cheese

Servings~ 👥👥
Cooking Time~ Twelve Minutes
Pan to Use: Divided, Mini or Base

Cooking Steps
A. Pre-heat and spray with cooking spray. Combined all ingredients.
B. Spoon 3/4 cup of mixture in each well, cook 7 minutes until golden. Repeat and cook the remaining two servings.

Hot Lobster Dip

Ingredients
- 1 5.2 oz. package boursin garlic and fine herbs cheese, softened
- ¼ cup mayonnaise
- ½ teaspoon dry mustard
- 1 tablespoon chopped salad pimentos, drained
- 1 tablespoon grated Asiago cheese
- 1 tablespoon shredded gruyere or Swiss cheese
- ¼ cup fresh or imitation lobster meat
- Melba toast rounds for serving

Servings~ 👤👤
Cooking Time~ Twelve Minutes
Pan to Use: Divided, Mini or Base

Cooking Steps
A. Gently combine all ingredients (except Melba toast) folding in lobster last.
B. Do not Pre-heat, but spray with cooking spray. Divide mixture evenly between cooking areas. Close cover; cook approximately 12 minutes until bubbly.
C. Serve on Melba toast rounds

Bean Dip

Ingredients
- ¾ cup refried beans
- 2 tablespoons salsa
- 2 tablespoons pepper jack cheese
- 2 tablespoons chopped pitted black olives
- Shredded lettuce, chopped red onions, sour cream, tortilla chips for serving

Servings~ 👤👤
Cooking Time~ Eight Minutes
Pan to Use: Divided, Mini or Base

Cooking Steps
A. Pre-heat and spray areas with non-stick cooking spray. Mix together first four ingredients.
B. Divide mixture evenly between wells. Close cover; cook 7 minutes until bubbly and cheese is melted. Serve warm with chips, topped with onions, lettuce and sour cream.

Pastelito de Guayaba

Ingredients
- 1 can refrigerator crescent rolls
- 1 ½ cups guava paste
- 1 tablespoon confectioner's sugar
- 1 tablespoon hot water

Servings~ 👤👤👤👤
Cooking Time~ Twelve Minutes
Pan to Use: Divided or Base

Cooking Steps
A. Pre-heat and spray with cooking spray. Separate crescents into 4 squares, pressing perforations together so there are no holes in dough. Divide equal amounts of guava paste onto center of each square. Fold over each dough square to make a triangle and delicately seal edges with fork. Spray top and bottom of each Pastelito with cooking spray.
B. Place one pastry in each cooking well; cover and cook for approximately 6 minutes. While that's cooking, dissolve sugar in 1 tablespoon of hot water to make simple syrup. After cooking 6 minutes, lightly brush top and bottom of each pastry with simple syrup. Cook 5-6 minutes more, until completely browned, and repeat for last 2 pastries

Huevos Ranchero

Ingredients
1 (7-inch) flour tortilla cut in half
½ cup salsa
2 eggs
2 tablespoons shredded cheddar cheese

Servings~ 👤👤
Cooking Time~ Ten Minutes
Pan to Use: Divided or Base

Cooking Steps
A. Pre-heat and spray with cooking spray.
B. Carefully fit half the tortilla into each well. Spoon ½ the salsa into each tortilla cup leaving room in the center for the egg. Crack an egg into the center of each well. Cook 8-10 minutes to desired degree of doneness.

Diner Style Eggs a'la King

Ingredients
3 hard boiled eggs, peeled
½ cup condensed cream of chicken soup with herbs
½ cup milk plus 1 tablespoon
2 tablespoons drained pimentos
3 slices white toast cut diagonally
Salt and pepper to taste

Servings~ 👤👤
Cooking Time~ Five Minutes
Pan to Use: Divided or Base

Cooking Steps
A. In a bowl mix soup, milk and pimentos, then slice eggs lengthwise. Pour enough mixture into wells to cover bottoms and plug in unit. Place 3 egg halves in each cooking area, then top with rest of mixture.
B. Close cover and cook 3-5 minutes. Serve eggs on toast, topped with sauce, salt and pepper.

Easy Frittatas

Ingredients
2 eggs beaten or 1/3 cup egg substitute
2 tablespoons mozzarella cheese
1 small roma tomato diced
1 green onion chopped
1 ounce chopped meat of choice
Salt and pepper to taste

Servings~ 👤👤
Cooking Time~ Seven Minutes
Pan to Use: Divided, Mini, or Base

Cooking Steps
A. Pre-heat and spray with cooking spray. In a medium bowl mix all ingredients.
B. Pour mixture in to cooking area and cook seven minutes

Cheese Sticks

Ingredients
2 mozzarella string cheese sticks
¼ cup flour for dredging
¾ cup Panko bread crumbs
1 tablespoon dried Italian seasoning
1 egg
Marinara sauce for dipping
(optional)

Servings~ 👤👤
Cooking Time~ Six Minutes
Pan to Use: Divided or Base

Cooking Steps
A. Cut each string cheese lengthwise so you have four cheese strips. Combine bread crumbs and seasoning. Beat egg in a bowl. Dredge each stick in flour, then dip in egg, then coat with bread crumbs. Repeat breading process again so each stick is breaded twice.
B. Pre-heat and spray with cooking spray. Place 2 cheese strips in each cooking well. Fry for 3 minutes; turn to brown top and cook 3 more minutes. Avoid overcooking or cheese will ooze out of coating. Serve with sauce, if desired.

Philly Stuffed Mushrooms

Ingredients
1 slice deli style roast beef, chopped
1 pound fresh mushrooms (about 12)
2 tablespoons butter or margarine
1½ tablespoons Italian breadcrumbs
2 ounces softened cream cheese
1 tablespoon finely chopped onion
1 dash garlic powder
¼ teaspoon seasoned salt

Servings~ 🙂🙂🙂🙂
Cooking Time~ Six Minutes
Pan to Use: Divided, Mini or Base

Cooking Steps
A. Remove mushroom stems and cut a thin slice off the top of each mushroom so it sits flat, and chop finely. Add 1 tablespoon of butter in each well. Plug in unit and add chopped stems to one well and remaining stems and onion in other. Close cover and sauté for 2 minutes.
B. Unplug and carefully scoop mushrooms and onions into a bowl, add remaining ingredients but not mushrooms, and mix. Fill each mushroom, cover and store in refrigerator until needed. To cook Pre-heat and spray with cooking spray. Place 2-3 mushrooms in each well. Close cover and cook for 3-4 minutes until heated and filling is bubbly, and repeat with remaining ingredients.

Tapas-Mini Pepper Empanadas

Ingredients
1 cup roasted red peppers
½ cup salsa or chili sauce
¼ teaspoon adobo seasoning
¼ teaspoon garlic
½ cup grated parmesan, Romano, and Asiago cheese blend (recommend Kraft blend)
1 lb. package pizza dough

Servings~ 🙂🙂🙂🙂🙂🙂🙂🙂
Cooking Time~ Ten Minutes
Pan to Use: Divided or Base

Cooking Steps
A. Mix all ingredients except pizza dough and set aside. Pre-heat and spray with cooking spray. Divide pizza dough into 10 equal pieces. On a lightly floured surface, roll each piece of dough into a 4 inch circle.
B. Spoon about 1 tablespoon of pepper mix onto each circle, fold over and pinch edges to close. Bake in batches of 2 per well, about 8-10 minutes at a time.

Puff Pastry Shells with Cheesy Bacon Filling

Ingredients
2 frozen puff pastry shells, trimmed to fit
1 tablespoon garlic herb cheese spread
2 tablespoons cream cheese
3 slices cooked bacon, chopped
2 tablespoons chopped cooked broccoli or spinach
2 tablespoons cooked mashed potatoes or rice

Servings~ 🙂🙂
Cooking Time~ Fifteen Minutes
Pan to Use: Divided or Base

Cooking Steps
A. Pre-heat and spray with cooking spray. Place frozen shells in wells, and cook for 10 minutes. Combine remaining ingredients.
B. Carefully remove center from shells and fill each with half of mixture. Cook 5 more minutes.

Chorizo Quesadillas

Ingredients
2 small flour tortillas
1 cup shredded Mexican cheese blend
2 tablespoons cooked chorizo
2 tablespoons chunky salsa
1 tablespoon chopped fresh cilantro
Extra salsa and sour cream for serving,

Servings~
Cooking Time~ Four Minutes
Pan to Use: Divided or Base

Cooking Steps
A. Pre-heat and spray with cooking spray. Top each tortilla with equal amounts of cheese chorizo, salsa and cilantro, leaving about 1/2 inch filling free border around each tortilla. Rub edges with a small amount of water and fold over being sure filling will not leak out. Cut edges if necessary to fit cooking wells and then spray outsides of tortilla with cooking spray.
B. Place one quesadilla into each cooking well close cover and cook approximately 4 minutes, looking for even browning halfway through cooking, cook until cheese is completely melted. Cut each quesadilla in half and serve with sour cream and salsa, if desired.

"Hot Pockets"

Ingredients
½ tablespoon yeast
½ tablespoon sugar
½ cup warm water
1 tablespoon olive oil
½ teaspoon salt
1½ cup flour
Filling of choice, anything you desire

Servings~
Cooking Time~ Twelve Minutes
Pan to Use: Divided or Base

Cooking Steps
A. Do not pre-heat but, spray wells with cooking spray. Then dissolve yeast in warm water with sugar let stand for a few minutes until foamy. Stir in oil, salt and flour. Turn dough out on floured board, knead 5 minutes, and then divide into four pieces and roll each into 6 inch circles. Place filling of choice on one side of each half pinching edges to seal.
B. Place two pockets in cold well, close cover and plug in then bake 12 minutes, turnover halfway through cooking to promote even browning. To cook other two carefully lift into hot machine and re-spray wells if needed. Cook for 10 minutes in heated unit.

Grilled Blue Cheese Apple Sandwich

Ingredients
4 slices date nut bread
1 cup crumbled blue cheese
1 Granny Smith apple, cored and seeded, sliced very thin
Butter

Servings~
Cooking Time~ Ten Minutes
Pan to Use: Divided or Base

Cooking Steps
A. Pre-heat and spray with cooking spray. Lightly butter one side each slice of bread. Then sprinkle the non-buttered side with half of cheese and top with a single layer of half the apple slices cover with other slice of bread and butter side up slice in half to fit wells
B. Cook seven to 10 minutes, turning half way through to ensure that bread is evenly toasted and cheese is thoroughly melted
C. Repeat for second sandwich, cover sandwiches with tin foil to keep warm while making additional batches.

Beef

Crescent Beef Bites

Ingredients
1 cup cooked ground beef
1 tablespoon dried onion flakes
½ teaspoon garlic salt
Mushrooms, finely chopped
1 cup softened cream cheese
1 cans refrigerator crescent rolls

Servings~ 👤👤👤👤
Cooking Time~ Ten Minutes
Pan to Use: Divided or Base

Cooking Steps
A. Pre-heat and spray with cooking spray. Separate crescents into 4 squares on cutting board, sealing triangle perforations by pressing with fingers. Stir all other ingredients together until smooth and divide between 4 squares, spreading to within ½ inch of edges. Roll up like a jelly roll and place 1, seam side down, in each well, lightly sprayed with non stick spray.
B. Close lid and bake 10 minutes, turning ¼ turn after 6 minutes to brown. Repeat with other 2 rolls. Slice into 4 or 5 diagonal slices and serve hot.

Steak au Poivre

Ingredients
2 (6-8 ounce) boneless rib eye steaks, 1 inch thick and trimmed to fit wells
2 tablespoons cracked peppercorns

Servings~ 👤👤
Cooking Time~ Fifteen Minutes
Pan to Use: Divided or Base

Cooking Steps
A. Pat meat dry. Press peppercorns into both sides of each steak. Place one in each well.
B. Cook 10 minutes for rare, 13 minutes for medium and 15 minutes for well done. Serve with béarnaise sauce in desired.

Stuffed Italian Shells

Ingredients
6 large shell pasta, boiled and drained
½ cup cooked ground beef
1 handful spinach leaves, finely chopped
½ cup ricotta cheese
½ teaspoon Italian seasoning
½ teaspoon garlic salt
1 small zucchini, sliced
½ cup marinara sauce
Parmesan cheese

Servings~ 👤👤👤👤
Cooking Time~ Ten Minutes
Pan to Use: Divided or Base

Cooking Steps
A. Pre-heat, spray wells with cooking spray. Mix together ground beef, spinach, ricotta and seasonings. Divide into 6 shells.
B. Put a layer of sliced zucchini in each well and place 3 shells on top of zucchini. Close cover and cook 10 minutes. To serve, cover with heated marinara sauce and parmesan cheese.

Quick Sesame Steak

Ingredients
Leftover steak, thinly sliced against the grain (preferably thick-cut)
2 packets soy sauce
2 tablespoons honey
2 tablespoons sesame oil
1 teaspoon minced garlic
1 chopped scallion (discard green top)
1 teaspoon sesame seeds (optional)

Servings~ 👤👤
Cooking Time~ Three Minutes
Pan to Use: Divided or Base

Cooking Steps
A. Combine first 4 ingredients in a one quart Ziploc plastic bag. Shake well to marinate. Pre-heat and spray with cooking spray. Divide equal portions into wells.
B. Cook for 2-3 minutes. Top with sesame seeds and scallions before serving.

Chili Enchiladas

Ingredients
1 cup prepared chili con carne
1 tablespoon canned or fresh jalapeno rings
¾ cup shredded cheddar cheese
2 jalapeno flavored wraps
¾ cup prepared enchilada or taco sauce
Sour cream, chopped green onions for serving

Servings~ 👤👤
Cooking Time~ Six Minutes
Pan to Use: Divided or Base

Cooking Steps
A. Pre-heat and spray with cooking spray. Combine chili, jalapenos and ½ cup of the cheddar and divide evenly between the two wraps. Fold in sides of wraps and roll to fit wells.
B. Put 1 tablespoon of enchilada sauce into each well. Place one enchilada into each well; top with the rest of the enchilada sauce and cheese. Cook 6 minutes until filling is hot and cheese is melted. Top with sour cream and green onions, if desired.

Hawaiian Beef Burgers

Ingredients
½ pound lean ground beef
½ teaspoon garlic salt
1 dash pepper
¼ cup pineapple tidbits
1 tablespoon real bacon bits
2 teaspoons soy sauce

Servings~ 👤👤
Cooking Time~ Ten Minutes
Pan to Use: Divided or Base

Cooking Steps
A. Pre-heat and spray with spray. Combine all ingredients, and shape into large round patty, about 5 inches round.
B. Cut in half and place half in each well, close cover and cook 8 to 10 minutes until beef is cooked through. Serve on split French rolls if desired.

Po Boy Sandwich

Ingredients
1, 5 inch sandwich roll split and trim to fit
1 large slice of deli roast beef
1 large slice Monterey jack cheese
1 tablespoon salsa or ranch dressing
Sliced tomato, cucumber, black olives, Lettuce, onion

Servings~ 👤
Cooking Time~ Six Minutes
Pan to Use: Divided or Base

Cooking Steps
A. Pre-heat, place roast beef, cheese and salsa on roll. Place in unit and cook for 5-7 minutes until filling is heated and roll is browned.
B. Open sandwich on a plate and garnish, alternating tomato and cucumber slices. Add olives, lettuce or onion as desired.

Empanadas

Ingredients
6 ounces ground beef
2 tablespoons chopped onions
1 clove garlic, crushed
1 tablespoon tomato sauce
1 teaspoon chipotle chili powder
½ teaspoon paprika
½ teaspoon salt
2 tablespoons shredded Monterey jack cheese
4 egg roll wrappers

Servings~ 👥
Cooking Time~ Six Minutes
Pan to Use: Divided or Base

Cooking Steps
A. Combine all ingredients except egg roll wrappers, spray wells lightly with cooking spray. Cook mixture until meat is well browned.
B. Allow mixture to cool before filling wrappers. Trim edges of wrappers to form a rough circle. Place 2 tablespoons mixture in center of each wrapper. Fold over and roll edges to seal, crimp edges.
C. Cook 3 minutes. Turnover and cook 3 more minutes. Repeat cooking process with remaining empanadas.

XRSG Steak

Ingredients
1 6 ounce rib eye boneless
½ small onion sliced
6 mushrooms sliced
Browning sauce
Salt and pepper
Garlic and steak seasoning to taste

Servings~ 👤
Cooking Time~ Seven Minutes
Pan to Use: Base

Cooking Steps
A. Brush one side of steak with browning sauce and place side down in base. Brush top of steak with browning sauce, season, and after 1 minute turn.
B. Season and top with mushrooms and onion slices. Close lid and cook 7 minutes depending on desired doneness.

Argentine Filet Mignon with Chimichurri Sauce

Ingredients
1 bunch fresh parsley stems removed
1 ½ cups Spanish olive oil
½ cup red wine vinegar
4 cloves fresh garlic, minced
1 tablespoon dried oregano
1 teaspoon paprika
1 teaspoon salt
1 tablespoon melted butter
2 4-6 oz. filet mignon steaks, about 2" thick, rested at room temperature for 30 min before cooking
Salt and pepper for seasoning

Servings~ 👥
Cooking Time~ Ten Minutes
Pan to Use: Divided or Base

Cooking Steps
A. To make chimichurri, combine first 7 ingredients, set aside at room temperature until serving.
B. Pre-heat and brush cooking surfaces with melted butter. Season both sides of filet mignon with salt and pepper. Place one steak into each well; steaks should be thick enough to touch the top cooking surfaces (if steaks are too thin to touch the top, turn during cooking for even browning). Cook 6-10 minutes for desired doneness. Serve drizzled with chimichurri and with remaining chimichurri for dipping.

Bite Size Burgers

Ingredients
4 ounces lean ground beef
½ cup plain bread crumbs
1 egg
1 tablespoon Heinz 57 or favorite BBQ sauce
¼ cup shredded cheddar cheese
1 tablespoon real bacon bits
4 potato bread dinner rolls
Optional toppings – raw onion, pickle chips, ketchup, mayonnaise, mustard, tomatoes

Servings~
Cooking Time~ Eight Minutes
Pan to Use: Divided or Base

Cooking Steps
A. Pre-heat and spray with cooking spray. Thoroughly mix together first 6 ingredients. Form into 4 burger patties to fit 2 patties in each well.
B. Close cover and cook burgers 3-4 minutes; flip and cook until desired doneness. Serve burgers on potato rolls topped with your favorite toppings.

Reuben Wrap

Ingredients
2 (8-inch) flour tortillas
2 teaspoons deli mustard
8 thin slices of corned beef
2 thin slices of Swiss cheese
2 tablespoons well-drained sauerkraut

Servings~
Cooking Time~ Eight Minutes
Pan to Use: Divided or Base

Cooking Steps
A. Spread half the mustard on each tortilla. Top each with half the corned beef, Swiss cheese and sauerkraut. Fold in sides of tortilla and roll.
B. Place one wrap in each well. Cook 7-8 minutes or until tops are well browned.

Mock Steak Diane

Ingredients
2 tablespoons butter
½ Vidalia onion, minced
2 button mushrooms, chopped
2 4 oz. pieces beef tenderloin
¼ cup heavy cream
¼ teaspoon Dijon mustard
Dash Worcestershire sauce
Fresh black pepper
Fresh parsley for serving

Servings~
Cooking Time~ Five Minutes
Pan to Use: Divided or Base

Cooking Steps
A. Pre-heat and melt ½ tablespoon butter in each well. Divide mushrooms and onions evenly between wells. Cook 3 minutes; remove from wells and set aside in a separate bowl to cool.
B. Divide remaining tablespoon of butter between wells. Place one steak piece into each well and cook 1 minute on each side; remove from wells. Slowly add heavy cream, mustard and Worcestershire to mushroom and onion mixture.
C. Divide sauce between wells and top each with a steak piece; cook until preferred doneness (1-2 minutes more). Serve steaks topped with pepper and parsley, if desired.

Mexican Stuffed Peppers

Ingredients
1 long, thin green pepper
½ cup cooked ground beef
½ cup bottled salsa, divided
¼ cup refried beans
½ teaspoon seasoned salt
½ cup instant rice
½ cup water
Grated cheese

Servings~ 👥
Cooking Time~ Ten Minutes
Pan to Use: Divided or Base

Cooking Steps
A. Slice pepper in half lengthways, clean out seeds and boil in small saucepan of water for 5 minutes until almost tender. Drain on paper towel and cool slightly. Mix together cooked ground beef, ¼ cup salsa, beans, salt, and stuff ½ into each green pepper.
B. Spray wells with cooking spray. Divide rice into wells of cold. Mix water and remaining salsa, pour half into each well over rice. Place pepper half on top of rice, close cover and plug in. Cook for 10 minutes. To serve, place pepper and rice on serving plate topped with grated cheese.

Italian Beef Rolls

Ingredients
2 3-4 ounce boneless beef chuck steaks
2 Italian sausage links, removed from casings
1 teaspoon fresh minced garlic
2 teaspoons fresh chopped parsley
Black pepper to taste
1 tablespoon grated parmesan cheese
1 tablespoon chopped or sliced black olives
2 cups prepared tomato sauce (jar or leftovers)
Cooked fettuccini for serving, optional

Servings~ 👥
Cooking Time~ Fifteen Minutes
Pan to Use: Divided or Base

Cooking Steps
A. Pre-heat and spray with cooking spray. Mix sausage with garlic, parsley, and black pepper in a bowl. Divide sausage mixture between wells. Cook for 3 minutes until gently browned. Turn off unit.
B. Remove crumbled sausage from wells; place in a small bowl and set aside to cool for 5 minutes. In the meantime, place steaks between two pieces of waxed paper or plastic wrap; pound very thin with a mallet. Spread half of sausage mixture onto each steak. Top each with 1 parmesan and olives.
C. Roll up each piece, jellyroll style, and secure with toothpick. Pre-heat again and spray with a small amount more of cooking spray.
D. Place one steak roll into each well. Brown on all sides (about 5 minutes total) and then add ½ cup tomato sauce over each roll. Cook 10 minutes more. Serve with additional tomato sauce over cooked fettuccini, if desired.

Beef Stew & Biscuit Bake

Ingredients
4 small or 2 large refrigerator biscuits
1 cup beef stew; remove any excess liquid
¼ cup shredded cheddar or Monterey jack cheese

Servings~ 👥
Cooking Time~ Ten Minutes
Pan to Use: Divided or Base

Cooking Steps
A. Press two small biscuits together or one large to form a 6 inch oval. Repeat with the remaining biscuits. Carefully fit the biscuits into the wells and spoon ½ the stew into each biscuit cup.
B. Cook 8-10 minutes or until biscuits are browned and puffy and stew is hot. Top with cheese.

Chili Taco Bowls

Ingredients
1 (8 inch) flour tortilla cut in half
1 cup canned or leftover sloppy Joe
2 tablespoons each cheddar and Monterey jack cheese
2 tablespoons each shredded lettuce and chopped tomato
2 teaspoons sour cream

Servings~ 👤👤
Cooking Time~ Five Minutes
Pan to Use: Divided or Base

Cooking Steps
A. Carefully fit the tortilla halves into wells forming 2 bowls. Spoon half of the mixture into each tortilla. Cook 5 minutes.
B. Remove and top with cheeses, lettuce, tomatoes and sour cream.

Hot Roast Beef on a Roll

Ingredients
4 pieces thinly sliced roast beef
½ cup prepared beef gravy
Splash Worcestershire sauce
Prepared horseradish sauce
1 cup raw fresh baby spinach or 2 romaine lettuce leaves
1 Kaiser Roll
Salt and pepper to taste

Servings~ 👤👤
Cooking Time~ Six Minutes
Pan to Use: Divided or Base

Cooking Steps
A. Combine gravy and Worcestershire sauce and pour equal amounts into each well. Put 2 slices roast beef into each well and cook for 3 minutes.
B. In the meantime, slice roll lengthwise without cutting all the way through. Spread liberally with horseradish sauce. Top with hot roast beef, salt and pepper, and spinach leaves.

Quick Beef Stew

Ingredients
1 package heat and serve beef tips and gravy
¼ cup canned mixed vegetables
2 tablespoons canned diced tomatoes, drained
1 teaspoon garlic powder
1 teaspoon Heinz 57 sauce

Servings~ 👤
Cooking Time~ Five Minutes
Pan to Use: Divided or Base

Cooking Steps
A. Pre-heat and spray with cooking spray.
B. Remove enough beef cubes from heat and serve tips to measure approximately ¾ cup (save or discard gravy). Mix with remaining ingredients. Divide stew evenly between wells. Cook for 5 minutes.

Toasted Bowls

Ingredients
1 (8-inch) flour tortilla cut in half
½ cup refried beans
½ cup cooked ground beef
2 tablespoons salsa
½ cup shredded cheese (cheddar, Colby, Jack)
Shredded lettuce
Chopped tomato
Chopped green onion

Servings~ 👤👤
Cooking Time~ Seven Minutes
Pan to Use: Divided or Base

Cooking Steps
A. Carefully fit the tortilla halves into each well forming 2 bowls. Fill each half with the beans, beef, salsa and shredded cheese.
B. Cook 6-7 minutes or until cheese is melted. Serve topped with lettuce, tomato, and green onion.

Steak and Peppers over Rice

Ingredients
½ cup beef broth, divided
Dash of Tabasco
Splash of Worcestershire sauce
Splash of red wine vinegar
Pinch of garlic powder
1 teaspoon Wondra flour
¼ cup minute rice
4 oz. leftover steak thinly sliced
½ cup fried peppers in a jar

Servings~ 👤
Cooking Time~ Five Minutes
Pan to Use: Divided or Base

Cooking Steps
A. Pre-heat. In the Shaker combine ¼ cup broth, Tabasco, Worcestershire, vinegar, garlic powder and flour. Shake vigorously so flour dissolves, and then pour mixture into left well.
B. In right well add remaining ¼ cup broth. Close cover and cook 1 minute. Open lid; add rice to right well and add steak and peppers to left well. Spray inner lid of unit with spray. Close cover; cook 5 minutes until rice is done and steak and peppers are heated through.

Hot Pastrami Wrap

Ingredients
2 8 inch flour tortillas
2 tablespoons mustard
4 ounces thinly sliced pastrami
Dill pickle slices
1 ounce mozzarella or provolone cheese

Servings~ 👤👤
Cooking Time~ Five Minutes
Pan to Use: Divided or Base

Cooking Steps
A. Pre-heat and spray with cooking spray. Lay out tortillas and spread with mustard. Pile on pastrami and pickle, top with cheese. Fold in sides of tortilla and roll.
B. Wraps will be thick and around 5 inches long. Place wraps in unit and cook 4-5 minutes or until lightly browned.

Grilled Meatloaf Sandwich

Ingredients
4 slices French bread about ½ inch thick
Leftover meatloaf, sliced
2 slices of cheese, optional
2 tablespoons garlic butter

Servings~ 👤👤
Cooking Time~ Six Minutes
Pan to Use: Divided or Base

Cooking Steps
A. Assemble two sandwiches with meatloaf and cheese. Spread garlic butter on the outside of sandwiches.
B. Place one sandwich in each well. Cook 4-6 minutes.

Salisbury Steak

Ingredients
10 ounces ground beef
1 teaspoon Worcestershire sauce
¼ teaspoon salt
1/8 teaspoon each pepper, garlic and onion powder
¼ cup onion slices
2 mushrooms, sliced
Prepared mushroom or brown gravy

Servings~ 👤👤
Cooking Time~ Thirteen Minutes
Pan to Use: Divided or Base

Cooking Steps
A. Combine beef, sauce and seasonings. Form mixture into two 3 x 4 inch ovals. Place 1 oval in each well. Cook 8 minutes.
B. Remove meat from wells and cover with foil to keep warm while mushrooms and onions are cooking. Place half of onions and mushrooms into each well. Cook 5 minutes. Spoon over meat and serve with hot gravy.

Sloppy Joes On Cornbread

Ingredients
½ cup corn muffin mix
1 egg
3 tablespoons milk
2/3 cups cooked sloppy Joe or taco meat
¼ cup salsa
2 tablespoons shredded cheddar or Jack cheese
2 teaspoons sour cream

Servings~ 👥
Cooking Time~ Eight Minutes
Pan to Use: Divided or Base

Cooking Steps
A. Pre-heat and spray with cooking spray. Combine muffin mix, egg and milk. Place Half of mixture in each well. Cook 3 minutes.
B. Spoon 1/3 cup meat into each partially cooked cornbread. Continue to cook for 5 minutes. Remove from wells and top with salsa, cheese and sour cream.

Burritos a'la Leftovers

Ingredients
2 (8 inch) flour tortillas
Cooked Steak, cut into thin strips
6 tablespoons chopped cooked potato, mushrooms and/or vegetables
4 tablespoons shredded cheese
2 tablespoons steak sauce

Servings~ 👥
Cooking Time~ Seven Minutes
Pan to Use: Divided or Base

Cooking Steps
A. Spread half the steak and vegetables in the center of each tortilla leaving 1 inch along perimeter. Top each with half the cheese and steak sauce. Rub a small amount of water along the perimeter of each tortilla to seal.
B. Fold each tortilla in half and place one in each cooking well. Cook 7 minutes.

Grilled Stuffed Burritos

Ingredients
2 (8 inch) flour tortillas
4 tablespoons refried beans, rice or combination
4 tablespoons shredded beef
2 tablespoons salsa
4 tablespoons shredded Monterey jack or cheddar

Servings~ 👥
Cooking Time~ Seven Minutes
Pan to Use: Divided or Base

Cooking Steps
A. Spread half the refried beans/rice in the center of each tortilla. Top each with half the shredded beef, salsa and shredded cheese. Fold in sides and roll tortillas.
B. Place one in each cooking well. Cook 5-7 minutes.

Asparagus & Beef Rollups

Ingredients
2 (4 ounce) thinly sliced top rounds sandwich steaks, pounded
2 slices Swiss cheese
4 asparagus spears, trimmed
Hollandaise sauce

Servings~ 👥
Cooking Time~ Seven Minutes
Pan to Use: Divided or Base

Cooking Steps
A. Place one piece of cheese on each piece of pounded beef. Add 2 asparagus spears to each. Roll up jellyroll fashion.
B. Place rolls seam side down into the wells. Cook 7 minutes or until well browned.
C. Serve with hollandaise or your favorite sauce.

Asparagus & Savory Beef Rollups

Ingredients
2 (4 ounce) thinly sliced top rounds sandwich steaks, pounded
2 tablespoons garlic spread
4 asparagus spears, trimmed

Servings~ 👥
Cooking Time~ Seven Minutes
Pan to Use: Divided or Base

Cooking Steps
A. Place Half of garlic spread on each piece of pounded beef. Add 2 asparagus spears to each. Roll up jellyroll fashion.
B. Place rolls seam side down into the wells. Cook 7 minutes or until well browned.

Stuffed Beef Rolls

Ingredients
¼ cup Italian flavored breadcrumbs
3 tablespoons water
1 tablespoon chopped onion
1 mushroom, chopped
2 (4 ounce) thinly sliced top round sandwich steaks
1 tablespoon grated parmesan cheese
1 tablespoon shredded mozzarella cheese
½ cup heated tomato sauce

Servings~ 👥
Cooking Time~ Seven Minutes
Pan to Use: Divided or Base

Cooking Steps
A. Combine the breadcrumbs, water, onion and mushrooms. Spread half the mixture on each slice of beef within ½ inch of the edges and top with cheese. Roll up jellyroll fashion.
B. Place the rolls seam side down into the wells. Cook 7 minutes or until browned. Serve topped with tomato sauce.

Indian Ground Beef

Ingredients
4 ounces ground beef
2 tablespoons frozen peas and carrots, thawed
1 tablespoon tomato paste
1 teaspoon water
½ teaspoon garam masala seasoning
2 tablespoons chopped fresh cilantro or to taste
1 tablespoon chopped fresh ginger
Pinch cayenne pepper
2 tablespoons plain yogurt for serving

Servings~ 👥
Cooking Time~ Twelve Minutes
Pan to Use: Divided, Mini or Base

Cooking Steps
A. Pre-heat and spray with cooking spray. Mix together all ingredients except yogurt.
B. Divide meat mixture evenly between cooking wells. Close cover; cook 10-12 minutes until meat is well browned, stirring once for even cooking. Serve topped with yogurt.

Easy to Make Frittatas

Ingredients
2 eggs beaten or 1/3 cup egg substitute
2 tablespoons mozzarella cheese
1 small roma tomato diced
1 green onion chopped
1 ounce chopped meat of choice
Salt and pepper to taste

Servings~ 👥
Cooking Time~ Seven Minutes
Pan to Use: Divided, Mini, or Base

Cooking Steps
A. Pre-heat and spray with cooking spray. In a medium bowl mix all ingredients.
B. Pour mixture in to cooking area and cook seven minutes.

Spaghetti Roll A Go-go

Ingredients
1 can spaghetti and meatballs
1 package refrigerator pizza dough
2 tablespoons shredded mozzarella cheese
2 tablespoons grated parmesan cheese, divided

Servings~ 👤👤
Cooking Time~ Ten Minutes
Pan to Use: Divided or Base

Cooking Steps
A. Pre-heat and spray with cooking spray. Heat spaghetti according to directions; drain any excess sauce and cool slightly. Remove dough from package and press out onto lightly floured surface; shape into 8 x 12 rectangles.
B. Mix spaghetti, mozzarella and 1 tablespoon of the parmesan. Spread spaghetti mixture onto dough; roll up jellyroll style. Cut into 4 equal sized portions
C. Spray all sides of rolls with cooking spray. Sprinkle tops with remaining parmesan. Place one roll in each cooking well; cook for 8-10 minutes, turning half way through to promote even browning. Repeat cooking process for second batch.

Beef Wellington's Pockets

Ingredients
1 sheet puff pastry, thawed
2 tablespoons canned mushroom pieces, drained
2 tablespoons hot dog onions and sauce from a jar
Dash Worcestershire sauce
4 thin slices rare deli roast beef

Homemade Horseradish Dipping Sauce
1 heaping tablespoon prepared horseradish
2 tablespoons mayonnaise
1 teaspoon heavy cream
Salt and pepper to taste

Servings~ 👤👤
Cooking Time~ Fourteen Minutes
Pan to Use: Divided or Base

Cooking Steps
A. Pre-heat and spray with cooking spray. Combine all dipping sauce ingredients; keep refrigerated until ready to use.
B. Roll out puff pastry dough according to general pocket maker instructions for making 2 pockets. Mix mushrooms, onion sauce and Worcestershire sauce. With dough in pocket maker spoon half of mushroom/onion mixture (discard excess liquid) into bottom section of dough circle; top with 2 slices roast beef. Close pocket maker; press down firmly to crimp pocket together.
C. Repeat steps to make second pocket. Place one pocket into each cooking well. Close cover; cook approximately 14 minutes until well browned. Serve hot with horseradish dipping sauce.

Liver & Onions

Ingredients
2 4ounce slices beef liver, washed, with any skin membranes removed
Seasoned salt to taste
2 tablespoons flour for dredging
½ onion, sliced very thin
1 pinch sugar
Dash Worcestershire sauce
2 tablespoons real bacon bit's
2 pats butter

Servings~ 👤👤
Cooking Time~ Five Minutes
Pan to Use: Divided or Base

Cooking Steps
A. Pre-heat and spray with cooking spray. Season both sides of liver with seasoned salt, then dredge liver in flour and set aside.
B. In a small bowl combine onion, sugar, Worcestershire sauce, and bacon bits. Divide onion mixture evenly between wells and cook two minutes. Open cover and place 1 pat of butter in each well, then place one piece of liver in each well, cook one to two more minutes on each side.

Mexican Burritos

Ingredients
2 8 inch flour tortillas
½ cup refried beans
½ cup beef cooked with taco seasoning or salsa
4 tablespoons grated cheddar or Mexican cheese
Salsa, guacamole and sour cream for garnish

Servings~
Cooking Time~ Five Minutes
Pan to Use: Divided or Base

Cooking Steps
A. Pre-heat and spray with cooking spray. Lay tortillas flat and spread each with half of beans. Top with meat and cheese. Fold in sides and roll; finished rolls will be thick and about 5 inches long.
B. Place rolls in unit and cook 5 minutes until brown and crispy. Serve with enchilada sauce, cheese, salsa, guacamole, and sour cream if desired.

RSG Steak & Cheese

Ingredients
1/4 tsp Olive oil
1/4 tsp Oregano
3-4 slices leftover Steak
2 slices Swiss cheese
1 tbsp Sautéed onions-optional
2 tbsp Sautéed mushrooms-optional
Salt and pepper -- to taste
2 slices bread

Servings~
Cooking Time~ Ten Minutes
Pan to Use: Divided or Base

Cooking Steps
A. Pre-heat and spray with cooking spray. Brush both sides of bread with oregano and oil. Stack the rest of ingredients and top with remaining bread.
B. Close cover and cook for 3-5 minutes.

Steak Pizzaialo Roll Up

Ingredients
2 Eye of Round thin Steaks
Fresh Spinach Leaves
Sliced mushrooms
Fat-Free Mozzarella cheese
Tomato sauce

Servings~
Cooking Time~ Seven Minutes
Pan to Use: Divided or Base

Cooking Steps
A. Pre-heat and spray with cooking spray. Lay steak out flat and place sauce and 10 spinach leaves then top with mushrooms and cheese.
B. Roll steak up and place seam side down in well. Cook for 7 minutes

Bread, Muffins, and Pastries

Cheesy Garlic Biscuits

Ingredients
2/3 baking mix, like Bisquick
1/3 cup milk
¼ cup shredded cheddar cheese
1 tablespoon melted butter
¼ teaspoon garlic powder

Servings~ 👤👤👤👤
Cooking Time~ Ten Minutes
Pan to Use: Divided or Base

Cooking Steps
A. Pre-heat and spray with cooking spray. Mix baking mix, milk and cheese and divide into each well. Close cover, bake 10 minutes.
B. Brush with garlic butter mixture and serve hot.

Homemade Dough

Ingredients
2¼ cups biscuit mix
½ cup milk

Servings~ 👤👤👤👤
Cooking Time~ Depends on recipe

Cooking Steps
A. Combine biscuit mix and milk and form into dough. Place the biscuit dough onto a lightly floured board or plastic wrap.
B. Sprinkle the top of the dough lightly with flour. Roll the dough into a 14 x 12 rectangle, press out 4 dough circles, and use the pocket maker.

Brown Sugar Muffins

Ingredients
1/2 cup quick oats
1/4 cup milk
1/3 cup brown sugar
2 tablespoons butter or margarine, softened
1 egg
1/2 cup flour mixed with
1 teaspoon baking powder
1/4 cup chopped walnuts or pecans

Servings~ 👤👤👤👤
Cooking Time~ Seven Minutes
Pan to Use: Divided, Mini or Base

Cooking Steps
A. Pre-heat and spray with cooking spray. Mixed together oats, milk and let stand for five minutes. Mix in sugar, butter and egg, stir, and then add flour, baking powder mixture.
B. Stir in nuts and divide mixture into each well. Close cover and bake 7 minutes.

Drizzle Frosting

Ingredients
1/3 cup powdered sugar
1 1/2 teaspoons warm water
2 drops vanilla extract

Servings~ 👤👤👤👤
Cooking Time~ Seven Minutes
Pan to Use: Divided, Mini or Base

Cooking Steps
A. Mix together until smooth and drizzle over warm pastry

Croissant Bread Pudding

Ingredients
3 cups chopped croissant pieces
1 (5 oz) can evaporated milk
1 egg, lightly beaten
1 teaspoon vanilla
1/4 teaspoon cinnamon
2 tablespoons dried cherries or raisins

Servings~ 👥
Cooking Time~ Ten Minutes
Pan to Use: Divided, Mini or Base

Cooking Steps
A. Pre-heat and spray with cooking spray. Combine all ingredients and allow mixture to sit until croissants soak up liquid, about two minutes.
B. Place half of mixture in each well, cook 10 minutes serve warm with whipped cream.

Chocolate Chip Muffins

Ingredients
1/2 cup baking mix (like Bisquick)
2 tablespoons sugar
1/2 cup milk
1 tablespoon melted butter
1 teaspoon vanilla
1/4 cup mini chocolate chips

Servings~ 👥
Cooking Time~ Eight Minutes
Pan to Use: Divided, Mini or Base

Cooking Steps
A. Pre-heat and spray with cooking spray. Combine mix, sugar, egg, milk, butter and vanilla, stir in chips, divide mixture into wells
B. Cook eight minutes or until nicely browned and toothpick inserted in center comes out clean.

Double Corn and Bacon Bread

Ingredients
1 (6 ounce) bag corn muffin mix
1 egg
2 tablespoons chopped onion
1/2 teaspoon salt
1/2 teaspoon garlic powder
1/4 cup milk
1/3 cup canned corn, drained
1 tablespoon oil
2 tablespoons shredded cheddar cheese
2 slices cooked bacon, chopped

Servings~ 👥
Cooking Time~ Eight Minutes
Pan to Use: Divided or Base

Cooking Steps
A. Pre-heat and spray with cooking spray. Combined all ingredients
B. Place half of mixture in each well. Cook 8 minutes or until toothpick inserted in center comes out clean.

Crusty Dinner Rolls

Ingredients
1 Package dinner rolls

Servings~ 👥
Cooking Time~ 1 Minutes
Pan to Use: Divided or Base

Cooking Steps
A. Place 2 small or 1 large dinner roll in each well.
B. Cook 1 minute until crusty on the outside and warm on the inside.

Pesto Crescent Rolls

Ingredients
1 tube refrigerated crescent rolls
2 tablespoons prepared pesto
2 tablespoons parmesan cheese

Servings~ 👤👤👤👤
Cooking Time~ Eight Minutes
Pan to Use: Divided or Base

Cooking Steps
A. Pre-heat and spray with cooking spray. Open Crescent rolls and separate into four rectangles. Press perforations firmly to seal, to make solid rectangles.
B. Mix pesto and cheese. Spread a thin layer of pesto mixture onto each rectangle. Roll up each rectangle, jellyroll style.
C. Place one roll into each well and cook about 8 minutes or until rolls are golden brown, turn if necessary, for even browning.

Strawberry Chocolate Kiss Crescents

Ingredients
1 tube refrigerated crescent rolls
Strawberry preserves
8 Hershey's chocolate kisses (substitute chocolate chips, if desired)
Can vanilla frosting
Pink and white candy sprinkles

Servings~ 👤👤👤👤 👤👤👤👤
Cooking Time~ Ten Minutes
Pan to Use: Divided or Base

Cooking Steps
A. Pre-heat and spray with cooking spray. Separate crescent rolls and lay on wax paper or cutting board. Spread a thin layer of preserves on each piece of dough and top with Hershey kisses. Gently fold up and pinch ends together to seal otherwise melted chocolate will seep out.
B. Place two roles in each well, close cover, cook 8 to 10 minutes until brown, turning half way through. Repeat with second batch.

Spicy Hush Puppy Sticks

Ingredients
1 6 ounce package corn muffin mix
1/3 cup canned corn niblets, drained
1 tablespoon chopped canned jalapeno peppers
1 tablespoon chopped pimentos
2 tablespoons shredded cheddar cheese
1/4 cup milk
1 egg
1 teaspoon liquid margarine or corn oil
1 teaspoon spicy seasoned salt
Maple syrup for dipping (optional)

Servings~ 👤👤👤👤 👤👤
Cooking Time~ Ten Minutes
Pan to Use: Divided or Base

Cooking Steps
A. Pre-heat and spray with cooking spray. Mix together all ingredients except maple syrup. Divide batter evenly between wells
B. Cook 10 minutes or until well brown (cakes are done when a toothpick inserted in center comes out clean.) Let cool five minutes and gently remove from wells. Slice each hush puppy lengthwise into three sticks. Serve with maple syrup for dipping.

Refrigerator Bran Muffins

Ingredients
1 1/2 cups whole bran cereal
1/2 cup boiling water
1 egg
1 cup buttermilk
1/3 cup salad oil
1 tablespoon molasses or honey
1 1/4 cups flour
1/2 cup sugar
1/4 teaspoon salt
1 1/4 teaspoons soda
1 cup chopped apple or raisins or dates or nuts, or any combination

Servings~ 👤 x 12
Cooking Time~ Twelve Minutes
Pan to Use: Divided, Mini or Base

Prep Steps
1. In large bowl with cover pour boiling water over cereal and stir to moisten. Set aside to cool.
2. Mix together dry ingredients in small bowl. Place liquid ingredients in shaker, mix and add to cereal. Stir together, add dry ingredients and mix until combined. Do not over mix. Fold in fruit
3. Cover and bake or refrigerate covered up to 2 weeks

Cooking Steps
A. Pre-heat and spray with cooking spray.
B. Place 1/3 cup batter in each well, close lid and bake 10 to 12 minutes. Allow to cool 5 to 10 minutes before serving

British Scones

Ingredients
2/3 cup Bisquick baking mix
1/3 cup half and half
1 tablespoon melted butter
2 tablespoons white sugar
2 tablespoons dried Conant's
2 tablespoons fresh grated orange rind

Servings~ 👤👤👤👤
Cooking Time~ Ten Minutes
Pan to Use: Divided or Base

Cooking Steps
A. Pre-heat and spray with cooking spray. Mix together all ingredients until well blended. Knead on a lightly floured surface until dough is no longer sticky shaped into a 5 Inch circle and cut into four wedges.
B. Place 2 wedges into each cooking well. Close cover, bake for 10 minutes. Serve warm, spread with butter and a drizzle of honey.

Beer Muffins

Ingredients
2 cups Bisquick baking mix
1 tablespoon sugar
6 ounces beer (1/2 can)

Servings~ 👤👤👤👤 👤👤👤👤
Cooking Time~ Nine Minutes
Pan to Use: Divided, Mini or Base

Cooking Steps
A. Pre-heat and spray with cooking spray. Mix all ingredients together and spoon 1/4 of batter into each well
B. Close cover, bake 8 to 10 minutes. Repeat with remaining batter

Muffin Mix

Ingredients
1 pouch (6.4 to 6.5 ounces) or one small box (7 to 8.5 ounces) any type muffin mix

Servings~ 👤👤
Cooking Time~ Eight Minutes
Pan to Use: Divided, Mini or Base

Cooking Steps
A. Mix muffin mix according to package directions. Divide batter between two wells, cook 6 to 8 minutes.

Pepper Jack Corn Cakes

Ingredients
1 package corn muffin mix (about 6-8.5 ounces)
2 tablespoons red pepper jelly
1 tablespoon shredded pepper jack cheese

Servings~
Cooking Time~ Ten Minutes
Pan to Use: Divided, Mini or Base

Cooking Steps
A. Spray cooking wells with cooking spray but do not Pre-heat. Prepare corn muffins according to package directions. Add jelly and cheese.
B. Divide batter evenly between cooking wells. Close cover; Plug in unit and cook 10 minutes, or until toothpick comes out clean when inserted into center.

Parmesan Dinner Muffins

Ingredients
1 1/3 cups baking mix (like Bisquick)
2 teaspoons sugar
1 tablespoon minced green onion
1/4 teaspoon each dried oregano, dill and basil
1 tablespoon butter, melted
1 egg
1/2 cup milk
2 tablespoons of parmesan cheese

Servings~
Cooking Time~ Ten Minutes
Pan to Use: Divided, Mini or Base

Cooking Steps
A. Pre-heat and spray with cooking spray. Combine baking mix, sugar, onion and spices in bowl and stir to mix. Add butter, egg and milk and mix well. Spoon 1/4 of mixture into each well, sprinkle top lightly with parmesan cheese
B. Close cover, bake for 9 to 10 minutes. Remove first 2 muffins, and repeat with remaining batter.

Parmesan Bagel Bake

Ingredients
2 eggs
1 tablespoon tarragon
Pinch of dried red pepper flakes
Salt to taste
2 teaspoons parmesan cheese
2 tablespoons shredded Provolone cheese
2 mini onion bagels split

Servings~
Cooking Time~ Ten Minutes
Pan to Use: Divided or Base

Cooking Steps
A. Pre-heat and spray with cooking spray. Place one half of each mini bagel into well.
B. Beat egg and next 4 ingredients with fork in a small bowl. Pour equal amounts onto each bagel half. Top each half with 1 tablespoon shredded provolone and other half of bagel. Close cover and bake for 10 minutes

Easy Garlic Refrigerator Crescent Rolls

Ingredients
1 can refrigerator crescent rolls
1/2 tablespoon parsley flakes
1 tablespoon parmesan cheese
1/2 teaspoon garlic powder

Servings~
Cooking Time~ Twelve Minutes
Pan to Use: Divided or Base

Cooking Steps
A. Pre-heat and spray with cooking spray. Separate 1/2 can of crescents into wedges, lightly spray with cooking spray and sprinkle with seasoning. Roll according to package directions. Place 2 crescents in each well at an angle so they fit.
B. Close cover, bake 10 minutes, and flip over after 6 minutes to promote even browning. Repeat with other 4 if desired or refrigerate for later use.

Hiker's Danish

Ingredients
1 tube refrigerator crescent rolls
8 tablespoons berry granola cereal
2 tablespoons chocolate chips
2 tablespoons cinnamon plus 2 teaspoons sugar

Servings~
Cooking Time~ Twelve Minutes
Pan to Use: Divided or Base

Cooking Steps
A. Pre-heat and spray with cooking spray. Unroll crescent rolls and divide into 4 rectangles but do not separate into triangles. Press perforations so each rectangle remains one piece.
B. For each Danish, top crescent triangle with 2 tablespoons granola, 1/2 tablespoon chocolate chips and 1/2 tablespoon cinnamon sugar; leaving about 1/4-inch border around the rectangle with no topping on it. Roll up rectangle jellyroll style. Crimp sides of rolls flat with fingers to seal in filling
C. Spray top of Danish with cooking spray and sprinkle with one teaspoon cinnamon sugar. Repeat process for other 3 triangles. Cook 2 rolls at a time for 10-12 minutes until rolls are well browned

Pepperoni Biscuits

Ingredients
2 individual-portion refrigerator home-style biscuits
2 teaspoons parmesan cheese
8 thin slices pepperoni

Servings~
Cooking Time~ Ten Minutes
Pan to Use: Divided or Base

Cooking Steps
A. Pre-heat and spray with cooking spray. Cut each biscuit in half like you would a roll, but do not slice all the way through. Pile 4 slices of pepperoni into each biscuit and top each with one teaspoon parmesan cheese.
B. Close biscuit and place one biscuit in each well. Close cover and bake for 8-10 minutes until golden brown.

Low Sugar Low Fat Banana Muffins

Ingredients
2/3 cup flour
1/4 cup Splenda
1/2 teaspoon baking powder
1/4 teaspoon baking soda
1 large mashed banana
1 1/2 teaspoons canola oil
1/4 cup low fat buttermilk
1 teaspoon vanilla
2 tablespoons chopped walnuts

Servings~
Cooking Time~ Eight Minutes
Pan to Use: Divided, Mini or Base

Cooking Steps
A. Pre-heat and spray with cooking spray. Mix dry ingredients together and set aside. Mix oil, buttermilk and banana in bowl, add vanilla, then fold in dry ingredients and nuts until just blended
B. Divide mixture into four parts. Cook 2 at a time for 7 to 8 minutes until brown.

Herb Cheese Biscuits

Ingredients
2 individual-portion refrigerator home-style biscuits
1 teaspoon Herbes de Provence
Molly McButter Natural Cheese Flavor Sprinkles

Servings~ 👥
Cooking Time~ Ten Minutes
Pan to Use: Divided or Base

Cooking Steps
A. Pre-heat and spray with cooking spray. Cut each biscuit in half like you would a roll, but do not slice all the way through. Sprinkle one side of open biscuit generously with cheese sprinkles. Close biscuit and sprinkle with 1/2 teaspoon Herbes de Provence
B. Place one biscuit in each well and bake 8-10 minutes until golden brown.

Sour Cream Muffins

Ingredients
1 cup Bisquick baking mix
1/2 cup sour cream
1/4 cup melted butter or margarine (1/2 stick)

Servings~ 👥
Cooking Time~ Ten Minutes
Pan to Use: Divided, Mini or Base

Cooking Steps
A. Pre-heat and spray with cooking spray. Mix all ingredients together, divide into wells.
B. Close cover and bake 10 minutes.

Pumpkin Muffins

Ingredients
2/3 cup Heart Smart Bisquick
1/2 cup canned pumpkin
3 tablespoons Splenda sweetener
1/4 cup reduced fat milk
1 tablespoon vegetable oil
1 1/2 tablespoons pumpkin pie spice
1/4 teaspoon cinnamon
2 tablespoons chopped pecans

Servings~ 👥👥👥
Cooking Time~ Eight Minutes
Pan to Use: Divided, Mini or Base

Cooking Steps
A. Pre-heat and spray with no stick cooking spray. Mix all ingredients together and spoon 1/3 of batter into each well, saving last 1/3 for a second batch
B. Close cover and bake 8 minutes until brown and puffed. Repeat with last 1/3 of batter using only 1 well. Cut each muffin in half making 6 muffins total.

Lite Biscuits and Gravy

Ingredients
2 patties reduced fat turkey sausage, chopped finely
1/2 cup skim milk
1/2 cup water
1 tablespoon flour
1/4 teaspoon pepper
2/3 cup Heart Smart Bisquick
1/2 cup reduced fat buttermilk or skim milk

Servings~ 👥
Cooking Time~ Ten Minutes
Pan to Use: Divided or Base

Cooking Steps
A. Pre-heat and spray with cooking spray. In small bowl mix baking mix and milk just until blended and spoon half of mixture into each well. Close cover and cook 10 minutes.
B. Meanwhile, place sausage into small saucepan and heat over medium heat for 2 minutes. Place water, milk and flour into shaker. Shake to blend and add to sausage, stirring until thickened.
C. To serve, split biscuits open and cover with gravy.

Refrigerator Sweet Muffins

Ingredients
2 1/4 cups flour
1/2 cup brown sugar
1/4 cup sugar
2 teaspoons baking powder
1/2 teaspoon baking soda
1/2 teaspoon salt
1 cup buttermilk
1/3 cup oil
1 teaspoon vanilla
2 eggs

Servings~ 🕴🕴🕴🕴
Cooking Time~ Ten Minutes
Pan to Use: Divided, Mini or Base

Cooking Steps
A. Combine dry ingredients in large bowl with cover and blend well. Combine liquids in shaker, mix, add to dry ingredients and stir until just moistened
B. Cover and refrigerate up to 1 week. To cook place 2/3 cup of batter in small bowl, add 1 of the following flavor ingredients.
   1. **Raisin spice**: fold in 1/4 cup raisins, 1/4 teaspoon Cinnamon, dash of nutmeg, Allspice, cloves.
   2. **Maple Walnut**: fold in 1/4 cup chopped walnuts and 1 tablespoon. Maple syrup.
   3. **Pina Colada**: fold in 1/4 cup each drained crushed Pineapple; coconut.
   4. **Chocolate Chip**: fold in 1/4 cup chocolate chips.
   5. **Mixed Fruit**: fold in 1/4 cup chopped mixed dried Fruit like raisins, dates, cranberries, cherries
C. Pre-heat and spray with cooking spray. Divide batter into wells. Close lid and bake for 10 minutes. Cool for 5 minutes before serving.

Garlic Spread

Ingredients
1/4 cup butter or margarine, softened
1 tablespoon minced fresh garlic
2 tablespoons parmesan cheese
1 teaspoon dry parsley

Servings~
Cooking Time~

Cooking Steps
1. Mix until well blended

Kristin's Cornbread

Ingredients
1/2 cup flour
1/2 cup cornmeal
2 tablespoons sugar
2 teaspoons baking powder
1/4 teaspoon salt
1 egg
1/2 cup milk
1 tablespoon vegetable oil

Servings~ 🕴🕴🕴🕴
Cooking Time~ Eight Minutes
Pan to Use: Divided, Mini or Base

Cooking Steps
A. Pre-heat and spray with cooking spray. Combine dry ingredients in small bowl. Beat egg, milk and oil in shaker. Add to dry ingredients, until just moistened
B. Divide into wells. Close cover, cook for 7 to 8 minutes until browned.

Cranberry Walnut Muffins

Ingredients
3/4 cup Bisquick baking mix
1/3 cup milk
3 tablespoons dried cranberries
3 tablespoons walnuts, chopped
1 tablespoon sugar

Servings~ 👤👤
Cooking Time~ Ten Minutes
Pan to Use: Divided, Mini or Base

Cooking Steps
A. Pre-heat and spray with cooking spray. Combine all ingredients, divide into wells.
B. Close cover; cook for 10 minutes.

Almond Bread

Ingredients
3/4 cup Bisquick baking mix
1/4 cup sugar
1/4 teaspoon baking soda
1 egg
1/4 cup buttermilk
1/3 cup toasted almonds

Servings~ 👤👤
Cooking Time~ Ten Minutes
Pan to Use: Divided, Mini or Base

Cooking Steps
A. Pre-heat and spray with cooking spray. Mix sugar and soda into Bisquick, add egg and buttermilk and blend. Stir in almonds, divide batter into wells.
B. Close cover and bake 8 to 10 minutes.

Bacon Cheese Muffins

Ingredients
1 3/4 cups flour
1/4 cup sugar
1 tablespoon baking powder
1 egg, beaten
3/4 cup milk
1/2 cup real bacon bits
1 cup shredded cheddar cheese
1/2 cup cereal nuggets, like grape nuts

Servings~ 👤👤👤👤 👤👤👤👤
Cooking Time~ eight minutes
Pan to Use: Divided, Mini or Base

Cooking Steps
A. Pre-heat and spray with cooking spray. Mix together flour, sugar and baking powder. Put egg and milk in shaker and blend, stir into dry ingredients. Add cheese, bacon and cereal, stirring until just moistened – batter will be lumpy.
B. Spoon 1/4 of mixture into wells and close cover. Bake 8 minutes then repeat with remaining batter.

Hawaiian Cornbread

Ingredients
1 pouch (6.4 to 6.5 ounces) or one small box (7 to 8.5
Ounces) corn muffin mix
1/2 cup well-drained crushed pineapple

Servings~ 👤👤👤👤
Cooking Time~ Ten Minutes
Pan to Use: Divided, Mini or Base

Cooking Steps
A. Mix corn muffin mix according to package directions. Fold in pineapple.
B. Fill each well with 1/2-cup batter. Cook 8-10 minutes or until toothpick comes out clean.

Mexican Cornbread

Ingredients
1 pouch (6.4 to 6.5 ounces) or one small box (7 to 8.5 Ounces) corn muffin mix
1/2 cup salsa

Servings~ 👤👤👤👤
Cooking Time~ Ten Minutes
Pan to Use: Divided, Mini or Base

Cooking Steps
A. Mix corn muffin mix according to package directions Reduce liquid in package directions to 1/4 cup. Fold in Salsa.
B. Fill each well with 1/2-cup batter. Cook 8-10 minutes or until toothpick comes out clean.

Cheese and Spinach Muffins

Ingredients
1 cup Bisquick baking mix
1/3 cup milk
1 egg
1/4 cup fresh spinach, chopped
1/4 cup shredded Swiss cheese
2 tablespoons parmesan cheese
1 tablespoon chopped green onions

Servings~ 👤👤
Cooking Time~ Ten Minutes
Pan to Use: Divided, Mini or Base

Cooking Steps
A. Pre-heat and spray with cooking spray. Mix all ingredients together, divide into wells.
B. Close cover, bake 10 minutes.

Glazed Strawberry Filled Gems

Ingredients
1 cup Bisquick baking mix
1 tablespoon sugar
1/4 cup melted butter or margarine
1/3 cup milk
1 tablespoon of strawberry preserves

Vanilla Glaze Recipe
1/4 cup powdered sugar
1 1/2 teaspoons warm water
1/4 teaspoon vanilla

Servings~ 👤👤👤👤
Cooking Time~ Ten Minutes
Pan to Use: Divided, Mini or Base

Cooking Steps
A. Pre-heat and spray with cooking spray. Mix together Bisquick and sugar, add butter and milk, stir until blended. Spread 1/4 of mixture in bottom of each well, spoon a line of jam down the center of each and top with remaining batter.
B. Close cover and cook 8 to 10 minutes until golden brown. Cut each cake in half to form 4 triangles. Glaze with vanilla glaze

Cherry Banana Loaf

Ingredients
8 Maraschino cherries
1 tablespoon cherry juice
2 tablespoons butter
1/3 cup brown sugar
1 egg
1 small ripe banana, mashed
3/4 cup flour
1 teaspoon baking powder
1/4 teaspoon salt
1/4 cup chopped nuts

Servings~ 👤👤👤👤
Cooking Time~ ten minutes
Pan to Use: Divided, Mini or Base

Cooking Steps
A. Pre-heat and spray with cooking spray. Combine flour, baking powder and salt; set aside. In a medium mixing bowl, combine butter, brown sugar, egg and cherry juice. Add flour mixture and mashed banana. Stir in cherries and nuts
B. Divide into wells. Close cover; cook 8 to 10 minutes until brown.

Calico Bell Pepper Muffins

Ingredients
2 tablespoons each finely chopped red and green pepper
2 tablespoons butter or margarine
1 cup flour
1 tablespoon sugar
1/2 teaspoon baking powder
1/2 teaspoon salt
1/4 teaspoon dried basil
1/2 cup milk
1 egg

Servings~ 👤👤👤👤
Cooking Time~ Eight Minutes
Pan to Use: Divided, Mini or Base

Cooking Steps
A. Pre-heat and spray with cooking spray. In a small skillet sauté bell pepper in butter until softened, about 2 to 3 minutes. Combine flour, sugar, baking powder, salt and basil in a mixing bowl. Mix egg, milk, peppers and any liquid in skillet in shaker, mix, add to dry ingredients and stir until moistened.
B. Divide into wells of unit. Close cover cook 7 to 8 minutes until brown.

Carrot Muffins with Cream Cheese Icing

Ingredients
Muffins
3/4 cup Bisquick baking mix
1/3 cup milk
1/4 cup shredded carrots
1 tablespoon Splenda brown sugar baking mix
3 tablespoons chopped pecans (reserve 1 tablespoon for garnish)
1 teaspoon pumpkin spice
Icing
2 oz. cream cheese, softened
1 1/2 tablespoons sweet butter, softened
1/2 cup confectioners' sugar
1/2 teaspoon vanilla extract

Servings~
Cooking Time~ Twelve Minutes
Pan to Use: Divided, Mini or Base

Cooking Steps
A. Pre-heat and spray with cooking spray. Combine all muffin ingredients except 1 tablespoon pecans; mix well.
B. Divide mixture evenly between wells. Close cover and cook 10-12 minutes, until golden brown.
C. Let cake cool completely before removing from wells. Fold all icing ingredients together. Spread icing on cooled muffins and top each muffin with 1/2 tablespoon reserved pecans

Onion Poppy Seed Rolls

Ingredients
1 tube refrigerator crescent rolls
1 medium-sized onion, sliced very thin
1 tablespoon sugar
1 teaspoon Worcestershire sauce
2 oz. butter
2 tablespoons poppy seeds

Servings~ 👤👤
Cooking Time~ eight minutes
Pan to Use: Divided or Base

Cooking Steps
A. Melt butter in small fry pan over low heat; add onions and sugar. Sauté until onions are translucent, being careful not to burn them. Mix in Worcestershire sauce; remove from heat and let cool. Separate crescent rolls into triangles as directed.
B. Spread a thin layer of onion mixture onto each triangle. Sprinkle with poppy seeds. Roll up each crescent, starting from bottom (wide) end of triangle
C. Bake in batches, 6-8 minutes, turning if necessary until rolls are golden brown.

Apple Express Muffinwich

Ingredients
1 split English muffin, lightly toasted
1 tablespoon butter
2 tablespoons orange marmalade
2 slices ready-to-serve Canadian bacon
2 slices cheddar cheese
3-4 thin apple slices (cored and peeled)

Servings~ 👤
Cooking Time~ Ten Minutes
Pan to Use: Divided or Base

Cooking Steps
A. Pre-heat and spray with cooking spray. Butter toasted English muffin and spread both sides with marmalade. Assemble sandwich on 1/2 muffin in the following order: 1 slice cheese, bacon, apple, 1 slice cheese. Top with other muffin half.
Spray outside of muffinwich with cooking spray. Cut sandwich in half and place half in each well. Grill approximately 10 minutes; flip after 5 minutes for even browning.

Pumpkin Apple Muffins

Ingredients
1/2 cup flour
2 tablespoons sugar
1/4 cup pumpkin
1 teaspoon pumpkin pie spice
1/4 teaspoon baking soda
1/4 teaspoon baking powder
2 tablespoons vegetable oil
1/2 small apple, peeled and chopped

Servings~ 👤👤👤👤
Cooking Time~ Eight Minutes
Pan to Use: Divided, Mini or Base

Cooking Steps
A. Pre-heat and spray with cooking spray. Mix dry ingredients in bowl. Add pumpkin, oil and apple and stir until combined
B. Spoon half of mixture in each side. Close cover and cook for 7 to 8 minutes.

Cheese Stuffed Garlic Breadsticks

Ingredients
1 box refrigerator garlic breadsticks
5 mozzarella string cheese sticks
Tomato sauce for dipping, heated in microwave

Servings~ 👤👤
Cooking Time~ twelve minutes
Pan to Use: Base

Cooking Steps
A. Unroll breadstick dough onto clean flat surface. Spread garlic spread evenly over dough, as directed. Cut dough at every other separation so that you have five double stick pieces. Put one mozzarella stick on each double dough stick. Fold dough over and seal well with fingertips.
B. Spray outside of breadsticks lightly with cooking spray. Bake one stick per well for 10-12 minutes until nicely browned, turning once during cooking to promote even browning; cheese should be soft and warm.

Foccacia Breads

Ingredients
1 almost instant pizza dough
1 teaspoon olive oil
Parmesan cheese
Filling of your choice: sliced olives, fresh Italian herbs, or roasted garlic

Servings~ 👤
Cooking Time~ Seven Minutes
Pan to Use: Base

Cooking Steps
A. Pre-heat and spray with cooking spray. Oil dough and knead filling of your choice into the dough. Poll dough in oil to coat and flatten.
B. Place in cooking base, sprinkle with garlic, basil, and parmesan cheese. Cook for 5 – 7 minutes.

Baby Elephant Ears

Ingredients
1 can refrigerated crescent rolls
Butter
Cinnamon sugar

Servings~ 👥
Cooking Time~ Two Minutes
Pan to Use: Base, Divided Pan

Cooking Steps
A. Pre-heat and spray with cooking spray. Separate crescent rolls into triangles. Brush each triangle with melted butter and sprinkle with cinnamon and sugar.
B. Close lid and cook for approximately 2-3 minutes or until golden brown.

Banana Walnut Bread

Ingredients
2/3 cup of Heart Smart Bisquick
1 Tbs. of Splenda
1/2 a banana - chopped
handful of chopped walnuts
1/3 cup skim milk
brown sugar

Servings~ 👥
Cooking Time~ Ten Minutes
Pan to Use: Base, Divided Pan

Cooking Steps
A. Pre-heat and spray with cooking spray. Mix all ingredients except brown sugar.
B. Close lid and cook for approximately 2-3 minutes or until golden brown.

Mini Parmesan Bites

Ingredients
1 Can refrigerated Biscuits
2 Tbs. Butter
1/8 tsp Garlic salt
1/3 Cup Parmesan cheese

Servings~ 👥
Cooking Time~ Ten Minutes
Pan to Use: Base, Divided Pan

Cooking Steps
A. Pre-heat and spray with cooking spray. Mix all ingredients except brown sugar.
B. Divide mixture between wells and sprinkle with brown sugar. Cook ten minutes

Breakfast

Heavenly Ricotta Pancakes

Ingredients
2/3 cup baking mix, like Bisquick
1/3 cup milk
¼ cup ricotta cheese
1 egg, beaten

Servings~
Cooking Time~ Nine Minutes
Pan to Use: Divided, Mini or Base

Cooking Steps
A. Pre-heat and spray with non stick spray. Mix all ingredients together and divide between wells.
B. Close cover and cook 9 minutes. Serve with butter and fruit syrup or fruit puree

Yesterday's Donuts Today's French Toast

Ingredients
2 1/2 cups of crumbled donuts
1 egg, beaten
3/4 cup milk
1/2 teaspoon vanilla
Cooking spray

Servings~
Cooking Time~ Eight Minutes
Pan to Use: Divided, Mini or Base

Cooking Steps
A. Combine all ingredients. Allow the mixture to stand for about a minute, or until the donut crumbs soften and soak up most of the liquid.
B. Spray wells lightly with cooking spray. Spoon half of the mixture into each well. Cook 8 minutes.

Strawberry Stuffed French Toast

Ingredients
2 Tablespoons egg substitute or 1/2 egg, lightly beaten
1/4 cup milk
1 teaspoon vanilla
1/4 teaspoon cinnamon
3 slices bread
2 tablespoons strawberry flavored cream cheese
Cooking spray

Servings~
Cooking Time~ Seven Minutes
Pan to Use: Divided or Base

Cooking Steps
A. Combine egg, milk, vanilla and cinnamon in small bowl. Spread half of cream cheese on one slice of bread, top with second slice. Spread remaining cream cheese and add another piece of bread to make triple-decker sandwich. Dip both sides and all ends of sandwich in egg mixture and allow it to soak in. With large serrated knife, cut sandwich in half, forming two triangles.
B. Spray wells lightly with cooking spray. Place one triangle in each well. Close cover and cook 7 minutes. Sprinkle with powdered sugar and serve with strawberry syrup.

Fruit and Almond Coffee Cakes

Servings~ 👤👤👤👤
Cooking Time~ Six Minutes
Pan to Use: Divided, Mini or Base

Ingredients
1/2 cup baking mix (like Bisquick), firmly packed
2 tablespoons sugar
2 tablespoons sour cream
1 egg, lightly beaten
1 teaspoon almond extract
Cooking spray

Topping Mixture
2 ounces almond paste, broken into pea-size pieces
4 tablespoons chopped dried fruits such as apricots,
Cherries or mixed berries
4 tablespoons sliced almonds
2 tablespoons sugar

Cooking Steps
A. Combine batter ingredients (batter should be very thick). In another bowl, combine topping mixture and reserve. Spray wells lightly with cooking spray. Place 2 tablespoons batter in each well. Spread to barely cover bottom of wells.
B. Cook 1 minute. Cover top of each cake with 1/4 each of almond paste, fruits, nuts and sugar. Cook 5 minutes more or until toothpick inserted in center comes out clean. Cool about 1 minute before removing. Repeat cooking process with remaining cakes.

Granola French Toast

Servings~ 👤👤
Cooking Time~ Nine Minutes
Pan to Use: Divided or Base

Ingredients
2 Tablespoons egg substitute or 1/2 egg, lightly beaten
1/4 cup milk
1 teaspoon vanilla
2 slices English muffin bread or thick-sliced bread
1/2 cup granola cereal, crushed
Cooking spray

Cooking Steps
A. Combine egg, milk and vanilla in small bowl. Dip each bread slice in mixture and allow it to soak into bread. Coat both sides of slices with cereal.
B. Spray wells lightly with cooking spray. Place one slice in each well. Cook six minutes. Serve with honey or maple syrup.

Cinnamon Rolls

Servings~ 👤👤👤👤 👤👤👤👤
Cooking Time~ Six Minutes
Pan to Use: Divided or Base

Ingredients
1 can (12.4 ounces) refrigerated cinnamon rolls
Cooking spray

Cooking Steps
A. Spray top of wells with cooking spray. Place 2 cinnamon rolls in each well.
B. Cook 6 minutes. Repeat with remaining 4 rolls or refrigerate for 24 hours. Frost and serve.

English Muffin French Toast

Ingredients
2 English muffins, split and halved
1 egg
1/4 cup milk
1/2 cup vanilla
1/4 teaspoon cinnamon
2 slices Canadian bacon

Servings~ 👥
Cooking Time~ Six Minutes
Pan to Use: Divided or Base

Cooking Steps
A. Pre-heat and spray with cooking spray. Place egg, milk, vanilla and cinnamon in shaker and mix. Pour into flat dish, sandwich the ham between English muffin halves and place in bowl with egg mixture until all egg is absorbed.
B. To cook place 1/2 muffin sandwich in each well, close cover and cook 5 to 7 minutes, turning half way through cooking to promote even browning repeat with other muffin.

Fruit Syrup

Ingredients
1 small box Jell-O or other flavored gelatin 1 cup water
1/2 cup sugar
2 tablespoons cornstarch

Servings~
Cooking Time~

Cooking Steps
A. Mix ingredients together in a small saucepan, bring to a roaring boil. Allow to cool until slightly thickened. Serve over pancakes or waffles, while still warm. This will thicken upon setting and cooling so you may wish to make half batch at a time.

Fluffy Pancakes with Fruity Syrup

Ingredients
1 cup Bisquick baking mix
1/2 cup milk
1 egg

Servings~ 👥
Cooking Time~ Seven Minutes
Pan to Use: Divided, Mini or Base

Cooking Steps
A. Pre-heat and spray with cooking spray. Put all ingredients in shaker and mix well.
B. Fill wells with batter, close cover and cook 7 minutes until done in center. Serve with fruity syrup (see recipe above) for dipping

Artichoke Omelet

Ingredients
3 eggs
1 tablespoon milk or cream
2 artichoke hearts, diced
2 ounces salsa, divided
1/4 cup shredded jack cheese, divided
Salt and pepper to taste

Servings~ 👥
Cooking Time~ Nine Minutes
Pan to Use: Divided or Base

Cooking Steps
A. Pre-heat and spray with cooking spray. Mix eggs, milk and seasonings in shaker and divide into wells. Mix artichokes with half the salsa and spoon in a line along center of egg in each well. Top with half the cheese
B. Close cover and cook 8 to 9 minutes until set. To serve, garnish with remaining salsa and cheese

Apple Sausage Pancake

Ingredients
4 brown and serve sausage links
2/3 cup baking mix, like Bisquick
1/3 cup milk
1 egg
1/4 cup finely chopped apple
Maple syrup

Servings~ 👥
Cooking Time~ Eight Minutes
Pan to Use: Divided or Base

Cooking Steps
A. Pre-heat and spray with cooking spray. Place two sausages in each well. Mix all other ingredients except maple syrup in shaker.
B. Pour half of batter in each well over sausage. Close cover and cook 8 minutes until pancake is puffed and done. Serve with maple syrup.

Mini Breakfast Casserole

Ingredients
12 tater tots, thawed
2 eggs, beaten
1/4 cup cheddar cheese, shredded
1 tablespoon real bacon bits

Servings~ 👥
Cooking Time~ Six Minutes
Pan to Use: Divided or Base

Cooking Steps
A. Do not Pre-heat but spray wells with cooking spray. Place 6 tator tots in each well, close cover and pre-heat for two to three minutes.
B. Open cover and place one beaten egg, half the cheese and bacon in each well, over potatoes. Close cover and cook six minutes until egg is set.

Zucchini Frittata

Ingredients
1 small zucchini, thinly sliced
1 tablespoon minced onion
1/2 cup baking mix, like Bisquick
2 tablespoons salad oil
2 tablespoons parmesan cheese
2 eggs
1 teaspoon dried oregano
1 tablespoon dried parsley
1/2 teaspoon garlic powder

Servings~ 👥
Cooking Time~ Ten Minutes
Pan to Use: Divided or Base

Cooking Steps
A. Pre-heat and spray with cooking spray. In bowl, beat eggs lightly with seasoning, add baking mix, oil, zucchini and cheese. Sir until blended.
B. Divide mixture between the wells close cover and bake 8 to 10 minutes until set and lightly browned

Mac and Cheese Omelet

Ingredients
1 package easy microwave macaroni and cheese
2 eggs, beaten with two tablespoons milk
1 wiener, cut into thin slices

Servings~ 👥
Cooking Time~ Six Minutes
Pan to Use: Divided or Base

Cooking Steps
A. Pre-heat and spray with cooking spray. Make macaroni and cheese according to package directions. Stir in Wiener slices. Place eggs and milk in shaker and mix well.
B. Divide into wells; add half of macaroni mixture to each well. Close cover and cook 6 minutes.

Biscuits and Gravy

Ingredients
2 patties of brown and serve sausage, diced finely
1/2 cup milk
1/2 cup water
1 tablespoon flour
1/4 teaspoon pepper
2/3 cup baking mix, like Bisquick
1/3 cup buttermilk or regular milk

Servings~ 👥
Cooking Time~ Ten Minutes
Pan to Use: Divided or Base

Cooking Steps
A. Pre-heat and spray with cooking spray. In a small bowl, mix baking mix and milk just until blended. Spoon half of mixture into each well. Close lid and cook 10 minutes
B. Meanwhile, place the sausage into small skillet and heat over medium heat for two minutes. Place water, milk and flour into shaker, shake to blend and add to sausage, stirring until thickened. To serve, split biscuits open, butter lightly as desired and cover with gravy.

Bagel French Toast

Ingredients
1 large bagel, split
1 ounce cream cheese, flavored or regular
1 egg
2 tablespoons milk
1/2 tablespoon sugar
Dash each vanilla and cinnamon

Servings~ 👥
Cooking Time~ Seven Minutes
Pan to Use: Divided or Base

Cooking Steps
A. Pre-heat and spray with cooking spray. Place egg, milk, sugar, vanilla and cinnamon in shaker and mix well. Pour into small deep bowl. Spread bagel with cream cheese, placed together like a sandwich and cut in half. Soak halves in egg mixture for several minutes, turning if necessary
B. Place one bagel half in each well close cover and cook 5 to 7 minutes. Serve with extra cream cheese and fruit

Apple Bacon Brunchers

Ingredients
2/3 cup Bisquick baking mix
1/2 cup milk
1 egg
1/2 cup shredded cheese
1/2 small apple, peeled, cored and thinly sliced
1 tablespoon sugar
2 tablespoons real bacon bits

Servings~ 👥
Cooking Time~ Ten Minutes
Pan to Use: Divided, Mini or Base

Cooking Steps
A. Pre-heat and spray with cooking spray. Place half of apple slices and sugar in each well, close cover and cook for 2 minutes. Mix Bisquick, milk and egg and cheese together. Open lid, divide batter into wells, pouring over apples. Sprinkle one tablespoon bacon on top of each.
B. Close cover and bake for 8 minutes until brown and puffed. To serve garnish with additional cheese and bacon.

Southwestern Hash Browns

Ingredients
1 cup shredded potato
1/2 cup egg substitute or 2 fresh eggs
1/2 teaspoon parsley flakes
1/2 teaspoon dried chives
1/4 teaspoon garlic powder
1/4 teaspoon salt
Salsa
Sour cream

Servings~ 👥
Cooking Time~ Ten Minutes
Pan to Use: Divided, Mini or Base

Cooking Steps
A. Pre-heat and spray with cooking spray. Place all ingredients except salsa and sour cream in mixing bowl and beat with electric mixer for one minute.
B. Divide batter into wells, close cover and cook 10 minutes. Serve with salsa and sour cream.

Hash and Egg

Ingredients
1/2 cup canned roast beef hash
2 eggs

Servings~ 👤👤
Cooking Time~ Eleven Minutes
Pan to Use: Divided, Mini or Base

Cooking Steps
A. Pre-heat and spray with cooking spray. Place 1/4 cup hash in each well. Close lid and cook 4 minutes. Place two eggs in shaker and mix. Pour over hash. Close cover and cook 7 minutes.

Egg Cups

Ingredients
8 slices heat and serve bacon
3 eggs
1/2 cup shredded cheddar cheese
1 tablespoon chopped pimentos
Seasoned salt to taste

Servings~ 👤👤
Cooking Time~ Ten Minutes
Pan to Use: Divided, Mini or Base

Cooking Steps
A. Do not Pre-heat, but spray with cooking spray. Line side walls of each well with bacon. Mix next four ingredients and pour equal amounts of mixture into each well.
B. Plug-in unit and cook 8 to 10 minutes until eggs are fully cooked. Egg cups should pop right out of well.

Western Omelet

Ingredients
3 large eggs
2 tablespoons finely chopped green and red bell peppers
2 tablespoons finely chopped onion
1 tablespoon milk
1/4 cup chopped cooked ham
1/4 teaspoon salt and dash of pepper

Servings~ 👤👤
Cooking Time~ Seven Minutes
Pan to Use: Divided, Mini or Base

Cooking Steps
A. Pre-heat and spray with cooking spray. Put all ingredients in shaker and mix well.
B. Pour 1/2 of egg mixture in each well. Close cover, cook 7 minutes until fluffy.

Easy Fruit Danish

Ingredients
2/3 cup Bisquick baking mix
1/3 cup milk
2 tablespoons butter or margarine, softened
1 tablespoon sugar
2 tablespoons any flavor fruit preserves

Servings~ 👤👤
Cooking Time~ Six Minutes
Pan to Use: Divided or Base

Cooking Steps
A. Pre-heat and spray with cooking spray. Mix all ingredients except preserves and divide into wells. Top each with one tablespoon preserves.
B. Close cover and cook for 6 minutes. Drizzle with glaze. Immediately wipe any preserves off top well with a wet rag.

Biscuit, Diced Ham and Eggs

Ingredients
1/2 cup baking mix, like Bisquick
1/4 cup milk
2 eggs, beaten with salt and pepper
Diced ham

Servings~ 👤👤
Cooking Time~ Seven Minutes
Pan to Use: Divided or Base

Cooking Steps
A. Pre-heat and spray with cooking spray. Combine baking mix and milk, stir and place in 1 well. Place diced ham in other well, close cover and cook 2 minutes.
B. Mix egg and seasoning in shaker pour over ham, add a little grated cheese if desired. Close cover and cook for 7 more minutes.

Fried Eggs

Ingredients
2 eggs
Salt & pepper

Servings~ 👤
Cooking Time~ Three Minutes
Pan to Use: Divided or Base

Cooking Steps
A. Pre-heat and spray with cooking spray. Carefully crack an egg into each well
B. Cook two to three minutes to desired doneness.

Mincemeat Pies

Ingredients
2 9 inch prepared pie crust, cut in half
3/4 cup prepared mincemeat
1/2 Granny Smith apple, peeled, cored, seeded and finely chopped
1 tablespoon raisins

Servings~ 👤👤
Cooking Time~ Fifteen Minutes
Pan to Use: Divided or Base

Cooking Steps
A. Do not Pre-heat, but spray with cooking spray. Carefully fit one half of pie crust into each cooking while. Mix together remaining ingredients and divide between pie crust in wells. Top each pie with remaining pie crust halves, pinch closed and nestle into cooking well (trim excess crust, if necessary and refrigerate for another recipe)
B. Poke holes in top of crust with fork to vent steam. Close cover, plug in unit and bake 12 to 15 minutes until browned serve warm.

Holiday French Toast

Ingredients
2 thick cut slices sweet bread, cut to fit wells
3/4 cup eggnog
1 egg
4 jellied spearmint leaves
6 red-hot candies
Powdered sugar for garnish

Servings~ 👤👤
Cooking Time~ Eight Minutes
Pan to Use: Divided or Base

Cooking Steps
A. Pre-heat and spray with cooking spray. Beat eggnog and egg together with fork. Soak bread slices and egg mixture until bread is saturated. Place one slice of bread into each well.
B. Close cover; cook 6 to 8 minutes, turning once to brown evenly. To serve top each slice with two Spearmint leaves and three red hots to form Holly leaves and douse with "snow" (powdered sugar)

Noodle Kugel (Hanukkah)

Ingredients
3/4 cup cooked wide egg noodles
1 teaspoon melted butter or margarine
1/4 cup fruit cocktail, drained
1 tablespoon golden raisins
2 tablespoons cottage cheese
1 tablespoon sour cream
2 teaspoon sugar
1/2 teaspoon vanilla extract

Servings~ 🧍🧍
Cooking Time~ Twenty Minutes
Pan to Use: Divided or Base

Cooking Steps
A. Pre-heat and spray with cooking spray. Mix noodles and melted butter. In a separate bowl, mix together all other ingredients, fold in noodles last.
B. Divide mixture evenly between wells. Close cover, cook 15 to 20 minutes until firm and browned.

Purim-Blintz Bake

Ingredients
1/4 cup sour cream
1 tablespoon apple juice
1 egg, beaten with fork
2 tablespoons cinnamon Home-style applesauce
2 tablespoons butter
2 frozen blintzes, slightly thaw to reduce cook time
1 tablespoon brown sugar

Servings~ 🧍🧍
Cooking Time~ Fifteen Minutes
Pan to Use: Divided or Base

Cooking Steps
A. Pre-heat and spray with cooking spray. Mix sour cream and apple juice. Fold in beaten egg and applesauce.
B. Melt one tablespoon butter in each cooking well. Place one blintz into each cooking well, top with equal amounts of sour cream mixture. Sprinkle with brown sugar. Close cover, cook approximately 10 to 15 minutes (cooking times may vary based on brand of blintzes used)

Scotch Eggs

Ingredients
4 oz sage flavored fresh rolls sausage
1 egg
1 cup Panko breadcrumbs
2 hard-boiled eggs, peeled and chilled
1/2 cup bottled horseradish sauce
1 tablespoon brown mustard
Hot sauce optional, to taste
Boston lettuce leaves

Servings~ 🧍🧍
Cooking Time~ Sixteen Minutes
Pan to Use: Divided or Base

Cooking Steps
A. Divide sausage in half. Beat uncooked egg with fork in small, shallow bowl. Pour breadcrumbs into another small shallow bowl. Press one portion of sausage meat around each hard-boiled egg (meat covering should be fairly thin, use more or less sausage depending on size of hard-boiled eggs). Roll each sausage covered egg in bread crumbs and dip in egg and roll in bread crumbs again
B. Let breaded eggs rest in refrigerator for 10 minutes before cooking. Pre-heat and spray with cooking spray. Place one prepared egg in each well. Close cover, cook about 16 minutes (turning to brown, as needed)
C. To make sauce combine horseradish, mustard and hot sauce if using, in small shallow bowl. To serve, slice fried eggs into wedges serve yolk side up on a bed of lettuce leaves, topped with horseradish sauce.

Strawberry Banana Pancakes

Ingredients
1/2 cup reduced fat pancake or baking mix
1 tablespoon honey
1 teaspoon vanilla
2 tablespoons egg substitute
1/2 cup skim milk
1/4 cup chopped strawberries
1/4 cup mashed bananas

Servings~ 👤👤
Cooking Time~ Ten Minutes
Pan to Use: Divided, Mini or Base

Cooking Steps
A. Pre-heat and spray with cooking spray. Combine all ingredients; divide batter between two wells
B. Cook 10 minutes or until well browned and a toothpick inserted in center comes out clean. Serve with honey or strawberry syrup

Natural French Toast Sticks

Ingredients
1-2 slices day old pound cake or banana bread
1 egg
2 tablespoons milk
1 teaspoon sugar Honey (warmed in microwave for five seconds)
1/2 teaspoon vanilla extract
1/2 teaspoons cocoa powder
Honey and butter for serving (optional)

Servings~ 👤👤👤👤
Cooking Time~ Six Minutes
Pan to Use: Divided or Base

Cooking Steps
A. Pre-heat and spray with cooking spray. Briskly beat egg, milk, honey, vanilla and cocoa together in small bowl. Cut cake or bread into four sticks. Soak in egg mixture until saturated.
B. Drain, place two sticks in each well. Close cover and cook two to three minutes, turn for even browning and cook an additional three minutes until golden brown. Top with butter and drizzle with more honey, if desired.

Salami and Eggs

Ingredients
1/2 cup beef bologna stick or salami of your choice cubed
3 large eggs
1 tablespoon milk or water
Solid pepper to taste

Servings~ 👤👤
Cooking Time~ Nine Minutes
Pan to Use: Divided, Mini or Base

Cooking Steps
A. Pre-heat and spray with cooking spray. Mix eggs, milk, salt and pepper shaker until frothy.
B. Divide equal amounts of salami into cooking wells. Cook two minutes until salami is browned. Pour half of egg mixture into each well. Close cover and cook seven minutes until eggs are solid and puffy.

Hot Cereal

Ingredients
1 cup grape nuts cereal
2/3 cup low-fat milk
2 teaspoons honey

Servings~ 👤👤
Cooking Time~ Seven Minutes
Pan to Use: Divided, Mini or Base

Cooking Steps
A. Pre-heat and spray with cooking spray. Place 1/2 cup cereal into each cooking well. Top each well with 1/3 cup milk and 1 teaspoon honey.
B. Close cover cook five to seven minutes until hot. Serve topped with slices of bananas for a healthy "good carb" breakfast loaded with essential vitamins and minerals.

Oatmeal Raisin Pancakes

Ingredients
1/2 cup reduced fat pancake or baking mix
1/4 cup oatmeal
1 teaspoon sugar
1/4 teaspoon cinnamon
1 teaspoon vanilla
1/4 cup egg substitute
1/2 cup skim milk
1/4 cup raisins

Servings~ 👨👨
Cooking Time~ Ten Minutes
Pan to Use: Divided, Mini or Base

Cooking Steps
A. Pre-heat and spray with cooking spray. Combined mix, oatmeal, sugar and cinnamon. Add vanilla, egg substitute, milk and raisins and stir until dry ingredients are moistened.
B. Divide batter between wells and cook 10 minutes or until well brown and toothpick inserted in center comes out clean. Serve with maple or flavored syrup.

Southwest Breakfast Bake

Ingredients
3 eggs
Salt and pepper to taste
2 tablespoons chopped chorizo
1 tablespoon chopped jalapenos
1 tablespoon sour cream
2 tablespoons shredded Jack or taco cheese
Prepare guacamole, salsa and additional sour cream for serving (optional)

Servings~ 👨👨
Cooking Time~ Seven Minutes
Pan to Use: Divided or Base

Cooking Steps
A. Pre-heat and spray with cooking spray. Beat eggs in small bowl with fork and season with salt and pepper. Mix in next three ingredients until well blended. Divide the mixture evenly between the two wells. Top with equal amounts of cheese.
B. Close cover and cook for five to seven minutes. Remove eggs and top with guacamole, salsa, or sour cream, if desired   Serve immediately.

Steak and Egg Omelet

Ingredients
1 piece of leftover grilled steak, chopped
1/2 leftover baked potato, chopped
Sautéed mushrooms, chopped
3 eggs beaten
2 tablespoons shredded cheese, optional

Servings~ 👨👨
Cooking Time~ Eleven Minutes
Pan to Use: Divided or Base

Cooking Steps
A. Pre-heat and spray with cooking spray. Place half of chopped steak, potatoes, and mushrooms in each well.
B. Pour half the beaten eggs into each well. Top with one tablespoon cheese. Cook 7 minutes until eggs are fluffy.

Low-fat Portabella Mushroom And Onion Omelet

Ingredients
3 baby bella mushrooms, sliced, or ½ cup Chopped Portabella mushrooms
2 tablespoons chopped onion
3/4 cup egg substitute
1/4 teaspoon each garlic powder, salt, pepper
2 slices fat-free cheese

Servings~ 👨👨
Cooking Time~ Eight   Minutes
Pan to Use: Divided or Base

Cooking Steps
A. Pre-heat and spray with cooking spray. Add mushrooms and onions to wells, cook three minutes. Or half of egg substitute into each well, season with garlic powder, salt, and pepper and top each with slice of cheese.
B. Cook 8 minutes.

Sausage & Cheese Strada

Ingredients
2 eggs, lightly beaten
2 tablespoons milk
1/2 teaspoon salt
1/8 teaspoon garlic powder
4 slices white bread
1 tablespoon chopped onion
2 ounces sliced cheddar cheese
2 ounces fully cooked breakfast sausage patties, chopped

Servings~ 👤👤
Cooking Time~ Seven Minutes
Pan to Use: Divided or Base

Cooking Steps
A. Pre-heat and spray with cooking spray. Combine eggs, milk, and salt and garlic powder. Soak bread slices in mixture.
B. Place one slice in each well, top each slice with half the onion, cheese and sausage. Place remaining soaked bread overfilling. Cook 7 minutes.

Quiche Lorraine

Ingredients
1/2 (9 inch) refrigerated pie crust, cut into two pieces
1 egg, lightly beaten
2 tablespoons chopped ham
1 tablespoon chopped onion
1 mushroom, chopped
1/3 cup shredded Swiss cheese
1/2 cup half-and-half or light cream
1/4 teaspoon garlic powder
1/8 teaspoon each salt and pepper

Servings~ 👤👤
Cooking Time~ Fifteen Minutes
Pan to Use: Divided or Base

Cooking Steps
A. Pre-heat and spray with cooking spray. Carefully fit pie crust in to wells, cook two minutes. Combine remaining ingredients and pour half of mixture into each pie crust.
B. Cook 15 minutes until mixture is set and a knife is inserted 1 inch from the center and comes out clean.
   1. **Broccoli and cheddar quiche** substitute 1/4 top chopped broccoli for ham and cheddar cheese for Swiss
   2. **Spinach and Muenster** substitute 1/4 cup chopped spinach for ham and Muenster cheese for Swiss

Breakfast Pigs in a Blanket

Ingredients
8 brown and serve sausages
1 package, complete pancake mix (6 ounces)
1 cup water

Servings~ 👤👤👤👤
Cooking Time~ Seven Minutes
Pan to Use: Divided or Base

Cooking Steps
A. Spray cooking wells with cooking spray. Before Pre-heating unit place four sausages in each well and cook two to three minutes until light goes out. Remove two sausages from each well. Meanwhile mix batter and water in bowl or shaker.
B. Place 1/4 cup batter in each well over sausage. Cook seven minutes, repeat with remaining sausages and batter serve warm with butter and syrup.

French Toast and Ham Wrap

Ingredients
1 egg, lightly beaten
1/4 cup milk
1/2 teaspoon cinnamon
1/4 teaspoon vanilla
2 large slices of cinnamon or raisin bread
2 slices ham

Servings~ 👥
Cooking Time~ Five Minutes
Pan to Use: Divided or Base

Cooking Steps
A. Pre-heat and spray with cooking spray. Combine the egg, milk, cinnamon and vanilla in a shallow bowl. Soak the bread slices in the mixture and allow the bread to soak up the liquid.
B. Place one slice of ham on each slice of bread and fold length wise to enclose the ham and place one in each well. Cook 5 minutes or until bread is browned.

Biscuit Breakfast Bake

Ingredients
2 large or 4 small refrigerator biscuits
2 whole eggs
1 slice American cheese, cut in half
2 slices pre-cooked bacon, cut in half

Servings~ 👥
Cooking Time~ Seven Minutes
Pan to Use: Divided or Base

Cooking Steps
A. Pre-heat and spray with cooking spray. Press one large or two small biscuits together to form a 6 inch oval. Repeat with remaining biscuit or biscuits, carefully fit one oval into each well.
B. Crack an egg onto each biscuit and top each with half the cheese and half the bacon. Cook seven minutes.
   1. **Scrambled Biscuit Breakfast Bake-**substitute beaten egg for whole egg
   2. **Canadian biscuit breakfast baked-**substitute two slices ham for the bacon
   3. **Sausage Biscuit Breakfast Bake** substitute pre-cooked breakfast sausages for the bacon
   4. **Low-cholesterol biscuit breakfast bake** substitute 1/2 cup egg substitute for the eggs, reduced fat cheese for the cheese and Canadian bacon for the bacon

Sloppy Joe and Egg Breakfast Pie

Ingredients
1/2 (9 inch) refrigerated pie crust, cut in two pieces
1/2 cup cooked or can Sloppy Joes
2 eggs
2 tablespoons salsa
2 tablespoons shredded cheddar cheese
2 tablespoons shredded Monterey Jack

Servings~ 👥
Cooking Time~ Nine Minutes
Pan to Use: Divided or Base

Cooking Steps
A. Pre-heat and spray with cooking spray. Carefully fit one piece of pie crust into each well cook for two minutes. Spoon half of meat mixture into the crust leaving room in the Center for the egg. Crack an egg into each shell.
B. Cook 7 minutes to desired doneness. Spoon salsa on and top with cheese.

Breakfast Burritos To Go

Ingredients
2 (8 inch) flour tortillas
3 brown and serve sausages, thinly sliced
2 eggs, beaten with two tablespoons milk and salt and pepper to taste
2 slices American cheese

Servings~ 👥
Cooking Time~ Ten Minutes
Pan to Use: Divided or Base

Cooking Steps
A. Pre-heat and spray with cooking spray. Place half the sausage slices in each well and cook two to three minutes. Divide beaten egg, milk and seasoning between two cooking wells cook two minutes. Stir slightly to scramble and cook two more minutes
B. Meanwhile place one cheese slice in the center of each tortilla. Top each with half the cooked eggs and sausage mixture. Rub a small amount of water along the perimeter to seal each tortilla. Fold each tortilla in half and place one in each cooking well. Cook four minutes and wrap in a napkin to serve.

Quickie Breakfast

Ingredients
2 eggs, beaten
2 large English muffins, split and cut in half vertically
2 slices Canadian bacon or precooked smoked bacon or one slice ham, cut in half
2 slices cheese

Servings~ 👥
Cooking Time~ Four Minutes
Pan to Use: Divided or Base

Cooking Steps
A. Pre-heat and spray with cooking spray. Pour half the egg into each cooking well, cook two minutes.
B. Meanwhile, put cheese and bacon or ham on one half of the English muffin. Remove egg and place over cheese and bacon or ham. Put on the other half of each English muffin. Put one muffin in each well cook about two minutes until cheese is melted and muffin is toasty.

Polenta, Sausage, Spinach and Cheese Snacks

Ingredients
4 (3/4 inch) slices of polenta flavored with sun-dried tomatoes, herbs or mushrooms
Salt, pepper and garlic powder to taste
8 baby spinach leaves
1 ounce Swiss cheese
4 fully cooked breakfast sausage patties

Servings~ 👥
Cooking Time~ Eight Minutes
Pan to Use: Divided or Base

Cooking Steps
A. Pre-heat and spray with cooking spray. Place two slices of polenta in each well, sprinkle with salt and pepper and garlic powder. Top with spinach leaves, cheese and sausage patties.
B. Cook for eight minutes or until hot.

Mixed Berry Corn Pancakes

Ingredients
1 package (8.5 ounces) corn muffin mix
1 egg
2 tablespoons melted margarine or corn oil
1/2 cup milk
1/2 cup mixed berries blueberries, raspberries, etc.

Servings~ 👤👤👤
Cooking Time~ Ten Minutes
Pan to Use: Divided, Mini or Base

Cooking Steps
A. Pre-heat and spray with cooking spray. Combine muffin mix, egg, margarine and milk. Stir in berries. Add 3/4 cup of mixture to each well. Cook 10 minutes or until well browned and a toothpick inserted into the center comes out clean.
B. Wrap in foil to keep warm or serve while making the last pancake. Serve with blueberry, raspberry or maple syrup.

Breakfast Hash

Ingredients
1 cup frozen, shredded hash brown potatoes
1/4 teaspoon garlic powder
2 tablespoons chopped onion
1/2 cup shredded cheddar cheese
2 fully cooked frozen breakfast sausage links, chopped
2 eggs, lightly beaten
1/2 teaspoon salt
1/4 teaspoon pepper

Servings~ 👤👤
Cooking Time~ Ten Minutes
Pan to Use: Divided, Mini or Base

Cooking Steps
A. Pre-heat and spray with cooking spray. Combine all ingredients, spoon half of the mixture into each well.
B. Cook 10 minutes or until well brown.
   1. **Vegetarian breakfast hash** substitute two tablespoons chopped broccoli or well-drained chopped spinach, one chopped mushroom and three chopped grape tomatoes for the sausage

Poached Eggs

Ingredients
1/2 cup water
2 eggs
Salt and pepper

Servings~ 👤👤
Cooking Time~ Three Minutes
Pan to Use: Divided or Base

Cooking Steps
A. Pre-heat and spray with cooking spray. Pour about half the water into each well, allow water to come to a boil about two minutes
B. Carefully crack an egg into each well, cook two to three minutes to desired doneness.

Egg Cheese and Canadian Bacon Bake

Ingredients
4 slices Canadian bacon
2 whole eggs
2 tablespoons shredded cheddar cheese

Servings~ 👤👤
Cooking Time~ Eight Minutes
Pan to Use: Divided or Base

Cooking Steps
A. Pre-heat and spray with cooking spray. Carefully place two slices Canadian bacon into each well. Crack one egg into each well cook seven to eight minutes. Sprinkle with cheese.
Scrambled egg, cheese and Canadian bacon substitute beaten eggs for whole.

Veggie and Cheese Omelet

Ingredients
3 eggs, lightly beaten
1 tablespoon milk
1 tablespoon chopped onion
2 mushrooms, chopped
2 tablespoons chopped red peppers
1 tablespoon chopped green peppers
1 slice cheese, chopped
1/4 teaspoon garlic powder
1/2 teaspoons salt
1/4 teaspoon pepper

Servings~ 👥
Cooking Time~ Ten Minutes
Pan to Use: Divided or Base

Cooking Steps
A. Pre-heat and spray with cooking spray. Combine all ingredients pour half of mixture into each well.
B. Cook 10 minutes or until omelets are puffing and well brown and a knife inserted into center comes out clean.
   1. **Cholesterol free omelet** substitute 1/2 cup egg substitute for the eggs and fat-free cheese for the cheese
   2. **Spinach and feta omelets** substitute 1/2 cup chopped fresh or well-drained cooked spinach for peppers and two tablespoons of feta cheese for the sliced cheese
   3. **Western omelet** substitute two tablespoons chopped ham for the cheese
   4. **Egg Foo Yong** substitute two tablespoons bean sprouts for peppers and two tablespoons chopped cooked shrimp, chicken or pork and 1/2 teaspoon soy sauce

Meat Lovers Omelet

Ingredients
3 eggs lightly beaten with one tablespoon milk
2 pre-cooked sausage links, cut into slices
1/4 cup diced ham
1 tablespoon sliced mushrooms
1 tablespoon chopped green pepper
1/2 cup shredded cheese

Servings~ 👥
Cooking Time~ Ten Minutes
Pan to Use: Divided or Base

Cooking Steps
A. Pre-heat and spray with cooking spray. Add sausage, ham, mushrooms, pepper and cheese to egg and milk mixture. Stir well. Divide between two wells.
B. Cook 10 minutes or until knife inserted into center comes out clean.

Low-Carb "Eggs Benedict"

Ingredients
1 package dry hollandaise sauce, prepared according to package directions
2 ½" inch thick slices beefsteak tomato
1 Pinch onion powder
2 slices Canadian bacon
2 eggs
Fresh tarragon leaves
Fresh lemon wedges for garnish

Servings~ 👥
Cooking Time~ Five Minutes
Pan to Use: Divided or Base

Cooking Steps
A. Pre-heat and spray with cooking spray. Pre-heat hollandaise sauce. Put tomato slices into each well, sprinkle with onion powder. Top tomato slice with bacon and crack egg over each
B. Close cover; cook five minutes or until desired doneness. To serve, drizzle with hollandaise sauce and top with garnish.

Breakfast Bagel Nosh

Ingredients
1 small or 1/2 large bagel, split and sliced in half vertically
2 eggs
2 slices Canadian bacon
1 slice American cheese

Servings~ 👥
Cooking Time~ Ten Minutes
Pan to Use: Divided or Base

Cooking Steps
A. Pre-heat and spray with cooking spray. Fit the bottom half of each bagel into well, carefully crack an egg onto each bagel
B. Top with half the cheese and half Canadian bacon and the top of the bagel. Cook 8 to 10 minutes.
   1. **Scrambled breakfast bagel Nosh** substitute two beaten eggs for whole eggs.

Caviar Omelet

Ingredients
3 eggs, lightly beaten
1 tablespoon milk
1 tablespoon chopped onion
2 mushrooms, chopped
2 tablespoons chopped red peppers
1 tablespoon chopped green peppers
1 slice cheese, chopped
1/4 teaspoon garlic powder
1/2 teaspoons salt
1/4 teaspoon pepper

Servings~ 👥
Cooking Time~ Seven Minutes
Pan to Use: Divided or Base

Cooking Steps
A. Do not Pre-heat, but spray with cooking spray. Mix all ingredients together in GT Shaker except sour cream and caviar.
B. Divide omelet mixture between wells. Plug-in and cook seven minutes.

Tortillas & Eggs

Ingredients
3 eggs lightly beaten with one tablespoon milk
2 pre-cooked sausage links, cut into slices
1/4 cup diced ham
1 tablespoon sliced mushrooms
1 tablespoon chopped green pepper
1/2 cup shredded cheese

Servings~ 👥
Cooking Time~ Ten Minutes
Pan to Use: Divided or Base

Cooking Steps
A. Pre-heat and spray with cooking spray. Place half the crushed tortilla chips in each well. Pour eggs beaten with milk over the top of chips, dividing equally between wells.
B. Top with cheese and meat. Cook 10 minutes.

Romantic Brunch Sweet Sandwiches

Ingredients
1/4 cup frozen strawberries, thawed and drained
3/4 cup powdered sugar
4 thin slices challah (or Hawaiian) bread, cut to fit
1/4 cup mascarpone cheese, softened
2 tablespoons egg substitute
1/4 cup half-and-half
1/2 teaspoon almond flavoring
2 pats butter
3 tablespoons slivered almonds for garnish

Servings~ 👥
Cooking Time~ Six Minutes
Pan to Use: Divided or Base

Cooking Steps
A. Purée strawberries in blender or food processor. Mix strawberries with powdered sugar to make serving sauce. Mix egg, half-and-half and vanilla in a small bowl. Spread equal amounts of Mascarpone cheese on two pieces of bread and top each with another slice of bread to make two sandwiches.
B. Pre-heat and spray with cooking spray. Melt one pat butter in each cooking well. Dip each sandwich in egg mixture until both sides of the bread are well coated
C. Place one sandwich in each cooking well and cook six minutes, turning after four minutes for even browning. Serve topped with strawberry glaze and slivered almonds.

Ham and Egg Breakfast Sandwich

Ingredients
2 eggs beaten
2 large English muffins split and cut in half vertically
1 slice of ham cut in half
2 slices of cheese

Servings~ 👥
Cooking Time~ Five Minutes
Pan to Use: Divided or Base

Cooking Steps
A. Pre heat and spray with cooking spray. Pour half the egg into each cooking area and cook 2-3 minutes. While waiting, put cheese and ham on one half and each English muffin.
B. Remove eggs and place eggs over cheese and ham. Put on the other half of each English muffin. Put muffins in cooking base. Cook about 2 minutes until cheese is melted and muffin is toasty.

Veggi & Cheese Omelet

Ingredients
¼ cup egg substitute
½ cup chopped sautéed mushrooms, bell peppers, tomatoes and zucchini
1 small scallion chopped
Salt and pepper to taste

Servings~ 👥
Cooking Time~ Five Minutes
Pan to Use: Divided or Base

Cooking Steps
A. Pre heat and spray with cooking spray. Add vegetables and scallion to pan and sauté.
B. Add egg substitute and cook for approx. 5 minutes or done to your taste.

Steak & Potato Omelet

Ingredients
1 piece of leftover steak chopped
½ leftover baked potato chopped
Sautéed mushrooms chopped
3 eggs beaten
2 tablespoons shredded cheese

Servings~ 👥
Cooking Time~ Seven Minutes
Pan to Use: Divided or Base

Cooking Steps
A. Pre heat and spray with cooking spray. Place the chopped steak, potato and mushrooms in unit. Pour the beaten eggs over steak, potato, and mushrooms.
B. Top each with 1 tablespoon cheese. Cook 7 minutes.

Eggs & Tortillas

Ingredients
3 eggs
1 tablespoon milk
½ cup shredded cheese
2 tablespoons crumbled cooked sausage or diced ham
6 large or 4 medium tortilla chips crushed

Servings~ 👤👤
Cooking Time~ Ten Minutes
Pan to Use: Divided, Mini or Base

Cooking Steps
A. Pre heat and spray with cooking spray. Place the crushed tortilla chips in unit.
B. Pour eggs beaten with milk over the top of chips. Top with meat and cheese. Cook for 10 minutes.

Cinnamon Pancakes

Ingredients
1 ¼ cup whole wheat flour
1 teaspoon baking soda
2 tablespoons splenda sweetener
1 cup skim milk
½ cup egg beaters
1 tablespoon vanilla extract
2 tablespoons cinnamon

Servings~ 👤
Cooking Time~ Seven Minutes
Pan to Use: Mini, Divided or Base

Cooking Steps
A. Pre heat and spray mini pan with cooking spray. Mix flour, baking soda, and splenda in a bowl. Mix milk, egg beaters, and vanilla in another bowl. Combine both bowls and mix roughly, stir in cinnamon last.
B. Fill Cooking areas with mix. Cook for 5-7 minutes or until desired doneness. Repeat with remaining mix until all batter is cooked.

Breakfast Potato Moons

Ingredients
1 cup shredded cheddar cheese
1 cup frozen hash browns -- thawed and excess moisture removed (you can just pat this dry on a paper towel)
1 large egg -- beaten
2 tsp baking powder
2 tblsp flour
1/3 cup each onion and green pepper – finely chopped
salt and pepper

Servings~ 👤👤
Cooking Time~ Seven Minutes
Pan to Use: Divided or Base

Cooking Steps
A. Pre heat and brush with butter. Combine ingredients and mix well.
B. Divide mixture between wells. Close cover and let cook 7-8 minutes or until golden brown.

Egg Tata tots

Ingredients
6 tator tots thawed
1 egg beaten

Servings~ 👤👤
Cooking Time~ Four Minutes
Pan to Use: Mini

Cooking Steps
A. Pre heat and spray mini pan with cooking spray. Place thawed tot into each cooking area.
B. Divide egg between the areas. Close cover and cook for 4 minutes.

Denver Omelet

Ingredients
2 Tbsp finely diced onion
2 Tbsp finely diced green pepper
4 oz chopped cooked ham
2 eggs
2 oz grated cheddar cheese
Salt and pepper
2 Tbsp water

Servings~ 👥
Cooking Time~ Seven Minutes
Pan to Use: Divided or Base

Cooking Steps
A. Pre heat and spray pan with cooking spray. Mix eggs and water then divide between wells.
B. Add half of each onion, pepper, and ham to each well, top with cheese. Cook seven minutes.

French Tomato Omelet

Ingredients
1/2 ripe tomato, diced fine
2 teaspoons olive oil
2 tablespoons red onion, diced fine
3 tablespoons minced chives
1 tablespoon chopped fresh basil leaves
Salt and pepper
2 large eggs
1/4 cup goat cheese, crumbled

Servings~ 👥
Cooking Time~ Six Minutes
Pan to Use: Divided or Base

Cooking Steps
A. Pre heat and spray pan with cooking spray. Mix eggs, chives, basil, salt, and pepper then divide between wells.
B. Add half of each red onion and top with crumbled goat cheese. Cook for 5-6 minutes.

Picante Omelet

Ingredients
1/4 cup picante sauce
1/2 cup shredded Monterey Jack cheese
1/2 cup shredded cheddar cheese
3 eggs
sour cream
tomato slices and chopped fresh cilantro

Servings~ 👥
Cooking Time~ Three Minutes
Pan to Use: Divided or Base

Cooking Steps
A. Pre heat and spray pan with cooking spray. Mix eggs, picante sauce, and cheese then divide between wells.
B. Close cover and cook for 2-3 minutes. After removing eggs to a plate garnish with tomatoes, cilantro and sour cream.

Eggs Benedict

Ingredients
1 English Muffin
4 slices Canadian bacon
½ cup steamed broccoli florets
2 eggs
Hollandaise Sauce

Servings~ 👥
Cooking Time~ 3 Minutes
Pan to Use: Divided or Base

Cooking Steps
A. Pre heat and spray pan with cooking spray. Split English muffin in half and place in the well. Cover with Canadian bacon and broccoli. Then crack an egg over the top of the muffin.
B. Close cover and cook for 2-3 minutes. After removing eggs to a plate pour Sauce over the eggs.

Sausage & Cheese Strata

Ingredients
3 eggs, lightly beaten
2 Tablespoons milk
1/2 teaspoon salt
1 clove minced garlic
4 slices bread
1 Tablespoon sliced green onion
2 slices American cheese (I prefer the white as it has no dyes)
2 ounces cooked sausage, crumbled

Servings~ 👥
Cooking Time~ 3 Minutes
Pan to Use: Divided or Base

Cooking Steps
A. Pre heat and spray pan with cooking spray. Combined eggs, milk, salt, and garlic. Soak bread slices in mixture. Put slices in well and brush top with oil. Top with onions, cheese and sausage.
B. Place a slice of bread on the top and close cover and cook for 2-3 minutes.

Puffy German Pancake

Ingredients
4 eggs
1 cup milk
1 cup flour
1 tsp vanilla

Servings~ 👥
Cooking Time~ 3 Minutes
Pan to Use: Divided or Base

Cooking Steps
A. Pre heat and spray pan with cooking spray. Combined eggs, milk, flower, and vanilla.
B. Use just enough to cover the base and cook for 7 minutes.

Deserts

Individual Pie or Quiche Crust

Ingredients
1 1/2 cups flour
1/2 cup butter or margarine
1 teaspoon salt
1/4 cup ice water

Servings~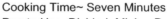
Cooking Time~ Seven Minutes
Pan to Use: Divided, Mini or Base

Cooking Steps
A. Place flour, butter and salt into a food processor and process until crumbly. Place flour mixture into a bowl, add water and mix with fork until it has a consistency that a small amount can be pressed into a ball with hands. Store in a plastic bag in refrigerator until ready to use
B. When ready to use, scoop a heaping ¼ cup measure from bag, place into wells of cold unit and press gently into well forming a shell. Prick holes in bottom with plastic fork or wooden toothpick. Close cover plug in unit and prebake for two minutes before adding filling. To make cooked shells allow baking until lightly browned, about seven minutes. Remove from unit, cool and fill with pudding our custard.

Cherry Cola Cake

Ingredients
1 cup chocolate cake mix, dry
1/2 diet Cherry Cola
1/4 cup chopped maraschino cherries
Whole cherries for garnish with screen

Servings~
Cooking Time~ Seven Minutes
Pan to Use: Divided, Mini or Base

Cooking Steps
A. Pre-heat and spray with cooking spray. Mix cake mix and cola until blended and pour about 1/4 of mixture into bottom of each well.
B. Distribute 1/2 of cherries evenly over cake mix in each well. Cover with remaining cake batter close cover and cook seven minutes. Serve warm with whipped cream and top with whole cherries.

Boston Cream Donuts

Ingredients
2 frozen puff pastry shells, thawed
2 ounces prepared putting
2 tablespoons hot fudge sauce

Servings~
Cooking Time~ Fifteen Minutes
Pan to Use: Divided, Mini or Base

Cooking Steps
A. Pre-heat and spray with cooking spray. Place one pastry shell in each well. Cook 15 minutes or until well browned and puffed
B. Fill injector with 2 ounces of pudding. Place the injector needle into the side of the cooked pastry shells and inject half the pudding. Repeat process with the second shell. Spread half the hot fudge sauce on the top of each donut.
   1. Variation: substitute jelly for pudding and sprinkle with powdered sugar.

Filo Wrapped Apple Pie

Ingredients
10 sheets frozen filo dough, thawed
1 can apple pie filling
1 teaspoon cinnamon
Butter flavor spray
Powdered sugar

Servings~ 👤👤
Cooking Time~ Ten Minutes
Pan to Use: Divided, Mini or Base

Cooking Steps
A. Layer five Filo sheets on flat surface, one at a time spreading lightly between each sheet with butter flavored non-stick spray. Do not spray top of last sheet. While apples are still in can and pass a sharp knife through them repeatedly to cut into smaller chunks. Pile about 1/2 apples in the lower right quadrant of dough sprinkle with cinnamon, and bring right corner of dough up over apples and fold in two side and rollup forming a package about 4 inches wide and 4 inches thick. Repeat with other five sheets of Filo dough and apples.

B. Pre-heat and spray with cooking spray and place one pie in each well. Close lid and bake for 8 to 10 minutes, turning 1/4 turn halfway through to promote even browning. Put on plate, cut on diagonal sprinkle with powdered sugar.

Individual Cheesecakes

Ingredients
Crust
8 full sheets graham crackers, crushed, or 1 cup crumbs
4 tablespoons sugar
4 tablespoons melted butter
1 teaspoon cinnamon
Filling
1 (8 ounce) package cream cheese
1/3 cup sugar
1 egg
1 tablespoon lemon juice
1 teaspoon vanilla

Servings~ 👤👤👤👤
Cooking Time~ Eight Minutes
Pan to Use: Divided, Mini or Base

Cooking Steps
A. Pre-heat and spray with cooking spray. Combine crust ingredients, set aside. With an electric mixer, combine the filling ingredients, beating well for three minutes or until thickened and fluffy.

B. Spoon 1/4 cup of the reserved crumb mixture into each well pressed down so that the crumbs adhere to the sides of the well. Top with 1/2 cup filling mixture; sprinkle 2 teaspoons of crumbs over each cake.

C. Cook eight minutes open the lid and allow to cool five minutes before removing. Refrigerate the cakes for several hours before serving and top with fruit if desired.

Mini Crumb Cake

Ingredients
Cake batter
1/2 cup baking mix firmly packed
2 tablespoons sugar
2 tablespoons milk
1 egg, lightly beaten
1/2 teaspoon vanilla
Crumb mixture
1/2 cup baking mix, firmly packed
1/2 cup dark brown sugar, firmly packed
3 tablespoons butter
1 teaspoon cinnamon

Servings~ 👤👤👤👤
Cooking Time~ Six Minutes
Pan to Use: Divided, Mini or Base

Cooking Steps
A. Pre-heat and spray with cooking spray. Combine batter ingredients (batter should be very thick). In another bowl, combine crumb mixture, forming into large crumbs and reserve. Place two tablespoons butter in each well, spread to barely cover bottom of wells.

B. Cook one minute, cover top of each cake with 1/4 cup large crumbs cook five more minutes or just until toothpick is inserted in center comes out clean. Cool about one minute before removing repeat cooking process for remaining cakes.

Pears in Chocolate Sauce

Ingredients
4 small can pear halves
2 teaspoons hot fudge sauce
2 teaspoons pear juice

Servings~
Cooking Time~ Five   Minutes
Pan to Use: Divided or Base

Cooking Steps
A. Pre-heat and spray with cooking spray. Place pear halves in each well. Place half of fudge sauce in center of each pair
B. Place juice in wells around pairs. Cook five minutes.

Raspberry Chantilly filled White Cake

Ingredients
3/4 cup white cake mix
1 egg
1/4 cup water
3 tablespoons frozen whipped topping, thawed
1 tablespoon seedless raspberry jam
Raspberry sauce
Powdered sugar

Servings~
Cooking Time~ Seven Minutes
Pan to Use: Divided, Mini or Base

Cooking Steps
A. Pre-heat and spray with cooking spray. Combine the cake mix, egg and water, spoon half of the batter into each well. Cook seven minutes or until a toothpick inserted in the center comes out clean. Allow cakes to cool completely before filling.
B. Combine the whipped topping and jam. Fill the injector tube with cream mixture. Place injector needle into the side of the cooled cake and inject half the cream. Repeat this process with second cake and top with raspberry sauce and sprinkle with powdered sugar.

Peach Flan

Ingredients
1/3 cup milk
1 egg
1/4 cup baking mix
3/4 cup peach slices

Servings~
Cooking Time~ Nine Minutes
Pan to Use: Divided, Mini or Base

Cooking Steps
A. Pre-heat and spray with cooking spray. Combine all ingredients except peaches place half the mixture into each well.
B. Cook three minutes. Then place half of peach slices over semi set batter in each well. Cook six more minutes. Unplug and allow to cool in well for five minutes before serving.

Bananas Foster

Ingredients
1 tablespoon butter or margarine
2 tablespoons brown sugar, divided
1/4 teaspoon cinnamon
2 small bananas cut in small pieces

Servings~
Cooking Time~ Five Minutes
Pan to Use: Divided or Base

Cooking Steps
A. Pre-heat and spray with cooking spray. Place half of butter in each well, sprinkle one tablespoon sugar over butter in each well.
B. Place half of bananas in each well sprinkle remaining sugar on bananas. Cook five minutes serve warm over vanilla ice cream or topped with whip cream.

Cherry Turnovers

Ingredients
1 (17.2 ounce) package frozen puff pastry sheets thawed for 30 minutes
2 cups cherries or flavored fruit pie filling
Powdered sugar

Servings~ 🚹🚹🚹🚹
Cooking Time~ Fourteen Minutes
Pan to Use: Divided or Base

Cooking Steps
A. Pre-heat and spray with cooking spray. Unfold the pastry dough onto a lightly floured board or plastic wrap. Sprinkle the top of dough lightly with flour. Press out two dough circles from each sheet. Combine all the remaining ingredients. Place a dough circle into the open pocket maker. Spoon about 1/2 cup of mixture into the bottom section of the dough circle. Close lid and press down firmly to crimp edges of the turnover.
B. Repeat the process for remaining dough and ingredients. Place one turnover in each well cook 14 minutes or until well browned.

Impossible Pecan Pie

Ingredients
1/3 cup baking mix, like bisquick
1 egg
1/2 cup milk
1 tablespoon brown sugar
1 tablespoon dark corn syrup
1 tablespoon butter, softened
1/8 teaspoon vanilla or rum extract
1/4 cup chopped pecans

Servings~ 🚹🚹
Cooking Time~ Fifteen Minutes
Pan to Use: Divided, Mini or Base

Cooking Steps
A. Pre-heat and spray with cooking spray. Combine all crust ingredients. Set aside. Mix cake batter with electric mixer place half of crust mixture into each well.
B. Then place half of filling mixture over crumbs in each well. Cook 15 minutes. Unplug and cool 10 minutes before removing from wells. Top with slices of strawberries and kiwi. Glaze with melted apricot jam if desired.

Strawberry Kiwi Cheesecake

Ingredients
Crust
10 vanilla wafers, crushed
1 tablespoon melted butter
1/4 teaspoon cinnamon
1/2 teaspoon sugar

Filling
1 egg
1/4 cup sugar
4 ounces strawberry flavored cream cheese
1 teaspoon flour

Servings~ 🚹🚹
Cooking Time~ Fifteen Minutes
Pan to Use: Divided, Mini or Base

Cooking Steps
A. Pre-heat and spray with cooking spray. Combine all crust ingredients. Set aside. Mix cake batter with electric mixer place half of crust mixture into each well.
B. Then place half of filling mixture over crumbs in each well. Cook 15 minutes. Unplug and cool 10 minutes before removing from wells. Top with slices of strawberries and kiwi. Glaze with melted apricot jam if desired.

Impossible Cranberry Pie

Ingredients
1 cup milk
1 egg
1/2 cup Bisquick baking mix
Mix all ingredients in Xpress Shaker extra batter can be refrigerated for up to two days

Filling
1/2 cup prepared pie batter
1 tablespoon white sugar
1/4 teaspoon vanilla
3/4 cup whole berry cranberry sauce
1/4 cup chopped dried apricots
1 tablespoon brown sugar
1/2 teaspoon cinnamon

Servings~ 👤👤
Cooking Time~ Ten Minutes
Pan to Use: Divided, Mini or Base

Cooking Steps
A. Pre-heat and spray with cooking spray. Mix batter with white sugar and vanilla. Divide batter evenly between wells. In a separate bowl, mix together cranberry sauce and apricots. Spoon equal amounts into each well.
B. Sprinkle pies with brown sugar and cinnamon. Close cover and cook for 10 minutes.

Caramel Apple Dessert

Ingredients
1 medium apple, peeled and sliced
2 tablespoons fat-free caramel sauce
4 tablespoons graham cracker or other cookie crumbs

Servings~ 👤👤
Cooking Time~ Seven Minutes
Pan to Use: Divided, Mini or Base

Cooking Steps
A. Pre-heat and spray with cooking spray. Combine apple slices and sauce
B. Divide mixture between two wells sprinkle with crumbs. Cook seven minutes serve with whipped topping or nonfat frozen yogurt if desired.

Easter Cake

Ingredients
3/4 cup dry strawberry cake mix
1 egg
1/4 cup water
Can vanilla frosting
Jelly beans
Coconut
Pastel cake sprinkles
Pink and green icing tubes

Servings~ 👤👤👤👤
Cooking Time~ Eight Minutes
Pan to Use: Divided, Mini or Base

Cooking Steps
A. Pre-heat and spray with cooking spray. Combine cake mix, egg and water and mix until smooth. Place half of batter into each well. Close cover, cook seven to eight minutes
B. Remove cakes and allow to cool completely. Put the two well shapes together to form a circle. Draw an egg on parchment paper and use as a trimming guide. Trim to form an Easter egg and ice with frosting. Decorate as desired with coconut, jelly beans, sprinkles and colored icing.

Peach Melba

Ingredients
Medium peaches, peeled and cut in half lengthwise
2 tablespoons fruit juice or water
4 teaspoons red raspberry jam

Servings~ 👤👤
Cooking Time~ Twenty Minutes
Pan to Use: Divided or Base

Cooking Steps
A. Pre-heat and spray with cooking spray. Place two peach halves in each well. Spoon fruit juice into well around peaches
B. Place 1 teaspoon jam in center of each half. Cook six minutes.

Cinnamon Twists

Ingredients
1/4, 9 inch refrigerated pie crust, cut into a square
2 tablespoons sugar
1 tablespoon cinnamon
Butter flavored cooking spray
2 tablespoons prepared vanilla icing softened for 30 seconds in microwave

Servings~ 👬
Cooking Time~ Ten Minutes
Pan to Use: Divided or Base

Cooking Steps
A. Do not Pre-heat, but spray with cooking spray. Lay pie crust on piece of wax paper or lightly floured surface for preparation. Evenly sprinkle cinnamon and sugar onto dough. Spray top with butter flavored cooking spray. Cut dough into four strips to fit wells. Twist each cinnamon strip holding ends.
B. Place two twisted strips into each well. Close cover cook five minutes on each side until golden brown. Let cool five minutes before handling. Serve warm, drizzled with melted icing.

Grilled Strawberry & Chocolate Sandwiches

Ingredients
2 thick slices pound cake
4 fresh strawberries
1 Hershey bar
1 ounce butter
Cinnamon sugar

Servings~ 👬
Cooking Time~ Three Minutes
Pan to Use: Divided or Base

Cooking Steps
A. Pre-heat and spray with cooking spray. Butter outer side of pound cake. Remove strawberry stems, wash and slice strawberries into 1/4 inch thick pieces. Cut pound cake slices in halves and place strawberries on two pieces. Break Hershey bar in half and place, each half on top of strawberries. Take remaining two halves of pound cake and place on top of strawberries and chocolate to create sandwiches
B. Grill sandwich halves until cake is browned and chocolate is melted, about three minutes. Remove from Wells and sprinkle with cinnamon sugar. Serve immediately.

Dessert Bruschetta

Ingredients
2 Anisette toasts
1 tablespoon peanut butter
1 tablespoon chocolate chips
2 teaspoons shredded almonds
2 teaspoons sweetened cocoa

Servings~ 👬
Cooking Time~ Five Minutes
Pan to Use: Divided or Base

Cooking Steps
A. Pre-heat and spray with cooking spray. Spread top of each anisette toast with peanut butter. Top with equal amounts of chips and almonds.
B. Place one toast into each well, close cover, cook 5 minutes until chips are melted. Top with coconut and serve.

Rocky Road Squares

Ingredients
1 package Pillsbury refrigerated triple chunk Brownies
1/2 cup mini marshmallows
1/4 cup crushed unsalted peanuts
2 tablespoons Baker's coconut
2 tablespoons sweetened condensed milk

Servings~ 👤👤
Cooking Time~ Twenty-Five Minutes
Pan to Use: Divided or Base

Cooking Steps
A. Do not Pre-heat but spray with cooking spray. Spread a layer of brownie dough in each well, about 1/4 full (save remaining brownies in fridge for another day). Mix remaining ingredients together and spread equal amounts of mixture on top of each brownie square.
B. Close cover cook approximately 25 minutes until toothpick comes out clean when inserted into brownies center.

Luau Pineapple Sundae

Ingredients
4 ounce can chunk pineapples (about 1/2 can)
1 tablespoon dark rum
4 tablespoons Splenda brown sugar blend
2 Pats butter, preferably unsalted
2 scoops coconut or vanilla bean ice cream
Coconut, crushed unsalted peanuts, whipped cream, and maraschino cherries for garnish

Servings~ 👤👤
Cooking Time~ Five Minutes
Pan to Use: Divided or Base

Cooking Steps
A. Pre-heat and spray with cooking spray. In a small bowl, combine first three ingredients and mix to coat. Divide pineapple mixture evenly between wells. Place one pat butter on top of each pineapple mixture.
B. Close cover; cook five minutes until pineapple is heated through. Serve immediately over ice cream. To garnish top with coconut, peanuts, whipped cream and cherries.

Peach, Plum and Kiwi Compote

Ingredients
1 medium peach, peeled and sliced
1 medium plum, sliced
1 kiwi, peeled and sliced
1 tablespoon honey
2 tablespoons apple juice

Servings~ 👤👤👤👤
Cooking Time~ Five Minutes
Pan to Use: Divided or Base

Cooking Steps

A. Pre-heat and spray with cooking spray.
B. Combine all ingredients spoon half of mixture into each well. Cook five minutes.

Hot Cini Minis

Ingredients
6 mini cinnamon Danish
1 can cream cheese icing for dipping

Servings~ 👤👤
Cooking Time~ Five Minutes
Pan to Use: Divided, Mini or Base

Cooking Steps
A. Pre-heat and spray with cooking spray. Place three mini danish into each well.
B. Close cover, cook five minutes until hot. Serve immediately with cream cheese icing for dipping.

Any Time Cookies

Ingredients
1/2 cup butter or margarine
1/2 cup sugar
1/2 cup brown sugar, packed
1 egg
1/2 teaspoon vanilla
1 3/4 cups flour
1/2 teaspoon baking soda
1/2 teaspoon salt
1/2 cup chopped nuts

Servings~ 👤👤
Cooking Time~ Twenty Minutes
Pan to Use: Divided, Mini or Base

Cooking Steps
A. In medium bowl, mix butter, sugars, eggs and vanilla, salt and baking soda. Stir in flour until well mixed, adding nuts last. Form into a log about 2 inches in diameter, wrap in plastic wrap and refrigerate at least three hours.
B. To bake, cut four slices, form into bottom well of cold GT express 101. But spray with cooking spray beforehand. Spray top well, close cover, plug in and bake 6 to 10 minutes to desired crisp and color.

Piña Colada Muffins

Ingredients
3/4 cup baking mix, like Bisquick
1/4 cup crushed pineapple
1/4 cup shredded coconut
2 teaspoons sugar
1 teaspoon vegetable oil
1/3 cup milk

Servings~ 👤👤👤👤
Cooking Time~ Ten Minutes
Pan to Use: Divided, Mini or Base

Cooking Steps
A. Pre-heat and spray with cooking spray. Mix all ingredients together
B. Divide in wells close cover and bake 8 to 10 minutes.

Root Beer Float Cake

Ingredients
Cake
1 cup classic white cake mix
1/2 cup root beer
1 egg
1/2 cup chopped maraschino cherries, dry
Drizzle icing
1/4 cup powdered sugar
1 1/2 tablespoons root beer
1/4 cup crushed root beer candies (for garnish)

Servings~ 👤👤
Cooking Time~ Ten Minutes
Pan to Use: Divided, Mini or Base

Cooking Steps
A. Pre-heat and spray with cooking spray. Combine all cake ingredients except one tablespoon cherries, mix well. Divide cake mixture evenly between wells. Close cover and cook 10 minutes, until cakes spring back when touched. Let cakes cool completely before removing from wells.
B. For icing, fold together powdered sugar and root beer and drizzle on cooled cakes. Top each cake with even amounts of candies and reserved cherries.

Apple Spice Snack Cake with Caramel Sauce

Ingredients
1/4 cup butter or margarine
1/2 cup sugar
1 egg
1/2 cup flour
1/2 teaspoon soda
1/2 teaspoon cinnamon
1 small apple, finally chopped
1/2 cup brown sugar
1/4 cup butter
1/4 cup whipping cream
Chopped pecans

Servings~ 🕴🕴🕴🕴
Cooking Time~ Eight Minutes
Pan to Use: Divided, Mini or Base

Cooking Steps
A. Pre-heat and spray with cooking spray. Cream together butter, sugar and egg until well blended. Then add flour, soda and cinnamon. Mix well then fold in apples and pecans. Divide batter into wells, close lid and bake for eight minutes.
B. While baking put brown sugar, butter and cream in small saucepan, bring to a boil stirring constantly and continue to cook for two minutes. To serve, pour caramel sauce over cooled cakes.

Mini Cinnamon Twists

Ingredients
1/2 can refrigerator crescent rolls (4)
2 tablespoon sugar
1 teaspoon cinnamon
2 large marshmallows, halved or eight mini marshmallows

Servings~ 🕴🕴🕴🕴
Cooking Time~ Ten Minutes
Pan to Use: Divided or Base

Cooking Steps
A. Pre-heat and spray with cooking spray. Separate crescents and lay on cutting board. Sprinkle with cinnamon and sugar. Place two mini or ½ large marshmallow on wide end and roll, pinching ands together to seal marshmallow in.
B. Place two rolls in each well, close cover and bake for 8 to 10 minutes until rolls are brown, turnover after six minutes if desired to promote even browning.

Pecan Ribbon Coffeecake

Ingredients
1 cup Bisquick baking mix
1/2 cup lemon lime, diet or regular soda
1/4 cup pecans, chopped
1/4 cup brown sugar, divided
1/2 teaspoon cinnamon

Servings~ 🕴🕴🕴🕴
Cooking Time~ Ten Minutes
Pan to Use: Divided, Mini or Base

Cooking Steps
A. Pre-heat and spray with cooking spray. Combine pecans, cinnamon and all but one tablespoon brown sugar, in small bowl and set aside. Mix baking mix and soda, spoon 1/4 of mixture into each well, distributing evenly over bottom, spoon half of pecan mixture into batter and top with remaining batter.
B. Divide remaining brown sugar and sprinkle on top of batter. Close cover and bake 10 minutes.

Fruit Filled No Roll Crepes

Ingredients
1/2 pie batter as found earlier in this section
1 tablespoon sugar
1 teaspoon cinnamon
1 cup apple, peach or cherry pie filling

Servings~ 👤👤
Cooking Time~ Ten Minutes
Pan to Use: Divided, Mini or Base

Cooking Steps
A. Pre-heat and spray with cooking spray. Mix batter with sugar and cinnamon, divide batter between wells about 1/4 cup each
B. Place pie filling in the center of batter until batter almost reaches the top of wells. Bake 10 minutes.

Caramel Nut Roll Cake

Ingredients
1 cup yellow cake mix, dry
1/2 cup lemon lime, ginger ale, diet or regular soda
4 squares caramel candy
1/4 cup chopped salted peanuts
Vanilla ice cream, Caramel sauce

Servings~ 👤👤👤👤
Cooking Time~ Six Minutes
Pan to Use: Divided, Mini or Base

Cooking Steps
A. Pre-heat and spray with cooking spray. Unwrap caramels and worked two at a time between fingers to form 3 inch roll, pressed into nuts to coat and set aside. In small bowl mix cake mix and soda with a wire whisk until well blended.
B. Pour enough cake mix to cover bottom of each well, set one caramel peanut roll on top of batter, sprinkle on any remaining peanuts. Cover with remaining batter. Close cover and bake seven minutes. To serve flip onto plate, place scoop of ice cream in center of each cake and drizzle with caramel syrup.

Almond Joy Cake

Ingredients
1 cup cake mix, chocolate, dried
1 egg
1/2 cup water
2 macaroon cookies
1/4 cup milk chocolate chips
Slivered almonds

Servings~ 👤👤👤👤
Cooking Time~ Seven Minutes
Pan to Use: Divided, Mini or Base

Cooking Steps
A. Pre-heat and spray with cooking spray. Mix cake mix, egg and water, with a wire whisk.
B. Place 1/4 of cake batter in each well. Break cookies in half and place end on end on the batter. Cover with remaining batter. Close lid and bake seven minutes. Remove and allow to cool slightly. Melt chips in microwave about one minute at 80% power. Stir until smooth, sprinkle over cake and garnish with almonds.

Frosted Apricot Cake

Ingredients
1 cup dry yellow cake mix
1/2 cup apricot nectar
1 egg
1/2 teaspoon apple pie spice or cinnamon
1 3 ounce package cream cheese,
2 teaspoons butter
1 cup confectioners' sugar

Servings~ 👤👤👤👤
Cooking Time~ Seven Minutes
Pan to Use: Divided, Mini or Base

Cooking Steps
A. Pre-heat and spray with cooking spray. Mix together cake mix, apricot nectar, egg and spice with wire whisk until well blended
B. Divide batter into Wells, close and cook for seven minutes. Mix cream cheese, butter and sugar for frosting. Allow cakes to cool and frost.

Black Forest Cake

Ingredients
1 cup dry chocolate cake mix
1/2 cup water
1 egg
1/2 cup cherry pie filling
Whipped topping
Maraschino cherries, for garnish

Servings~ 👤👤👤👤
Cooking Time~ Seven Minutes
Pan to Use: Divided, Mini or Base

Cooking Steps
A. Pre-heat and spray with cooking spray. Mix cake mix, water and egg with whisk until well blended. Divide batter into wells, close and bake seven minutes.

Cool cakes and split in half to form two layers. Spread half of cherry pie filling on top of each bottom half. Top with layer of whipped cream and cake top. Add whipped cream and cherry for garnish.

Ruby Scones

Ingredients
2/3 cup baking mix, like Bisquick
1/3 cup milk
2 tablespoons sugar
1 tablespoons butter, melted
10 maraschino cherries, chopped

Servings~ 👤👤👤👤
Cooking Time~ Ten Minutes
Pan to Use: Divided, Mini or Base

Cooking Steps
A. Pre-heat and spray with cooking spray. Mix baking mix, milk, sugar, butter and cherries just until blended. Turn on a floured kneading board until loses stiffness. Pat into 5 Inch Circle, cut into four wedges. Place two wedges in each well.
B. Close cover and bake 10 minutes. Serve with butter and jam or split and drizzle with maraschino syrup.

Banana Split Cake

Ingredients
1 cup dry yellow cake mix
1/2 cup lemon lime, diet or regular soda
1/2 banana, chopped
1/4 cup milk chocolate chips
Vanilla ice cream
Chocolate syrup

Servings~ 👤👤👤👤
Cooking Time~ Seven Minutes
Pan to Use: Divided, Mini or Base

Cooking Steps
A. Pre-heat and spray with cooking spray. Mix chocolate chips and banana together and set aside. In a small bowl, mix cake mix and soda with wire whisk until well blended. Pour enough batter in each well to cover bottom, pile half of banana mixture on top of cake topped with last of batter covering banana
B. Close lid and bake seven minutes. To serve flip over onto plate top with scoop of ice cream and drizzle with chocolate syrup.

Pineapple Outside-in Cake

Ingredients
3/4 cup yellow cake mix
1 egg
1/4 cup water
3 tablespoons dried crushed pineapple
1 tablespoon brown sugar

Servings~ 👤👤👤👤
Cooking Time~ Ten Minutes
Pan to Use: Divided or Base

Cooking Steps
A. Pre-heat and spray with cooking spray. Mix cake mix, egg and water in a bowl or shaker.
B. Divide mixture between wells. Mix pineapple and brown sugar, spoon into center of cake batter. Cook 9 minutes.

Wapple Pie

Ingredients
4 round frozen waffles, like Eggo
2/3 cup apple pie filling, cut up.
4 tablespoons seedless raspberry jam, melted
1/2 teaspoon cinnamon
Powdered sugar

Servings~ 👤👤👤👤
Cooking Time~ Five Minutes
Pan to Use: Divided or Base

Cooking Steps
A. Pre-heat and spray with cooking spray. Pass a sharp knife through pie filling to cut apples into smaller chunks. Mix in cinnamon. Cut about 1 inch off each waffle to make a flat side, and place one waffle in each well, layer apples, cut off piece, more apples and top with second waffle.
B. Close lid and cook for five minutes or until waffle is brown and filling his bubbly. To serve drizzle plate with zigzag of raspberry sauce, place pie on top. Sprinkle with powdered sugar and another drizzle of syrup.

Raspberry Shortcake

Ingredients
2/3 cup baking mix, like Bisquick
2 tablespoon sugar
1 tablespoon cocoa powder
1/3 cup light cream
1 package fresh raspberries
1/2 cup seedless raspberry jelly, regular or light

Servings~ 👤👤👤👤
Cooking Time~ Ten Minutes
Pan to Use: Divided, Mini or Base

Cooking Steps
A. Pre-heat and spray with cooking spray. Mix baking mix, sugar, cocoa, and cream together to form dough. Knead on floured board until dough loses its stiffness and then pat into 5 inch Circle. Cut in half and place, each half in each well.
B. Close cover and bake 10 minutes. Place jelly in microwave safe bowl and microwave for 15 to 20 seconds. Stir in raspberries, crushing berries to release juice. Split cooked cakes in half spread with berries and top with whipped cream.

Mocha Frappuccino Cake

Ingredients
1 cup dry chocolate cake mix
1 egg
1/2 cup strong black coffee
Dreyer's French silk ice cream in round carton
Whipped cream, chocolate syrup or sprinkles

Servings~ 👤👤👤👤
Cooking Time~ Seven Minutes
Pan to Use: Divided, Mini or Base

Cooking Steps
A. Pre-heat and spray with cooking spray. Mix cake mix, egg and coffee with wire whisk. Divide batter into wells, close and cook seven minutes. Remove and cool
B. Slice cakes in half to form two layers. Cut 1 inch slice of ice cream. Divide ice cream into two halves and place between cake layers forming a sandwich. Wrap in plastic wrap and freeze at least one hour. To serve, cut into four wedges. Garnish with chocolate syrup, whipped cream and sprinkles.

Black Cherry Pie Turnovers

Ingredients
1/2 sheet prepared pie crust, cut in half
1 cup pitted fresh Bing cherries
2 heaping tablespoons brown sugar
2 shakes Wondra flour
1 teaspoon lemon zest
1/2 teaspoon lemon juice

Servings~ 👨👨👨👨
Cooking Time~ Twenty   Minutes
Pan to Use: Divided, Mini or Base

Cooking Steps
A. Pre-heat and spray with cooking spray. Mix cherries, brown sugar, flour, and lemon zest and lemon juice together in small bowl. For each turn over, lay one piece of pie crust on clean lightly floured surface. Take half of cherry filling mixture and place on bottom of unbaked crust quarter. Fold crust over and pinch firmly closed with fingertips or a fork. Prick top of turnover with a fork to let air escape. Repeat for second turnover
B. Place one turnover in each well, close cover and bake 10 minutes carefully turn for even browning and bake an additional 10 minutes. Let rest for a few minutes before removing from well. Serve with vanilla ice cream.

Mushroom Clouds

Ingredients
4 slices angel food cake, cut to fit wells
4 tablespoons marshmallow fluff
2 tablespoons white chocolate chips
2 tablespoons Baker's coconut
2 tablespoons slivered almonds

Servings~ 👨👨
Cooking Time~ Seven Minutes
Pan to Use: Divided, Mini or Base

Cooking Steps
A. Pre-heat and spray with cooking spray. For each "cloud" but two tablespoons marshmallow fluff on one side of cake (this is too difficult to spread). Sprinkle with one tablespoon each chocolate chips, coconut and almonds. Top with another slice of cake, repeat with other two slices of sponge cake
B. Lay one assembled "cloud" into each well and spray top of "cloud" with cooking spray. Close cover and cook five to seven minutes. Sponge cake should be golden brown and filling completely melted.

Braised Pears with Pomegranate Juice

Ingredients
2 organic canned pear halves
6 cloves
1/3 cup pomegranate juice
1 tablespoon honey
1 tablespoon lemon juice
Pinch pumpkin pie spice
2 tablespoons chopped almonds
(hazelnuts and walnuts make excellent substitutions)

Servings~ 👨👨
Cooking Time~ Ten   Minutes
Pan to Use: Divided or Base

Cooking Steps
A. Pre-heat and spray with cooking spray. Stack three cloves into each pear half, place one pear half into each well
B. Combine remaining ingredients except nuts, mix well. Pour equal amounts of mixture over pear halves. Close cover, cook 10 minutes, serve sprinkled with nuts.

"Almost Instant" Coconut Custard Pies

Ingredients
1 egg
1/4 cup coconut
1/4 cup baking mix
1/2 cup milk
2 tablespoons sugar
1 tablespoon butter or margarine, softened
A few drops of vanilla extract

Servings~ 👤👤
Cooking Time~ Ten Minutes
Pan to Use: Divided or Base

Cooking Steps
A. Pre-heat and spray with cooking spray. Mix all ingredients in a bowl, blender or shaker.
B. Divide mixed ingredients between the two cooking wells. Cook 10 minutes and cool.

Pineapple Outside-in Cake

Ingredients
3/4 cup yellow cake mix
1 egg
1/4 cup water
3 tablespoons dried crushed pineapple
1 tablespoon brown sugar

Servings~ 👤👤👤👤
Cooking Time~ Ten Minutes
Pan to Use: Divided or Base

Cooking Steps
C. Pre-heat and spray with cooking spray. Mix cake mix, egg and water in a bowl or shaker.
D. Divide mixture between wells. Mix pineapple and brown sugar, spoon into center of cake batter. Cook 9 minutes.

Ice Cream Cakewich

Ingredients
2 cakes (flavor of your choice) cooled and split horizontally
Half gallon your favorite flavor of ice cream in a round carton

Servings~ 👤👤👤👤
Cooking Time~

Cooking Steps
A. Remove cover from ice cream carton. Using a sharp knife, slice a one-inch slice from the top of the carton including the ice cream replace lid on carton of ice cream and return to freezer. Remove carton from ice cream around.
B. Cut ice cream in half horizontally to fit cake. Place half the ice cream round between two layers of cake forming a sandwich.

Cake for 2

Ingredients
3/4 cup any flavor cake mix
1 egg
1/4 cup water

Servings~ 👤👤👤👤
Cooking Time~ Seven Minutes
Pan to Use: Divided, Mini or Base

Cooking Steps
A. Pre-heat and spray with cooking spray. Mix all ingredients until smooth
B. Divide between wells and cook seven to eight minutes or until toothpick inserted in center comes out clean.

Savory Brunch Cakes

Ingredients
1 6 ounce package pancake mix
1 cup water
4 sun-dried tomatoes without oil, chopped
2 tablespoons grated parmesan cheese
1 pinch dried red pepper flakes
1 teaspoon garlic salt
1 tablespoon dried Italian seasoning mix

Servings~ 👤👤👤👤
Cooking Time~ Seven Minutes
Pan to Use: Divided, Mini or Base

Cooking Steps
A. Pre-heat and spray with cooking spray. Mix all ingredients in shaker.
B. Place ¼ cup batter into each cooking well. Close cover, cook seven minutes until done. Repeat with remaining batter.

Chocolate Cake for 4

Ingredients
1 small box chocolate cake mix prepared according to package directions

Servings~ 👤👤👤👤
Cooking Time~ Eight Minutes
Pan to Use: Divided, Mini or Base

Cooking Steps
A. Pre-heat and spray with cooking spray. Place 1/4 of batter in each cooking well.
B. Cook seven to eight minutes or until toothpick inserted in the center comes out clean. Repeat with remaining batter allow to cool. Dust with powdered sugar.
   1. **Chocolate Soufflé** add one snack size candy bar (Milky Way, Snickers, or Three Musketeers) to the center of the batter in each well before cooking
   2. **Cookies N' Cream** crumbled two chocolate filled cookies on top of batter in each well before cooking **Chipper Cake** at 1/4 cup chocolate chip or peanut butter chips to the batter in each well before cooking
   3. **Split Banana Cake add** half of a peeled banana to the center of the batter in each well before cooking
   4. **Chocolate Cake with Peanut Butter Filling** add half a peanut butter cup to the center of the batter in each well before cooking.

Angel Food Cake

Ingredients
1/2 cup angel food cake mix
3 tablespoons water
3 tablespoons sliced berries, optional

Servings~ 👤👤
Cooking Time~ Seven Minutes
Pan to Use: Divided, Mini or Base

Cooking Steps
A. Pre-heat and spray with cooking spray. Mix cake mix with water until thoroughly blended fold in berries, if desired
B. Divide batter between two wells. Cook seven to eight minutes until dark brown. Remove carefully, cakes will be soft. Cool and serve.

Lemon Cherry Pies

Ingredients
1/2 (9 inch) refrigerated pie crust, cut in half
1/2 cup prepared lemon pie filling
1/4 cup prepared cherry pie filling

Servings~ 👤👤
Cooking Time~ Eight Minutes
Pan to Use: Divided or Base

Cooking Steps
A. Pre-heat and spray with cooking spray. Carefully fit one piece of pie crust into each well. Cook eight minutes. Allow to cool completely before filling
B. Spoon half of lemon filling in to each of the shells and top with the cherries. Chill if desired.
   1. **Lemon Cream** substitute whipped cream or whipped topping for cherries
   2. **Chocolate Banana Cream pies** substitute prepared chocolate pudding for pie filling and bananas for cherries top with a dollop of whipped cream before serving
   3. **Vanilla Berry Cream pies** substitute prepared vanilla pudding for lemon pie filling and fresh raspberries or blueberries for cherries. Top with a dollop of whipped topping
   4. **Yogurt and Fruit pies** substitute your favorite fruit yogurt for lemon pie filling and fresh berries for cherries
   5. **Banana Split pies** substitute ice cream for lemon pie filling, omit cherries. Top with chocolate or caramel syrup, sliced bananas, whipped cream and a cherry

Heath Bar Cheesecake Tarts

Ingredients
2 frozen puff pastry shells, trimmed to fit
1/4 cup, Philadelphia brand "chocolate ready to eat." Prepared cheesecake filling
1 heath bar, crushed (reserve one teaspoon for topping)
1 tablespoon chocolate syrup
2 maraschino cherries for garnish

Servings~ 👤👤
Cooking Time~ Ten Minutes
Pan to Use: Divided or Base

Cooking Steps
A. Pre-heat and spray with cooking spray. Place one frozen pastry shell into each well, cook 10 minutes. Allow shells to cool slightly, and gently remove from wells and allow to cool completely before filling or filling well melt
B. Just prior to serving fold Heath bar (except 1 teaspoon) into chocolate cheese filling and spoon mixture into prepared shells. To serve, drizzle with Hershey's syrup, sprinkle with reserved crushed Heath bar and top with maraschino cherry.

Oatmeal Cookie Pies

Ingredients
1 (1 pound 1.5 ounces) add oatmeal cookie mix
1 egg
1/3 cup vegetable oil
3 tablespoons water
4 tablespoons marshmallow cream

Servings~ 👤👤👤👤 👤👤👤👤
Cooking Time~ Ten Minutes
Pan to Use: Divided, Mini or Base

Cooking Steps
A. Do not Pre-heat, but spray with cooking spray. Combined all ingredients except cream. Spoon 1/4 cup dough into each well. Spoon one tablespoon cream over dough in wells.
B. Top each with 1/4 cup dough. Cook 10 minutes allow pies to cool one minute. Repeat cooking process with remaining 6 pies.

Mini Cannoli Layer Cakes

Ingredients
1 1/2 cup chocolate cake mix
2 eggs
1/2 cup water (omit any oil as per package directions)
2 tablespoons crushed almonds
2 tablespoons dried candied fruit

Cannoli filling
1 cup ricotta cheese
1/4 cup confectioners' sugar
1/4 teaspoon almond extract
2 tablespoons chocolate chips

Servings~ 👤👤
Cooking Time~ Eight Minutes
Pan to Use: Divided or Base

Cooking Steps
A. Do not Pre-heat, but spray with cooking spray. Mix together first three ingredients until batter is smooth. Fold in nuts and dried fruit. Place 1/4 of batter into each cooking well. Close cover, plug in and cook seven to eight minutes until done (when done, toothpick should come out clean when inserted into center of cakes). Repeat with remaining batter.
B. Allow cakes to cool completely before filling or filling will melt. While cakes are cooling, prepare filling by folding all the ingredients together and refrigerating the mixture until ready to use.
C. Place equal amounts of filling on two cakes. Then top each with another cake. Serve dusted with additional confectioners' sugar (optional).

Chocolate Biscotti Dessert Strata

Ingredients
2 cups chocolate nut biscotti broken into medium sized pieces
1 1/4 cups each sugar and butter
1 egg
1 cup heavy cream
1/2 tablespoon almond extract
1/2 teaspoon pumpkin spice
2 scoops vanilla bean ice cream for garnish
Slivered almonds for garnish
1 biscotti broken in half for garnish

Servings~ 👤👤
Cooking Time~ Ten Minutes
Pan to Use: Divided or Base

Cooking Steps
A. Pre-heat and spray with cooking spray. Combine all ingredients except garnishes, let mixture sit approximately 5 minutes so biscotti pieces will soften.
B. Divide mixture evenly between wells. Cook 7 to 10 minutes (should have consistency of bread pudding). Let cool and remove from well. Serve warm with ice cream, one half biscotti and almonds.

Apple Tartlets

Ingredients
½ cup pie crust (recipe found earlier in this section)
1 cup apple pie filling, chopped
½ teaspoon cinnamon
¼ cup brown sugar
¼ cup rolled oats
2 tablespoons chopped pecans

Servings~ 👤👤
Cooking Time~ Twelve Minutes
Pan to Use: Divided, Mini or Base

Cooking Steps
A. Follow directions for pie crust recipe from earlier in this section. . Pressing into COLD well. Plug in unit and bake for 2 minutes. After 2 minutes pre bake, add half of apple pie filling mixed with cinnamon into each shell. Close cover and cook for 5 minutes.
B. While this is baking mix brown sugar, oats and pecans together. After 5 minutes, spreads half over each pie, close cover and continue to bake for an additional 5 minutes. Serve with ice cream or whipped cream. Each pie may be halved to make 4 smaller servings.

Fresh Peach Shortcake

Ingredients
1 cup dry pound cake mix (about 1/3 of box)
¼ cup lemon lime, diet or regular soda
1 fresh peach, peeled and diced
1 tablespoon sugar or Splenda
1 teaspoon cinnamon
Whipped Cream

Servings~ 🕴🕴🕴🕴
Cooking Time~ Eight   Minutes
Pan to Use: Divided, Mini or Base

Cooking Steps
A. Pre-heat. Mix pound cake mix and soda until smooth. Mix chopped peach with cinnamon and sugar. Lightly spray wells with cooking spray. Spread ½ of cake mixture into each well.   Pile half of peach chunks in center of batter. Close lid.
B. Bake 8 minutes. Unplug machine. Do not open machine. Let stand for 10 minutes. Remove cakes carefully. Serve with whipped cream.

Low-Fat Snack Cake

Ingredients
1/3 cup Splenda
2 tablespoons brown sugar
1 cup egg substitute
1/3 cup natural unsweetened applesauce
1 teaspoon vanilla extract
1 teaspoon soft butter
1/3 cup flour
1/4 teaspoon baking powder
1/4 teaspoon baking soda

Servings~ 🕴🕴🕴🕴
Cooking Time~ Seven Minutes
Pan to Use: Divided, Mini or Base

Cooking Steps
A. Pre-heat and spray with cooking spray. Combined all ingredients and divide into wells.
B. Close cover and bake for seven minutes.

Brownie Overload

Ingredients
¼ cup butter or margarine, softened
½ cup sugar
½ teaspoon vanilla
1 egg
¼ cup flour
3 tablespoons unsweetened cocoa powder
¼ tablespoons salt
¼ teaspoon baking powder
¼ cup chopped walnuts
2 tablespoons milk chocolate chips

Servings~ 🕴🕴🕴🕴
Cooking Time~ Seven   Minutes
Pan to Use: Divided, Mini or Base

Cooking Steps
A. Pre-heat and spray with cooking spray. Mix butter, sugar, vanilla and egg with a wire whisk until smooth. Add flour, cocoa, salt and baking powder. Mix until well moistened. Stir in walnuts and divide mixture into wells evenly.
B. Close cover and cook for seven minutes. Remove from Wells and immediately place one tablespoon chips on each section allows to sit two to three minutes spread frosting, cut in half.

Lo-Cal Cherry Angel Food Pudding

Ingredients
1 ½" inch thick slice angel food cake, torn into pieces
2/3 cups canned cherry pie filling with Splenda
Pinch cinnamon
2 tablespoons nondairy with topping

Servings~ 👤👤
Cooking Time~ Five Minutes
Pan to Use: Divided, Mini or Base

Cooking Steps
A. Pre-heat and spray with cooking spray. Divide equal amounts of cake between wells. Mix cinnamon and pie filling together
B. Top angel food cake with equal amounts of pie filling mixture. Close cover, cook five minutes until bubbly. Serve hot with a dollop of whipped cream.

Low Fat Mini Brownies

Ingredients
1 box reduced sugar chocolate cake mix
1 15 ounce can pumpkin
¼ cup egg substitute
¼ cup water
6 single serve packages splenda

Servings~ 👤👤👤
Cooking Time~ Five Minutes
Pan to Use: Divided, Mini or Base

Cooking Steps
A. Pre-heat and spray with cooking spray. Mix together cake mix, egg, and pumpkin.
Spoon batter into cooking area. Bake about 5 minutes. Refrigerate left over batter.

Mini Pumpkin Muffins

Ingredients
1 cake mix, carrot or spice
1 15 ounce can pumpkin
1 egg or ¼ cup egg substitute

Servings~ 👤👤👤
Cooking Time~ Five Minutes
Pan to Use: Mini

Cooking Steps
A. Pre-heat and spray mini muffin pan with cooking spray. Mix together cake mix, egg, and pumpkin.
B. Spoon batter into cooking areas. Bake about 5 minutes.

Giant Cookie

Ingredients
3 tablespoons butter or margarine softened
1/3 cup brown sugar packed
4 teaspoons egg substitute
2/3 cup bisquick baking mix regular or reduced fat
½ teaspoon vanilla
Ice Cream and Toppings of your choice.

Servings~ 👤👤👤👤
Cooking Time~ Five Minutes
Pan to Use: Base

Cooking Steps
A. Pre-heat and spray base with cooking spray. Mix first 5 ingredients together and spread in unit carefully with the back of a spoon sprayed with non stick spray. Put topping of your choice on. Cook 5 minutes.
B. Turn off unit and remove cookie, being careful bottom will be soft. Do not cook to long as it will burn easy. Cut cookie into four wedges.

This is a base recipe you could do this with any cookie batter.

Chocolate Cheese Dream Roll

Ingredients
14 tablespoons whipped cream cheese
1/2 teaspoon almond extract
2 tablespoons slivered almonds
1/2 cup chocolate chips
1 tube refrigerator crescent rolls

Servings~ 👤👤
Cooking Time~ Ten Minutes
Pan to Use: Divided or Base

Cooking Steps
A. Pre-heat and spray with cooking spray. Mix cream cheese and almond extract. Unroll crescent rolls and divide into four rectangles do not separate into triangles. Crimp perforations so each rectangle is one piece. Spread equal amounts of cream cheese mixture onto each rectangle, being careful not to spread it all the way to the edges (soften cream cheese in microwave for five seconds, if necessary, for easier spreading). Top cream cheese with equal amounts chocolate chips and slivered almonds. Rollup rectangles jellyroll style and crimp sides of rolls flat with fingers or fork to seal in filling
B. Cook two rolls at a time for six to eight minutes, turning once, if necessary to promote even browning. Cool slightly before eating, filling will be very hot.

Quick and Simple Phyllo Pies

Ingredients
5 sheets Phyllo dough
Pie filling of your choice

Servings~ 👤👤👤👤
Cooking Time~ Five Minutes
Pan to Use: Divided, Mini, or Base Unit

Cooking Steps
A. Pre-heat and spray base with cooking spray. Lay out stack of 5 sheets of Phyllo dough and cut off one end to make a square. If using the mini pan cut into smaller pieces. Sprat dough lightly with cooking spray on both sides.
B. Center dough squares in unit and fill with ½ can pie filling of your choice. Fold edges in over filling after full. Close cover and cook five minutes. Remove from unit and sprinkle with powdered sugar.

Banana Marshmallow Delight

Ingredients
1 small banana, peeled and sliced
2 oz. marshmallows, chopped
1 oz. dark cooking chocolate, grated
2 slices raisin bread, buttered on one side

Servings~ 👤👤
Cooking Time~ Two Minutes
Pan to Use: Mini

Cooking Steps
A. Pre-heat and spray pan with cooking spray. Mix together banana, marshmallow, and chocolate. Butter one side of each bread, place one in the well and place filling on it. Top with other piece of bread.
B. Close lid and cook for 2 minutes.

Pumpkin Fluff Pockets

Ingredients
pumpkin bread, sliced
Fluff
nutella

Servings~ 👤👤
Cooking Time~ Two Minutes
Pan to Use: Base

Cooking Steps
A. Pre-heat and spray base with cooking spray. Spread fluff and Nutella on the bread and top with other piece of bread.
B. Cook for 2 minutes.

Pie Batter

Ingredients
1 cup milk
1 egg
1/2 cup baking mix

Servings~
Cooking Time~

Cooking Steps
A. Mix all ingredients together in a covered Shaker.
B. Extra can be stored in the fridge for two days.

Pizza

Pepperoni Calzone

Ingredients
½ loaf frozen bread dough, thawed
2 ounces softened cream cheese
2 ounces shredded mozzarella cheese
2 ounces sliced pepperoni
1 green onion, chopped
1 clove garlic minced
¼ teaspoon dried thyme

Servings~ 👤👤
Cooking Time~ Twelve Minutes
Pan to Use: Divided or Base

Cooking Steps
A. Pre-heat and spray with cooking spray. Combine cream cheese and mozzarella in bowl, add onion and spices. Divide dough into two pieces and roll a 6 inch circle. Spread each round with half the cheese mixture to within an inch of edge. Layer pepperoni over cheese. Fold and seal edges with tines of fork
B. Brush each calzone with all of oil and place in well. Close cover and bake 10 to 12 minutes until crust is browned.

Pizza Parlor Stromboli

Ingredients
1 package refrigerator pizza dough
½ bulk sausage
½ pound lean ground beef
1 teaspoon fennel seed
¼ teaspoon salt
¼ teaspoon pepper
1 tablespoon olive oil
¼ cup grated Romano cheese
1 teaspoon dried oregano

Servings~ 👤👤👤👤
Cooking Time~ Ten Minutes
Pan to Use: Divided or Base

Cooking Steps
A. Combine sausage, beef, fennel seed, salt and pepper in a skillet and cook until meat is browned and crumbly about 10 minutes. Drain if necessary and cool slightly. Remove dough from can and press out on flat oiled surface into 8 x 12 rectangle. Spread meat over dough to within 1 inch of edges, sprinkle cheese over meat and roll up from long edge like a jelly roll
B. When finished role should be 12 inches long. Brush with remaining olive oil sprinkle with oregano and cut into 4 equal sections, pressing ends together slightly to seal.
C. Pre-heat and spray with cooking spray. Bake 8-10 minutes until brown rolling quarter turn after five minutes to promote even browning and repeat with last two sections.

Stuffed Spaghetti Pies

Ingredients
2 cups chopped cooked spaghetti, coated with tomato sauce, divided
2 tablespoons grated mozzarella cheese
1 tablespoon grated parmesan cheese
6 small meatballs

Servings~ 👤👤
Cooking Time~ Eight Minutes
Pan to Use: Divided, Mini or Base

Cooking Steps
A. Pre-heat and spray with cooking spray. Combine spaghetti and cheeses, spoon half of spaghetti mixture into each well. Top with meatballs. Spoon half of spaghetti over the meatballs in each well.
B. Cook 8 minutes or until well browned served with additional sauce if desired.

Pepperoni Pizza Wrap

Ingredients
2 (8 inch) flour tortillas
2 tablespoons tomato sauce
¾ ounces sliced pepperoni
¼ cup shredded mozzarella cheese
2 tablespoons grated parmesan cheese
¼ teaspoon each dried oregano and garlic powder

Servings~ 👥
Cooking Time~ Eight Minutes
Pan to Use: Divided or Base

Cooking Steps
A. Pre-heat and spray with cooking spray. Spread half of tomato sauce on each tortilla. Top each with half the remaining ingredients
B. Fold in sides and roll. Place one wrap each well. Cook seven to eight minutes or until tops are well browned.

Hawaiian French Bread Pizza

Ingredients
1 4" inch piece day old French baguette, cut in half lengthwise
Olive oil
¼ cup honey BBQ sauce
Garlic powder to taste
Black pepper
2 tablespoons canned pineapple chunks, drain
2 tablespoons diced boiled ham
½ cup shredded white cheddar cheese

Servings~ 👥
Cooking Time~ Eight Minutes
Pan to Use: Divided or Base

Cooking Steps
A. Pre-heat and spray with cooking spray. Rub bottom of bread pieces with oil and place one piece in each cooking well, oil side down. Spread BBQ sauce on top of each piece of bread and sprinkle with garlic powder and pepper
B. Top with equal amounts of pineapple and ham and cheddar cheese. Cook six to eight minutes until hot and cheese is completely melted.

Meatball Pockets

Ingredients
1 package refrigerator pizza dough
½ bulk sausage
½ pound lean ground beef
1 teaspoon fennel seed
¼ teaspoon salt
¼ teaspoon pepper
1 tablespoon olive oil
¼ cup grated Romano cheese
1 teaspoon dried oregano

Servings~ 👥👥
Cooking Time~ Eight Minutes
Pan to Use: Divided or Base

Cooking Steps
A. Pre-heat and spray with non-stick cooking spray. Cut dough into four equal sections and roll out into circles. Combine rest of ingredients. Place a dough circle in the open pocket maker. Spoon about ½ cup of mixture into the bottom section of the dough circle. Close lid and press down firmly to crimp edges of sandwich
B. Repeat with remaining dough and ingredients. Place one in each well and cook eight minutes or until golden brown.
   1. Variation: Pepperoni Pizza -- substitute 1 cup chopped pepperoni for meatballs.

Italian Chicken Pizza Bake

Ingredients
1/3 cup baking mix, like Bisquick
2 tablespoons egg substitute
1 tablespoon water
¼ teaspoon garlic powder
¼ cup chopped pepper and onion
¼ cup chopped cooked chicken
1 small Roma tomato, diced
¼ teaspoon Italian seasoning
¼ cup shredded mozzarella cheese

Servings~ 👥
Cooking Time~ Six Minutes
Pan to Use: Divided or Base

Cooking Steps
A. Do not Pre-heat, but spray with cooking spray. Mix baking mix, egg, water and garlic powder to form a thick batter, split between wells and spread with back of spoon to cover bottom of wells. In a small pan sprayed with cooking spray. Sauté onion and pepper and tomato until tender, add chicken, seasoning and stir to mix.
B. Plug in unit, and after two minutes. Add chicken mixture to top of crust. Close cover, bake five minutes. Spray top of wells with cooking spray and top pizza with cheese. Cook one more minute until cheese melts. Remove pizzas, and wipe way any melted cheese.

Just About Instant Pizza Dough

Ingredients
2 cups warm water
4 cups all purpose flour
1 envelope yeast (2 ½ teaspoons)
1 teaspoons salt

Cooking Steps
A. Place warm water, yeast, and salt in mixing bowl and stir. Add flour, mixing until combined and scraping into ball in bottom of bowl. Cover and let stand 2 hours.
B. Dough is now ready to use or store. Scrape down sides of bowl, dump mixture onto floured surface, turn to coat with flour and flatten for easy measuring. Divide dough into 12 sections. To store, place a ball of dough into a small bag, twist closed and store in refrigerator for up to 2 weeks. When fresh, dough flattens best using floured surface.
C. When cold, dough flattens best using lightly oiled surface like plastic cutting mat or paper plate with about 1 teaspoon of olive or cooking oil on surface. Roll dough in oil to coat and flatten.
D. To use: flatten into a 6 inch round, place in unit and add toppings as desired.

Meatballs Parmigianino Crescent Style

Ingredients
1 (8 ounce) package refrigerated crescent rolls
4 meatballs, sliced
2 tablespoons shredded mozzarella cheese
1 tablespoon grated parmesan cheese
¼ cup tomato sauce

Servings~ 👥
Cooking Time~ Eight Minutes
Pan to Use: Divided or Base

Cooking Steps
A. Pre-heat and spray with cooking spray. Carefully unroll dough. Press to connect triangles together until the dough forms a rectangle, repeat with remaining dough. Place meatball slices on each rectangle and top with cheeses.
B. Fold two sides together to cover filling and then fold opposite sides over to complete each pocket. Place one pocket into each well, cook four minutes. Then turning cook four minutes longer.

Mexican Pizza Rollups

Ingredients
2 8" flour tortillas
¼ cup refried beans
½ cup diced cooked chicken or ground beef
¼ cup grated cheddar jack cheese
2 tablespoons salsa
Sour cream for dipping if desired

Servings~ 👥
Cooking Time~ Five Minutes
Pan to Use: Divided or Base

Cooking Steps
A. Pre-heat and spray with cooking spray. Spread each tortilla with half of the beans to within an inch of the edge. Cover beans with a layer of salsa and then a layer of meat and cheese.
B. Fold in sides until tortilla is about 4 inches wide, then roll from bottom enclosing filling. Place seam side down in well close cover and cook four to five minutes. Serve with sour cream for dipping.

Torta Rustica Pockets

Ingredients
1 frozen puff pastry sheet thawed
Flour
1 egg, beaten with fork
1/4 cup cubed stick salami or pepperoni
1 cup leftover cooked rigatoni, ziti or penne (with or without sauce)
1 tablespoon grated parmesan cheese
1 tablespoon ricotta cheese
1 tablespoon shredded mozzarella cheese
1 tablespoon minced fresh parsley
Pinch garlic powder

Servings~ 👥
Cooking Time~ Fifteen Minutes
Pan to Use: Divided or Base

Cooking Steps
A. Pre-heat and spray with cooking spray. Unfold puff pastry sheet on to lightly floured surface and lightly dust top with flour. Press out 2 circles from dough sheet. Mix together all remaining ingredients. Divide pasta mixture in half and mount half onto each dough circle.
B. Fold circles over into half-moon shape and crimp edges together with fork. Fit one dough pocket in each well cook 12 to 15 minutes until filling well is warm and outside is browned.

Dough Batter

Ingredients
1 cup milk
1 egg
1/2 cup baking mix

Servings~
Cooking Time~

Cooking Steps
A. Mix all ingredients together in a covered Shaker.
B. Extra can be stored in the fridge for two days.

Hawaiian Pizza

Ingredients
1 6 inch pita bread round
1 tablespoon pizza sauce
3 slices Canadian bacon
5 pineapple chunks cut in half
2-3 tablespoons shredded mozzarella cheese

Servings~ 👥
Cooking Time~ Five Minutes
Pan to Use: Base

Cooking Steps
A. Pre-heat and spray with cooking spray. Warm pita bread a few seconds in microwave to make more pliable, place in preheated unit. Spoon sauce on pita and spread with back of spoon. Quarter Canadian bacon slices and arrange over pita. Top with pineapple and cheese.
B. Spray inside lid with non stick spray. Close and cook 5 minutes.

Deep Dish Sicilian Pizza

Ingredients
6 ounces pizza dough, cut into pieces
1/4 cup tomato sauce
2 tablespoons parmesan cheese

Servings~ 👥
Cooking Time~ Eight Minutes
Pan to Use: Divided or Base

Cooking Steps
A. Pre-heat and spray with cooking spray. Form each piece of dough into 5 x 3 inch oval.
B. Fit one oval into each well and top with tomato sauce and cheeses. Cook eight minutes.

Stromboli

Ingredients
1/2 pound pizza dough cut in half
1/2 cup chopped broccoli
1/2 teaspoon garlic powder
2 tablespoons chopped onion
1/4 cup shredded cheddar cheese

Servings~ 👥
Cooking Time~ Twelve Minutes
Pan to Use: Divided or Base

Cooking Steps
A. Pre-heat and spray with cooking spray. Roll dough into 7 Inch circles. Combine remaining ingredients and place half of mixture in center of each dough circle
B. Rollup and fold ends under to seal seam. Place in well cook for 12 minutes.

Greek Pizza Wedges

Ingredients
1 small no pocket whole wheat pita
2 tablespoons each prepared eggplant caponata
and feta cheese
2 ounces leftover cooked chicken reheated in microwave
1 tablespoon pitted Greek olives, chopped
1 teaspoon dried Greek seasoning
Olive oil

Servings~ 👥
Cooking Time~ Eight Minutes
Pan to Use: Divided or Base

Cooking Steps
A. Pre-heat and spray with cooking spray. Spread one side of pita with Caponata, chicken, feta, olives and seasoning. Cut pizza in half and coat bottom of cooking Wells with olive oil.
B. Place one half pizza in each cooking well, tucking to fit wells. Cook eight minutes until cheese is melted, cut in wedges.

Pizza Burritos

Ingredients
2 8" flour tortillas
2 tablespoons pizza sauce
6 tablespoons mozzarella cheese
6 tablespoons cooked ground beef, sausage or sliced pepperoni

Servings~ 👥
Cooking Time~ Seven Minutes
Pan to Use: Divided or Base

Cooking Steps
A. Pre-heat and spray with cooking spray. Spread half of pizza sauce in the center of each tortilla leaving 1 inch around perimeter. Top each with half the cheese and ground beef. Rub small amount of water along parameter of each tortilla to seal.
B. Fold each tortilla in half and place one in each cooking well. Cook seven minutes.

Calzones

Ingredients
8 ounces pizza dough, cut into pieces
1 cup ricotta cheese
2 tablespoons grated parmesan cheese
1/2 cup shredded mozzarella cheese
1 ounce pepperoni, chopped
1/4 teaspoon each salt, garlic powder and onion
Tomato sauce, optional

Servings~ 👥
Cooking Time~ Seven Minutes
Pan to Use: Divided or Base

Cooking Steps
A. Pre-heat and spray with cooking spray. Stretch each piece of dough into a 7 Inch Circle. Combine remaining ingredients, spoon half of the mixture into the center of each round dough. Fold the dough over to form a half-moon. Roll edges and crimp being sure to seal well and place into the wells.
B. Cook seven minutes or until evenly brown. Remove and serve with tomato sauce if desired.
   1. **Spinach Calzone** substitute 1/4 cup chopped fresh spinach for pepperoni
   2. **Sausage Calzone** substitute 1/4 cup chopped cooked sausage for pepperoni

Pizza Pita

Ingredients
1 six-inch pita bread, sliced in half vertically forming pockets
½ cup pizza sauce
10 pepperoni slices, coarsely chopped
1 tablespoon green pepper, chopped
1 thin slice onion, separated into rings
¾ cup shredded mozzarella cheese

Servings~ 👥
Cooking Time~ Three Minutes
Pan to Use: Divided or Base

Cooking Steps
A. Pre-heat and spray with cooking spray. Mix sauce, pepperoni, and cheese together in a small bowl. Divide the mixture in half and stuff into each pocket
B. Place one half in each well cook two to three minutes until cheese is melted.

Veggie Pizza

Ingredients
1/2 pound pizza dough cut in half
1/2 cup chopped broccoli
1/2 teaspoon garlic powder
2 tablespoons chopped onion
1/4 cup shredded cheddar cheese

Servings~ 👥
Cooking Time~ Ten Minutes
Pan to Use: Divided or Base

Cooking Steps
A. Pre-heat and spray with cooking spray. Divide vegetables between two wells and cook one minute and divide sauce and cheese between the two wells.
B. Pour batter over ingredients fill each well to the top cook 10 minutes.

Pizza Burger Pies

Ingredients
1/2 cup ground beef, cooked and drained
2 tablespoons pizza sauce
1/2 cup shredded mozzarella cheese
1/2 cup pie batter

Servings~ 👥
Cooking Time~ Ten Minutes
Pan to Use: Divided or Base

Cooking Steps
A. Pre-heat and spray with cooking spray. Place half of ground beef and half pizza sauce in each cooking well, add half the cheese to each cooking well
B. Pour "pie" batter over ingredients filling each well to the top. Cook 10 minutes.

Traditional Pizza Pies

Ingredients
1/2 cup total of any of the following: reduced-fat pepperoni, cooked drained sausage, diced ham, olives, well drained pineapple chunks
2 tablespoons pizza sauce
½ cup mozzarella cheese
½ cup pie batter

Servings~ 👥
Cooking Time~ Ten Minutes
Pan to Use: Divided or Base

Cooking Steps
A. Pre-heat and spray with cooking spray. Divide pizza toppings between the two cooking wells. Divide the pizza sauce.
B. Divide cheese between the two wells. Pour "pie" batter over ingredients filling each well to the top. Cook 10 minutes.

Veggi White Pizza Pies

Ingredients
1 Almost instant pizza dough
1 tablespoon ranch dressing
Shredded cooked chicken
Cooked broccoli
Mushrooms
Onion
2-3 tablespoons shredded mozzarella cheese

Servings~ 👥
Cooking Time~ Seven Minutes
Pan to Use: Base

Cooking Steps
A. Pre-heat and spray with cooking spray. Pour small amount of cooking or olive oil on plastic cutting mat, roll dough in oil and press flat into 6 inch round. Place dough in to unit.
B. Spread ranch dressing over dough and top with toppings. Close cover and bake for seven minutes

White Pizza

Ingredients
1 Almost instant pizza dough
1 tablespoon pizza sauce
13 slices turkey pepperoni
6 pitted black olives
2-3 tablespoons shredded mozzarella cheese

Servings~ 👥
Cooking Time~ Seven Minutes
Pan to Use: Base

Cooking Steps
A. Pre-heat and spray with cooking spray. Carefully place dough pressed into 6 inch round into base. Spoon sauce onto dough and spread evenly with back of spoon. Top with pepperoni, cheese and olives.
B. Spray inside lid with non stick spray. Close and bake 7 minutes.

White Asparagus and Tomato Pizza

Ingredients
1 Almost instant pizza dough
¼ cup shredded mozzarella
1 tablespoon ricotta cheese
3 cooked asparagus spears chopped
3 cherry or grape tomatoes diced
¼ cup parmesan cheese
Pinch of red pepper flakes
Pinch of garlic salt

Servings~ 👥
Cooking Time~ Ten Minutes
Pan to Use: Base

Cooking Steps
A. Pre-heat and spray with cooking spray In a small bowl mix ricotta, parmesan, asparagus, tomatoes, and seasonings. Carefully place dough pressed into 6 inch round into base. Spoon asparagus mixture onto crust and spread evenly with back of spoon. Top with mozzarella.
B. Spray inside lid with non stick spray. Close and bake 7 minutes.

Mexican Stacked Pizza

Ingredients
2 6 inch corn or flour tortillas
2 tablespoons refried beans
¼ cup seasoned taco meat
2 tablespoons grated cheddar cheese
Shredded lettuce
Diced tomato
Crushed taco chips

Servings~ 👤👤
Cooking Time~ Ten Minutes
Pan to Use: Base

Cooking Steps
A. Pre-heat and spray with cooking spray. Place 1 tortilla spread with beans in preheated cooking base. Top with 2nd tortilla and spread taco meat and cheese evenly over top.
B. Close cover and cook 4 minutes. Remove to plate, top with lettuce and tomato, sprinkle with crushed chips and serve.

Pepperoni and Provolone Roll Ups

Ingredients
2 teaspoons mustard
1 (8 ounce) package refrigerated crescent rolls
4 ounces thinly sliced package pepperoni
4 ounces thinly sliced provolone cheese

Servings~ 👤👤👤👤
Cooking Time~ Ten Minutes
Pan to Use: Divided or Base

Cooking Steps
A. Pre-heat and spray with cooking spray. Separate crescent rolls at perforations forming triangles. Spread top side of the triangle with mustard. Place 1/2 of each pepperoni and cheese on dough. Starting at point carefully rollup dough fold edges under to seal rolls completely.

Pepperoni Hot Pocket

Ingredients
1 (8 ounce) package refrigerated crescent dinner rolls
½ cup pizza sauce
1 cups shredded mozzarella cheese
4 oz sliced pepperoni
Grease and Preheat the Redi Set Go

Servings~ 👤👤👤👤
Cooking Time~ Seven Minutes
Pan to Use: Divided or Base

Cooking Steps
A. Pre-heat and spray with cooking spray. Separate crescent rolls in to 4 rectangles and seal seams. Divide Sauce, cheese, and pepperoni on one half of each of the 4 rectangles.
B. Close and pinch sides closed. Place in well and close cover, cook for seven minutes.

Pork

Pork and Potato Croquettes

Ingredients
1 medium roast potato, peeled and cooked
2 tablespoons butter
1 medium onion, chopped
1 clove garlic, chopped
1 cup ground pork
1 teaspoon salt, divided
½ teaspoon pepper, divided
1 egg
4 ounces mushroom, sliced
¼ cup white wine or chicken broth
¼ cup sour cream

Servings~ 👤👤
Cooking Time~ Twelve Minutes
Pan to Use: Divided or Base

Cooking Steps
A. Pre-heat and spray with cooking spray. Mash cooked potato and set aside. Heat butter in skillet and sauté onion and mushrooms with salt and pepper until tender, about five minutes. In a bowl place about ¼ of onion, mushroom mixture and using paring knife and fork chopped into small pieces, add pork and potato and mix well. form into two balls
B. Place pork mixture in wells using fork to distribute mixture evenly. Close cover and cook 12 minutes. Heat pan with remaining mushrooms. Add wine and sour cream stirring to make sauce. Serve sauce over croquettes.

Sausage Corn Muffins

Ingredients
1 box corn muffin mix, like Jiffy
1 egg
1 tablespoon maple syrup
2 patties or links brown and serve sausage chopped
¼ cup sour cream

Servings~ 👤👤👤👤
Cooking Time~ Eight Minutes
Pan to Use: Divided, Mini or Base

Cooking Steps
A. Pre-heat and spray with cooking spray. Mix all ingredients together, divide into Wells
B. Close cover and bake 8 minutes.

Lite Cheese and Sausage Biscuits

Ingredients
2/3 cup heart smart Bisquick
1/3 cup low-fat buttermilk
2 slices fat-free cheese
2 patties, reduced fat turkey sausage, crumbled, like Jimmy Dean

Servings~ 👤👤
Cooking Time~ Eight Minutes
Pan to Use: Divided or Base

Cooking Steps
A. Pre-heat and spray with cooking spray. Blend Bisquick and buttermilk, divide and pat out on floured board 2, 6 inch circles.
B. Place one slice of cheese on each round, top with crumbled sausage, fold, press edges together and place in wells. Close cover bake 8 minutes.

Hot Dog Wraps

Ingredients
1 package canned crescent rolls (4)
4 hot dogs or wieners

Servings~ 👤👤
Cooking Time~ Eight Minutes
Pan to Use: Divided or Base

Cooking Steps
A. Pre-heat and spray with non-stick cooking spray. Separate crescents into four squares and wrapped each along a hot dog.
B. Cook to at the time for 8 minutes.

Hot Ham Rocks

Ingredients
4 round dinner rolls
1 cup small ham cubes
½ cup shredded cheddar cheese
¼ cup green onion tops, chopped
1½ tablespoons Dijon mustard

Servings~ 👤👤👤👤
Cooking Time~ Five Minutes
Pan to Use: Divided or Base

Cooking Steps
A. Pre-heat and spray with cooking spray. Cut a small circle on top of each role, reserving the tops. Hollow out the rolls leaving a small border of bread.
B. Stir together remaining ingredients and spoon into rolls. Replaced tops, place one roll it each well. Close cover and cook five minutes until filling is heated. Repeat with remaining two rolls.

Three Alarm Chili Dog Bake

Ingredients
1 cup canned chili
2 dogs, cut into bite sized pieces
2 tablespoons shredded cheddar cheese
1 teaspoon cayenne pepper
1 teaspoon black pepper
1 tablespoon hot sauce
2 tablespoons crushed Fritos corn chips

Servings~ 👤👤
Cooking Time~ Seven Minutes
Pan to Use: Divided, Mini or Base

Cooking Steps
A. Pre-heat and spray with cooking spray. Mix together all ingredients except Fritos. Divide chili mixture between cooking wells.
Close cover and cook approximately 5 minutes. Open cover top both wells with equal amounts of crushed Fritos. Cook 2 more minutes, until hot and bubbly and cheese is completely melted.

Spicy Barbecued "Fried" Boneless Pork Chop

Ingredients
2 tablespoons repaired barbecue sauce
1 teaspoon hot pepper sauce
1 teaspoon lemon juice
2 (6 ounce) boneless center cut pork chops, 1 inch thick
3 tablespoons flavored bread crumbs

Servings~ 👤👤
Cooking Time~ Fifteen Minutes
Pan to Use: Divided or Base

Cooking Steps
A. Pre-heat and spray lightly with cooking spray. Combine first three ingredients and spoon in to injector tube. Inject the liquid into the side of the meat in several places.
B. Cook the pork with bread crumbs. Place one piece in each well, cook 15 minutes.

Pot Stickers

Ingredients
¼ pound ground pork
¼ pound ground beef
2 scallions, chopped
1 clove garlic, crushed
1 mushroom, finely chopped
1 tablespoon soy sauce
1 teaspoon cornstarch
2 tablespoons chopped spinach
4 egg roll wrappers

Servings~ 👤👤
Cooking Time~ Seven Minutes
Pan to Use: Divided or Base

Cooking Steps
A. Pre-heat and spray with cooking spray. Combined all ingredients except egg roll wrappers. Trim edges of wrappers to form circles. Place two tablespoons mixture in center of each wrapper. Fold over and roll edges to seal and crimp edges with fork.
B. Place one pot sticker in each well cook three minutes. Turn and cook 3 more minutes. Repeat process for remaining pot stickers.

Pork Egg Rolls

Ingredients
1 mushroom, finely chopped
1 clove garlic, crushed
1 tablespoon finely chopped scallions
2 tablespoons finely chopped spinach
2 tablespoons finely chopped bamboo shoots
2 tablespoons finely chopped water chestnuts
2 tablespoons finely chopped pork or chicken
1 teaspoon cornstarch
¼ teaspoon ground ginger
2 egg roll wrappers

Servings~ 👥
Cooking Time~ Ten Minutes
Pan to Use: Divided or Base

Cooking Steps
A. Pre-heat and spray with cooking spray. Combined all ingredients except egg roll wrappers. Place three tablespoons filling diagonally across the center of each wrapper. Fold top of triangle over meat and then fold sides into each other forming an envelope.
B. Place one egg roll in each well. Cook 5 minutes turn and cook 5 more minutes.

Biscuits Stuffed with Ham and Cheese

Ingredients
1 (7.75 ounce) bag three cheese biscuit mix
½ cup water
2 (3/4 ounce) slices of American cheese
1 (1 ounce) slice, thin slice deli cut ham

Servings~ 👥
Cooking Time~ Eight Minutes
Pan to Use: Divided or Base

Cooking Steps
A. Pre-heat and spray with cooking spray. Combined mix and water, place 1/4 of mixture on bottom of each well. Place cheese on top of ham slices and rollup.
B. Place ham rolls on batter in wells. Spoon remaining batter over rolls cook 7 minutes.

Ham and Cheese Pockets

Ingredients
2 (2 ounce) slices deli cut ham
2 (1 ounce) slices Muenster cheese
½ teaspoon horseradish mayonnaise
¼ teaspoon mustard
½ (9 inch) prepared, refrigerated pie crust, cut into 2 pieces

Servings~ 👥
Cooking Time~ Sixteen Minutes
Pan to Use: Divided or Base

Cooking Steps
1. Pre-heat and spray with cooking spray. Spread ham with mayonnaise and mustard place cheese on top of ham and rollup. Place ham rolls lengthwise on pie triangles.
2. Fold top of triangle over meat and then fold sides into each other forming an envelope. Rollup to form pocket. Place one pocket in each well cook eight minutes. Turn and cook eight more minutes.

Chicago Style Brat Wrap

Ingredients
2 6inch corn tortillas
4 slices deli pepper jack cheese
Yellow mustard to taste
2 tablespoons sweet pickle relish
2 heat and eat bratwurst
4 Port peppers (substitute pepperoncini if unavailable in your area)
4 tomato wedges
¼ cup thinly sliced the Vidalia onions
Celery salt to taste

Servings~
Cooking Time~ Seven Minutes
Pan to Use: Divided or Base

Cooking Steps
A. Pre-heat and spray with cooking spray. To build the wrap, layer 2 slices cheese, mustard, one tablespoon relish, one brat, two peppers and two tomato wedges on each tortilla.
B. Top with raw onions and celery salt. Rollup; tuck in size to fit wells. Grill five to seven minutes until wraps are brown.

Monster Grilled Sandwich

Ingredients
1 extra-large hamburger bun, split and halved
1 tablespoon butter or margarine
1 slice cheese
1 ounce thin slice deli ham

Servings~
Cooking Time~ Three Minutes
Pan to Use: Divided or Base

Cooking Steps
A. Pre-heat and spray with cooking spray. Butter both sides, cut in half, and place halves in with butter side down. Grill for 2-3 minutes until lightly toasted. Assemble sandwich halves with half slice of cheese and half the ham on each side place in butter side down.
B. Return to machine close cover and heat 2-3 minutes more, until cheese is melted and ham is heated. Use any favorite sandwich filling pastrami mustard and pickle or roast beef and cheddar.

Mini Pork and Potato Loafs

Ingredients
1 medium russet potato peeled and cooked
2 tablespoons butter
1 medium onion, chopped
1 clove garlic, chopped
1 cup ground pork
1 teaspoon salt, divided
½ teaspoon pepper, divided
1 egg
4 ounces mushrooms, sliced
¼ cup white wine or chicken broth
¼ cup sour cream

Servings~
Cooking Time~ Twelve Minutes
Pan to Use: Divided or Base

Cooking Steps
A. Pre-heat and spray with cooking spray. Mash cooked potato and set aside. Heat butter in skillet and sauté onion and mushroom with salt and pepper for about five minutes, in bowl place about ¼ of onion, mushroom mixture and using a paring knife and fork chop into small pieces. Add pork and potato and mix well and form two balls. place pork mixture in wells using fork to distribute mixture evenly
B. Close cover and cook for 12 minutes. Heat pan with remaining mushrooms, add white wine and celery, stirring to make sauce. Serve sauce over croquettes.

Broccoli Ham Roll Ups

Ingredients
4 4x6 slices boiled ham
2 4x6 slices mozzarella cheese
¼ onion chopped
¼ cup broccoli
¼ cup seasoned bread crumbs, divided
2 tablespoons butter or margarine, melted
1 tablespoon parmesan cheese

Servings~ 👥
Cooking Time~ Six Minutes
Pan to Use: Divided or Base

Cooking Steps
A. Pre-heat and spray with cooking spray. Sauté onion and broccoli in one tablespoon butter over low heat until tender. Add 2 tablespoons breadcrumbs, next and set aside. Layer two ham slices with one sliced mozzarella and place half broccoli mixture in center. Rollup, dip in remaining melted butter and roll in remaining bread crumbs mixed with parmesan cheese to coat. Repeat with remaining ingredients
B. Place one role in each well, seems site down close cover and cook six minutes until lightly browned and filling it is hot.

Steamed Dumplings

Ingredients
4 ounces ground pork
2 tablespoons chopped onion
1 clove garlic, crushed
2 teaspoons hoisin sauce
1 mushroom, finely chopped
4 egg roll wrappers
1/3 cup chicken broth

Servings~ 👥
Cooking Time~ Eight Minutes
Pan to Use: Divided or Base

Cooking Steps
A. Pre-heat and spray with cooking spray. Combined all ingredients except egg roll wrappers and chicken broth. Place two tablespoons mixture into center each wrapper. Gather up edges and twist to close.
B. Pour half of broth in each well place two dumplings in each well. Cook eight minutes serve with soy or duck sauce.

Marinated Pork Tenderloin

Ingredients
1 10-12 ounce pork tenderloin
¼ cup soy sauce
1 tablespoon red wine vinegar
2 tablespoons salad oil
1 teaspoon dried parsley
¼ teaspoon pepper
1 teaspoon minced garlic
½ teaspoon seasoned salt

Servings~ 👥
Cooking Time~ Fifteen Minutes
Pan to Use: Divided or Base

Cooking Steps
A. Place all marinade ingredients in plastic bag. Cut tenderloin in half pierce with fork numerous times and place in bag with marinade. Seal refrigerate for 30 minutes up to overnight.
B. Pre-heat and spray with cooking spray. Place tenderloins in wells. Close cover and cook for 15 minutes

Sloppy Dogs

Ingredients
2 hot dogs cut into bite size pieces
1 can manwich sloppy Joe sauce
½ cup shredded cheddar cheese
Finely chopped sweet white onion, and corn chips for serving (optional)

Servings~ 👥
Cooking Time~ Seven Minutes
Pan to Use: Divided or Base

Cooking Steps
A. Pre-heat and spray with cooking spray. Place equal amounts of hot dogs in each well. Cover with manwich (save left over for another meal). Top with cheddar cheese.
B. Cook seven minutes until heated through and cheese is melted. Serve topped with chopped onion and corn chips, if desired.

Boneless Oriental Pork Chops

Ingredients
2 (6 ounce) boneless, center cut pork chops 3/4 inch thick
1 tablespoon hoisin
1 teaspoon ketchup
1 teaspoon honey
½ teaspoon black bean and garlic sauce

Servings~ 👥
Cooking Time~ Ten Minutes
Pan to Use: Divided or Base

Cooking Steps
A. Pre-heat and spray with cooking spray. Pat meat dry place one chop in each well.
B. Cook five minutes, combined remaining ingredients and brush both sides of chops. Continue to cook two more minutes. Remove chops. Add remaining sauce mixture to Wells and cook two minutes spoon over chops and serve.

Oktoberfest Bratwurst

Ingredients
2 3-4 ounce fully cooked bratwurst, cut in half lengthwise, but not all the way through
½ cup canned sauerkraut
¼ cup chunky applesauce
½ teaspoon Caraway seeds
½ teaspoon celery salt

Servings~ 👥
Cooking Time~ Eight Minutes
Pan to Use: Divided or Base

Cooking Steps
A. Do not pre-heat but spray with cooking spray, fit one cut bratwurst, flat side down, into each well, mix together remaining ingredients, mount equal amounts of sauerkraut mixture on top of brats.
B. Close cover and plug in unit and cook for eight minutes. Serves with brown mustard and rye bread.

Italian Porketta Wrap

Ingredients
2 8-inch sun dried tomato wraps
1 ½ tablespoons mayonnaise
2 Tablespoons Classico Sun-Dried Tomato Pesto
4-6 thin slices deli roast pork

Servings~ 👥
Cooking Time~ Five Minutes
Pan to Use: Divided or Base

Cooking Steps
A. Pre-heat and spray with cooking spray. Spread each wrapped with mayo and one tablespoon sun-dried tomato pesto. Pile on equal amounts of pork, tuck in corners and roll up.
B. Close cover, cook five minutes until wrapped his grilled to a golden brown and filling is warm.

Kielbasa & Kraut

Ingredients
2 (3 ounce), Polish kielbasa links
1 (3/4 ounce) sliced American cheese, cut in half lengthwise
¼ cup sauerkraut
¼ teaspoon Worcestershire sauce
1/8 teaspoon each garlic and onion powder

Servings~ 👥
Cooking Time~ Six Minutes
Pan to Use: Divided or Base

Cooking Steps
A. Pre-heat and spray with cooking spray. Cut lengthwise slit in top of each link did not cut through completely. Place cheese in slit. Combine sauerkraut and seasonings place half of Kraut in each link and place one in each well
B. Cook six minutes top with mustard.

Brats In Beer

Ingredients
2 (3-4 ounce) fully cooked bratwurst
1/2 cup sliced onion
1/4 cup low carbohydrate beer
1 teaspoon mustard
1 teaspoon Worcestershire sauce
1/4 teaspoon garlic powder

Servings~ 👥
Cooking Time~ Ten Minutes
Pan to Use: Divided or Base

Cooking Steps
A. Pre-heat and spray with cooking spray. Place one bratwurst and half of onions in each well.
B. Cook five minutes combined remaining ingredients pour half of mixture in each well. Cook five more minutes.

Oriental Sesame Pork Buns

Ingredients
6 ounces bread dough, cut in half
3 ounces cooked pork or chicken sliced
1 teaspoon hoisin sauce
¼ teaspoon mustard
1 scallion, chopped
½ clove garlic, crushed
2 teaspoons sesame seeds

Servings~ 👥
Cooking Time~ Ten Minutes
Pan to Use: Divided or Base

Cooking Steps
A. Pre-heat and spray with cooking spray. Roll dough into 2 5x7 inch ovals. Combined pork, hoisin sauce, mustard and scallions, fold two sides together and then fold opposite side to seal, shape roles in to 4x2 inch logs and roll in sesame seeds
B. Place one in each well cook 10 minutes serve with soy or duck sauce.

Ham and Swiss Frittata

Ingredients
2 eggs
1 tablespoon milk
1/8 teaspoon each garlic powder and onion powder
¼ teaspoon salt
1 ounce ham, chopped
1 out Swiss cheese, chopped

Servings~ 👥
Cooking Time~ Five Minutes
Pan to Use: Divided or Base

Cooking Steps
A. Pre-heat and spray with cooking spray. Combined eggs, milk, garlic and onion powder and salt, place half of mixture in each well cook for two minutes.
B. Sprinkle half of ham and cheese over semi set eggs in wells. Continue cooking three more minutes or until eggs are puffy and set.

Monte Cristo sandwich

Ingredients
4 slices Italian bread
2 teaspoons mayonnaise
2 teaspoons mustard
2 slices ham
2 slices Swiss cheese
1 egg, lightly beaten
3 tablespoons milk
1/8 teaspoons each onion powder, garlic powder, pepper

Servings~ 👥
Cooking Time~ Five Minutes
Pan to Use: Divided or Base

Cooking Steps
A. Pre-heat and spray with cooking spray. Spread the bread with mayo and mustard place cheese and ham on bread and top with second slice of bread, combined eggs, milk and seasonings. Dip each sandwich into mixture, allowing the bread to soak up all the liquid
B. Carefully fit the sandwiches into each well cook five minutes or until the bread is golden brown allow the sandwiches to cool for a few minutes before serving, because the filling is extremely hot.

French Poodles
(Parisian-style hot dogs)

Ingredients
2 hot dogs
4 ounce sauerkraut, drained of excess water
2 thin slices Gruyere or Swiss cheese
2 tablespoons Dijon mustard
2 pieces baguette cut to fit hot dog length

Servings~ 👤👤
Cooking Time~ Eight Minutes
Pan to Use: Divided or Base

Cooking Steps
A. Pre-heat and spray with cooking spray. Hollow out middle of baguette pieces without cutting sides. Spread inside of bread. "Tubes" with mustard. place cheese into tube to make a "cheese lining"
B. Place one hot dog and 2 ounces of sauerkraut in each cooking well. Cook six to eight minutes until completely heated through. Stuff hot dogs and sauerkraut into bread and serve.

Stuffed Dogs and Taters

Ingredients
2 hot dogs, split lengthwise, but not cut all the way through
1½ cups refrigerated hash browns
½ can cream of celery soup
¾ cup crushed potato chips
½ cup shredded Swiss cheese
¼ cup prepared onion dip made with sour cream

Servings~ 👤👤
Cooking Time~ Eight Minutes
Pan to Use: Divided or Base

Cooking Steps
A. Pre-heat and spray with cooking spray. Mix together hash browns, soup, ½ cup of crushed chips, and ¼ cup of cheese. Spread equal amounts of potato mixture into cooking wells. Arrange one hot dog on top of each well, split site up.
B. Close cover and cook eight minutes or until heated through. Open cover fill the hot dogs with remaining cheese and sprinkle the remaining crushed chips. Cook two more minutes until cheese is completely melted.

Hot Dog Macaroni

Ingredients
3/4 cup cooked corkscrew or wagon wheel pasta
1 dog, sliced into bite size pieces
2 tablespoons frozen peas, thawed
1 cup Ragu doubled cheddar sauce

Servings~ 👤👤
Cooking Time~ Five Minutes
Pan to Use: Divided, Mini or Base

Cooking Steps
A. Pre-heat and spray with cooking spray. Mix together all ingredients. Divide macaroni mixture into wells, cook for five minutes.

Hot Dog and Mashed Potato Bake

Ingredients
2 hot dogs
¾ cup mashed potatoes

Servings~ 👤👤
Cooking Time~ Seven Minutes
Pan to Use: Divided or Base

Cooking Steps
A. Pre-heat and spray with cooking spray. Cut the dogs lengthwise, being careful not to completely cut through
B. Fill each well with mashed potatoes. Place one hotdog in each well. Cook five minutes or until the potatoes are well brown and the hotdog is heated through.

Cajun Style Pork Tenderloin with Citrus BBQ Sauce

Ingredients
1 (1 pound), pork tenderloin cut to fit
1 tablespoon Cajun or pan blackening spices or spice rub
Sauce
1/3 cup hickory smoked barbecue sauce
2 tablespoons orange juice
1 teaspoon each lemon and lime juice
1 teaspoon soy sauce
1/8 teaspoon garlic powder

Servings~ 🕴🕴🕴🕴
Cooking Time~ Fifteen Minutes
Pan to Use: Divided or Base

Cooking Steps
A. Pre-heat and spray with cooking spray. Sprinkle rub over pork and press into surface of meat place half of pork in each well.
B. Cook 15 minutes. Meanwhile combine sauce ingredients and heat in microwave. Serve pork cut into 1/2 inch thick strips with sauce.

Rich Girl Sandwich

Ingredients
1 5 inch sandwich roll, split and trimmed to fit if needed
1 large slice deli Virginia ham
1 tablespoon Catalina or honey mustard
Brie cheese
Cooked asparagus spears
Tomato and cucumber slices

Servings~ 🕴
Cooking Time~ Seven Minutes
Pan to Use: Divided or Base

Cooking Steps
A. Pre-heat and with cooking spray. Place ham, cheese and dressing on roll and top with asparagus spears.
B. Place in well and cook five to seven minutes until filling is heated and roll is nicely browned. Open sandwich on a plate and garnish, alternating tomato and cucumber slices.

Vienna Sausage and Bean Dip

Ingredients
1 5oz. can Vienna sausages, cut into pieces
½ cup canned refried beans
2 tablespoons prepared salsa
Hot sauce optional
½ cup shredded taco cheese mix
1 bag tortilla chips

Servings~ 🕴🕴
Cooking Time~ Six Minutes
Pan to Use: Divided or Base

Cooking Steps
A. Pre-heat and spray with cooking spray. Mix sausage pieces with beans, salsa and hot sauce.
B. Divide dip evenly between cooking wells. Top each well with equal amounts of cheese. Heat for six minutes until cheese is melted.

Chili Dog Burrito's

Ingredients
2 8 in flour tortillas
1 cup canned chili
2 hot dogs
¼ cup shredded Monterey Jack cheese
1 tablespoon chopped onion

Servings~ 🕴🕴
Cooking Time~ Five Minutes
Pan to Use: Divided or Base

Cooking Steps
A. Pre-heat and spray with cooking spray. Spread half of chili on the lower center of each tortilla.
B. Place a dog on chili, sprinkle with cheese and onion and roll out, tucking in sides to fit well. Place one wrap in each well, close cover and cook five minutes cool before eating.

White Beans and Ham

Ingredients
1 cup small white canned beans
¾ cup cooked ham, cut into small cubes
2 tablespoons Italian style stewed tomatoes
1 teaspoon dehydrated onion flakes
¼ teaspoon dried Rosemary
¼ teaspoon dried parsley
Olive oil and grated parmesan cheese for serving

Servings~ 👤
Cooking Time~ Five Minutes
Pan to Use: Divided or Base

Cooking Steps
A. Pre-heat and spray with cooking spray. Combined all ingredients except oil and cheese in a small bowl. Divide bean mixture evenly between wells.
B. Close cover: cook five minutes until heated through. Drizzle with olive oil and top with parmesan if desired and serve immediately.

Glazed Ham Steak

Ingredients
¼ cup apricot preserves
¼ cup brown and spicy mustard
Pinch of ground allspice
1 tablespoon orange juice
1 small ham steak, cut in half to fit

Servings~ 👤👤
Cooking Time~ Seven Minutes
Pan to Use: Divided or Base

Cooking Steps
A. Pre-heat and spray with cooking spray. Mix together first four ingredients in a small bowl to make glaze, brush both sides of ham with glaze
B. Heat ham steaks four minutes turn to promote even browning and cook three minutes longer

Sweet and Sour Spam

Ingredients
2 ½ inch thick slices of spam, cut bite sized cubes
¼ cup crushed pineapple, drained
4-5 slices canned carrots
4 suite gherkin pickles, stems removed cut in half
½ cup sweet and sour sauce
Dash soy sauce

Servings~ 👤
Cooking Time~ Seven Minutes
Pan to Use: Divided or Base

Cooking Steps
A. Pre-heat and spray with cooking spray. mix together all ingredients in a small bowl.
B. Divide mixture evenly between cooking area, cook 5-7 minutes until heated through.

Italian Stuffed Pork Roast

Ingredients
1 small pork tender loin 6"-8" long
4 slices Italian prosciutto
4 Slices provolone cheese
1 cup thawed spinach, squeeze excess water
2 tablespoons Pesto
1 tablespoon minced garlic
2 tablespoons pine nuts
Pinch of dried Italian seasonings
Olive oil

Servings~ 👤👤
Cooking Time~ Twenty Minutes
Pan to Use: Divided or Base

Cooking Steps
A. Pre-heat and spray with cooking spray. Slice pork tenderloin lengthwise without cutting completely through, open flat and spread with prepared pesto. Lay prosciutto and provolone to cover pork. In a separate bowl, mix spinach, garlic and pine nuts; spread mixture across prosciutto and provolone. Roll up pork jelly roll style, cut in half to fit wells.
B. One tablespoon of water in each well, place one half of stuffed tenderloin in each well, brush exposed outer pork with olive oil and sprinkle with Italian seasonings. Close cover and cook 15 to 20 minutes until pork is no longer pink.

Ham Salad Poppers

Ingredients
4 wonton wrappers (similar to, but smaller than, egg roll wrappers)
½ cup prepared ham salad
½ teaspoon hot mustard
2 teaspoons whipped cream cheese

Servings~
Cooking Time~ Four Minutes
Pan to Use: Divided or Base

Cooking Steps
A. Pre-heat and spray with cooking spray. Mix together all ingredients (except wrappers). Divide filling mixture into four equal portions and spoon onto center of each wrapper. Fold up sides making little sacks, twisted and pinch to seal.
B. Spray each popper with cooking spray, cook two poppers in each well with three to four minutes.

Oriental Pork Cutlets

Ingredients
½ tablespoon cornstarch
1 tablespoon soy sauce
¼ teaspoon ground ginger
½ teaspoon brown sugar
1 tablespoon water
2 4 ounce boneless pork cutlets
¼ a sesame seeds
2 teaspoons oil for frying
Dash sesame seed oil
Sliced green onion for garnish

Servings~
Cooking Time~ Eight Minutes
Pan to Use: Divided or Base

Cooking Steps
A. Pre-heat and spray with cooking spray. Mix first five ingredients together in a small bowl. Put sesame seeds onto a saucer or piece of waxed paper. Dip cutlets in soy marinade, then press both sides into seeds to coat lightly, put 1 teaspoon of oil into each well.
B. Place one cutlet into each well, dividing any remaining marinade and sesame seeds between wells. Cook 10 minutes, turning after five minutes to brown tops (actual cooking time will vary depending on thickness of pork). Serve topped with green onion and a dash were two of sesame oil, if desired.

Quick Thai Brown Curry Pork

Ingredients
Olive oil for frying
2 4 ounce boneless pork cutlets
½ cup regular or light coconut milk
1 tablespoon Pad Thai seasoning
Dash fish sauce
Dash cinnamon
Dash dried cumin
½ cup baby carrots (cooked fresh or thawed frozen)
Sliced scallions for garnish (optional)

Servings~
Cooking Time~ Fifteen Minutes
Pan to Use: Divided or Base

Cooking Steps
A. Pre-heat and pour a small amount of olive oil into each well. Put one cutlet into each cooking well; and sear for five minutes.
B. In the meantime, to make sauce, combined all the remaining ingredients except scallion garnish. After five minutes, turn pork cutlets over. So brown side is up and top each with equal amounts of sauce. Close lid and cook 10 more minutes until pork is tender.

Pork Roll & Cheese Croissant

Ingredients
1 piece sliced pork roll cut to fit Wells
2 slices, Munster cheese
1 croissant
Spicy brown mustard

Servings~ 👤
Cooking Time~ Eight Minutes
Pan to Use: Divided or Base

Cooking Steps
A. Pre-heat and spray with cooking spray. Cut pork roll into pieces, and fry each half in each well for two minutes on each side. Cut croissant in half lengthwise and spray inside of croissant liberally with mustard. Fold one cheese sliced in half and place on bottom side of sandwich, top with pork roll, then second slice of cheese and other half of croissant.
B. Spray entire outside of croissant was cooking spray. Cut croissant in half and place one half in each well. Close cover and Grill for 8 minutes turned for even browning.

Orange Glazed Smoked Pork Chops

Ingredients
2 tablespoons orange juice concentrate
2 tablespoons start around sugar
1 teaspoon soy sauce
¼ teaspoon garlic powder
2 (4-6 ounces) boneless smoked pork chops cut 1 inch thick

Servings~ 👤👤
Cooking Time~ Six Minutes
Pan to Use: Divided or Base

Cooking Steps
A. Pre-heat and spray with cooking spray. Combined all ingredients except chops. Brush both sides of each chop with mixture, reserve remaining mixture for serving.
B. Cook six minutes heat remaining sauce and spoon over chops before serving.

Ham & Cheese Panini

Ingredients
2 slices white Italian bread
1 tablespoon Dijonaise or mayo mustard mix
2 slices tomato
2 ounces deli slices ham
1 ounce provolone or Swiss cheese
Olive oil

Servings~ 👤👤
Cooking Time~ Four Minutes
Pan to Use: Base

Cooking Steps
A. Pre-heat and spray with cooking spray. Spread the bread with Dijonaise or mayo mustard. Place cheese and ham on bread, top with tomato. Top with second slice of bread and brush with olive oil.
Brush top with olive oil. Close cover and cook for 4 minutes until golden brown.

Corn Dogs

Ingredients
1 pouch (6.4 to 6.5 ounces) or one small box (seven to 8 1/2 ounces) corn muffin mix
3 hot dogs whole or cut in to pieces

Servings~ 👤👤
Cooking Time~ Ten Minutes
Pan to Use: Divided, Mini or Base

Cooking Steps
A. Pre-heat and spray with cooking spray. Mix corn muffin mix according to package directions. Fill Wells half full with muffin batter. Place one whole hotdog or pieces into each well.
B. Add enough muffin batter to fill Wells. Cook eight to 10 minutes or until toothpick inserted into the center comes out clean. Repeat with remaining hot dogs and batter.

Spring Lamb Salad

Ingredients
Leftover cooked lamb equal to one serving
1 tablespoon extra virgin olive oil
1 teaspoon minced garlic
1 tablespoon lemon juice
2 sprigs fresh rosemary (strip leaves from stems)
1 teaspoon fresh ground pepper
For the Salad
2 cups salad mix
½ cup pitted kalamata olives
½ cups crumbled feta cheese
1½ tablespoons balsamic vinegar
Salt and pepper to taste

Servings~ ♦
Cooking Time~ Five Minutes
Pan to Use: Divided or Base

Cooking Steps
A. Pre-heat and spray with cooking spray. Mix lamb and the next five ingredients together, and set aside, toss all salad ingredients together and set aside.
B. Divide lamb mixture between wells, close cover and cook five minutes until heated through. Toss heated lamb with greens mixture. Top with the an additional lemon juice if desired.

Lamb Burger Loaves With Yogurt Sauce

Ingredients
½ pound ground lamb
½ teaspoon lemon pepper
Salt to taste
½ cup yogurt
1 tablespoon minced garlic
½ teaspoon dried mint or for chopped mint leaves
Fresh lemon slices (optional garnish)

Servings~ ♦♦
Cooking Time~ Twenty Minutes
Pan to Use: Divided or Base

Cooking Steps
A. Pre-heat and spray with cooking spray. Combine first three ingredients, divide mixture in half and form it into a ball. Shape each ball into an elongated burger patty.
B. Cook 15 to 20 minutes to desired wellness, turning to brown evenly. Mix together yogurt and garlic. Remove patties and garnish with fresh mint, if desired and/or two thin lemon slices and serve with yogurt sauce.

Franks & Beans Burrito

Ingredients
2 8 inch corn tortillas
1 cup canned pork and beans
1 tablespoon BBQ sauce
1 tablespoon real bacon bits
2 tablespoons finely chopped onions
2 hot dogs
Ketchup and mustard, if desired

Servings~ ♦♦
Cooking Time~ Five Minutes
Pan to Use: Divided or Base

Cooking Steps
A. Pre-heat and spray with cooking spray. Slice hot dogs in half lengthwise, lay two hot dog halves on each tortilla. Mix together beans, barbecue sauce and bacon bits. Divide the mixture evenly on top of hot dogs on tortillas and sprinkle with even amounts of onion. Fold in sides of tortilla and rollup(rub small amount of water along top flap of tortilla after rolling to help seal)
B. Place 1 burrito in each well, tucking tortilla to fit. Close cover and cook five minutes, until filling is heated through. Serve with ketchup or mustard for dipping.

American Panini

Ingredients
2 thick slices sourdough bread
4 slices bologna
4 slices yellow American cheese
2 thin slices tomato
1 teaspoon mustard
1 teaspoon sweet pickle relish
Butter or margarine

Servings~ 👤👤
Cooking Time~ Ten Minutes
Pan to Use: Divided or Base

Cooking Steps
A. Pre-heat and spray with cooking spray. Spread on one side of each slice of bread with butter or margarine. To assemble Panini, spread inside of one slice of bread with mustard. Place two slices of cheese on bread, then two slices of bologna, tomato, two slices of bologna, two slices of cheese, pick relish. Top with other slice of bread, butter size will touch cook surface.
B. Cut sandwich in half and put one half in each well. Grill for 10 minutes until Panini is golden brown.

Cheatin' Boston Baked Beans

Ingredients
3 tablespoons ketchup
1 teaspoon brown mustard
1 tablespoon maple syrup
2 teaspoons brown sugar
1 teaspoon Worcestershire sauce
1 cup canned Pinto beans, rinsed, drain thoroughly
1 tablespoon chopped onion
4 slices heat and serve bacon

Servings~ 👤👤
Cooking Time~ Twenty Minutes
Pan to Use: Divided or Base

Cooking Steps
A. Pre-heat and spray with cooking spray, mix together first five ingredients, add beans and onion mix to bowl. Divide equal amounts of bean mixture between wells.
B. Top each well with two slices of bacon and cook for 20 minutes. Serve with pumpernickel bread and butter.

Ham and Scallop Potatoes

Ingredients
1 cup sliced canned potatoes
2 tablespoons chopped Canadian bacon
½ cup heavy whipping cream
2 teaspoons butter
2 tablespoons shredded Swiss cheese
1/8 teaspoon onion powder
Paprika, salt and pepper to taste

Servings~ 👤👤
Cooking Time~ Twelve Minutes
Pan to Use: Divided or Base

Cooking Steps
A. Do not Pre-heat, but spray with cooking spray. Place ½ cup potato slices in one tablespoon bacon in to each well. Mix heavy cream with onion powder, salt and pepper in a small bowl. Pour equal amounts of cream mixture over potato.
B. Top each well with one tablespoon shredded Swiss cheese and sprinkle with paprika. Plug in unit and cook for 10 to 12 minutes.

Honey Mustard Smoked Pork Chops

Ingredients
2 (4 ounce) smoked pork chops, ¾ thick
1 tablespoon mustard
1 teaspoon honey
½ teaspoon soy sauce
1/8 teaspoon garlic powder

Servings~ 👤👤
Cooking Time~ Six Minutes
Pan to Use: Divided or Base

Cooking Steps
A. Pre-heat and spray with cooking spray. Place one pork chop in each well cook three minutes. Combine remaining ingredients.
B. Brush both sides of chops continue to cook for three minutes. Spoon liquid from Wells over chops before serving.

Polenta Panini's

Ingredients
4 ½ inch slices prepared polenta
6 slices salami
2 slices fontina cheese
1 egg
½ cup Italian flavored bread crumbs
1 teaspoon butter

Servings~ 👤👤
Cooking Time~ Ten Minutes
Pan to Use: Divided or Base

Cooking Steps
A. Pre-heat and spray with cooking spray. For each polenta Panini, top one piece of polenta with three slices salami and one slice cheese, and top with another piece of polenta. Beat egg in small bowl with fork. Place bread crumbs on small plate. dip both sides of each Panini in egg, then dredge in bread crumbs to cover both sides.
B. Place 1 teaspoon butter into each well and let melt. Place one Panini into each well, cook five minutes on each side until golden brown and cheese is melted.

Blue Cheese and Bacon Frittata

Ingredients
3 large eggs
1 tablespoon half and half
3 strips, fully cooked bacon, chopped
¼ cup thinly sliced mushrooms
¼ cup finely chopped onion
2 tablespoons crumbled blue cheese
Dash of garlic powder
Salt and black pepper to taste

Servings~ 👤👤
Cooking Time~ Ten Minutes
Pan to Use: Divided or Base

Cooking Steps
A. Pre-heat and spray with cooking spray. Add all ingredients into Shaker and mix well.
B. Divide frittata mixture evenly between wells. Cook eight to 10 minutes (frittatas should be slightly brown on top and not running).

Whole Wheat Ham Pitawich

Ingredients
1 cup sliced canned potatoes
2 tablespoons chopped Canadian bacon
½ cup heavy whipping cream
2 teaspoons butter
2 tablespoons shredded Swiss cheese
1/8 teaspoon onion powder
Paprika, salt and pepper to taste

Servings~ 👤👤
Cooking Time~ Five Minutes
Pan to Use: Divided or Base

Cooking Steps
A. Pre-heat and spray with cooking spray. Spread half the mustard on the inside of each of the pitas fill with remaining ingredients.
B. Place one half in each well cook five minutes.

Mini Pigs in a Blanket

Ingredients
8 brown n serve sausages chopped
1 6 ounce package pancake mix
1 cup water

Servings~ 👤👤👤👤
Cooking Time~ Four Minutes
Pan to Use: Mini

Cooking Steps
A. Pre-heat and spray with cooking spray. Mix batter and water in bowl. Place a piece of sausage into each cooking area and cover with pancake batter.
B. Cook 4 minutes. Repeat with remaining sausages and batter. Serve warm with butter and syrup.

Sausage Tortellini Bake

Ingredients
Refrigerator sausage tortellini
1 jar prepared Alfredo sauce
½ cup thawed frozen peas and carrots
2 tablespoons shredded mozzarella
Parmesan cheese and minced fresh or dried parsley for serving

Servings~ 🧍
Cooking Time~ Fifteen Minutes
Pan to Use: Divided or Base

Cooking Steps
A. Pre-heat and spray with cooking spray. Fill Wells with tortellini, save any extra for another meal. Pour enough Alfredo sauce into each well to cover tortellini, but be careful not to overfill (with the sauce on top will brown like it was baked in the oven). Divide mozzarella peas and carrots between wells.
B. Cover; cook approximately 15 minutes until pasta is cooked al dente or to desired softness. Transfer to serving plate and sprinkle with parmesan and parsley.

Pork Tenderloin Stuffed with Dried Fruit and Herb Stuffing

Ingredients
1 (1 pound), pork tenderloin
¼ cup finely chopped mixed dried fruit
½ cup herb flavored stuffing mix or stovetop stuffing
1 tablespoon butter
½ cup apple juice
Glaze
1 tablespoon apricot jam
1 tablespoon chicken broth or water
½ teaspoon mustard
½ teaspoon soy sauce
1/8 teaspoon garlic powder

Servings~ 🧍🧍
Cooking Time~ Twelve Minutes
Pan to Use: Divided or Base

Cooking Steps
A. Pre-heat and spray with cooking spray. Cut split lengthwise in pork, being careful not to cut completely through. Combined fruits stuffing mix butter and juice. Stuff into slit in pork using cotton string to tie pork every 2 inches. cut meat roll in half crosswise placed each half in wells cook 12 minutes
B. Meanwhile, combine glaze ingredients brush meat with glaze and continue to cook three more minutes. Remove meat from Wells and add remaining glaze to Wells heat about 30 seconds' spoon juices over meat before serving.

Ham & Cheese Mini Frittatas

Ingredients
½ cup chopped onion
2/3 cup chopped ham
1/3 cup shredded cheddar cheese
2 tablespoons chopped fresh chives
½ teaspoon each dried thyme and black pepper
4 large egg whites
1 whole egg

Servings~ 🧍🧍🧍🧍 🧍🧍🧍🧍
Cooking Time~ Fifteen Minutes
Pan to Use: Divided and Mini

Cooking Steps
A. Place divided pan in unit and pre-heat and spray with cooking spray. Add onion; sauté for 2 minutes or until crisp, add ham to onion; sauté for 3 minutes. Remove divided pan and let cool for 5 minutes.
B. Combine remaining ingredients in a large bowl and stir. Add ham mixture and stir. Place mini pan inside unit and spray with non stick spray and preheat. Spoon mixture into mini pan and cook 10 minutes and until set. Mixture should make around 24 frittatas.

Pork Tenderloin w/ Sweet Potatoes

Ingredients
1 pork tenderloin
½ cup canned sweet potato
¼ small apple peeled and sliced thin
2 tablespoons brown sugar
1 small pat of butter
Bottled teriyaki marinade

Servings~ 👤👤
Cooking Time~ Seven Minutes
Pan to Use: Mini

Cooking Steps
A. Pre-heat and spray with cooking spray. Place pork tenderloin in plastic bag with marinade. Seal and marinade a few hours if possible overnight.
B. Slice 4 medallions of tenderloin and lay in one area overlapping to fit. Mix sweet potato, apple, and brown sugar together and place in other area. Place pat of butter on top. Close lid and cook 7 minutes.

Ham & Cheese Dijon

Ingredients
1 tablespoons butter or margarine, melted
1/2 teaspoon Dijon mustard
Dash Worcestershire sauce
2 slices Red Onion
Several strips of roasted red pepper
2 slices bread
1 thick slice cooked ham
1 slice Swiss cheese

Servings~ 👤
Cooking Time~ Five Minutes
Pan to Use: Base

Cooking Steps
A. Pre-heat and spray with cooking spray. In a small bowl combined butter, Dijon mustard, and Worcestershire sauce. Brush butter mixture on one side of each slice of bread. Then place a slice of bread butter side down in the base of unit.
B. Place ham, cheese onion and red peppers on, then top with other slice of bread butter side up. Close lid and cook 4-5 minutes.

Poultry

Italian Chicken Rolls

Ingredients
2 5oz. boneless, skinless chicken breasts
1 slice Swiss cheese – halved
1 slice prosciutto or lean ham – halved
¼ cup Italian bread crumbs
1 tablespoon parmesan cheese
¼ teaspoon garlic salt
½ teaspoon Italian seasoning or ¼ teaspoon each basil and oregano
2 tablespoons melted butter

Servings~ 👤👤
Cooking Time~ Fifteen Minutes
Pan to Use: Divided or Base

Cooking Steps
A. Pound each breast until about ¼ inch thick. Layer ½ cheese slice and prosciutto on chicken and roll to encase filling. Mix remaining ingredients except butter in shallow dish, dip each chicken roll in butter and then in crumbs to coat
B. Place seam side down in Pre-heated unit and sprayed with cooking spray. Close cover cook 15 minutes.

Crispy Potato Chicken

Ingredients
2 4-5 ounce boneless, skinless chicken breasts, seasoned with ½ teaspoon seasoned salt
1 medium potato, peeled and shredded
1 teaspoon olive oil
Salt, pepper and garlic powder
½ teaspoon dried parsley flakes

Servings~ 👤👤👤👤
Cooking Time~ Fifteen Minutes
Pan to Use: Divided or Base

Cooking Steps
A. In small bowl mix shredded potato with seasonings and olive oil. Pre-heat and spray wells with non stick spray. Place small amount of potato mixture in each well, top with seasoned chicken, then place half of remaining potato on top of chicken, spreading to cover evenly.
B. Close cover and cook 15 minutes, until potato topping is crisp and chicken is done.

Chicken Pot Pie to Go

Ingredients
2 slices whole grain bread
½ cup mixed vegetables
½ cup chopped cooked chicken, beef or pork
1 cup mashed potatoes, divided
¼ cup of grated cheddar or Swiss
Cooking spray

Servings~ 👤👤
Cooking Time~ Eight Minutes
Pan to Use: Divided or Base

Cooking Steps
A. Pre-heat and spray with cooking spray. Place a slice of bread into each well. Top each with half of the vegetables and meat.
B. Spoon the potatoes over the mixture and top with cheese. Cook 8 minutes.

Chicken Croquettes

Ingredients
¾ cup prepared or leftover mashed potatoes
1 egg
½ teaspoon poultry seasoning
1 5-oz. can chunk white meat chicken
1 cup prepared chicken gravy, heated as directed

Servings~ 👤👤
Cooking Time~ Eight Minutes
Pan to Use: Divided or Base

Cooking Steps
A. Mix all ingredients together (except gravy). Form into 2 loaf-shaped patties.
B. Pre-heat and spray with cooking spray. Close cover; cook 8 minutes until heated through. Remove, serve ladled with gravy.

Barbecued Chicken and Corn Pockets

Ingredients
1 (11-ounce) refrigerated French bread dough or 1 (13.8oz) refrigerated pizza crust dough
1 ½ cups of chopped cooked chicken
1 cup barbecue sauce
1 cup cheddar cheese
1 cup canned or frozen corn, defrosted

Servings~ 👤👤👤👤
Cooking Time~ Eight Minutes
Pan to Use: Divided or Base

Cooking Steps
A. Unroll bread or pizza dough onto a lightly floured board or plastic wrap. Sprinkle the top of the dough lightly with flour. Press out four dough circles. Combine the remaining ingredients. Place a dough circle into the opened pocket maker. Spoon about ½ cup of the mixture into the bottom section of the dough circle. Close the lid and press down firmly to crimp the edges of the sandwich. Repeat the process with remaining dough and ingredients. Spray wells lightly with cooking spray
B. Place one in each well. Cook 8 minutes or until well browned. Cook remaining 2 pockets.

Note: Sandwiches can be partially cooked for 4 minutes and refrigerated for reheating at a later time. To reheat, spray the wells lightly with cooking spray and heat for four minutes.

Coca-Cola Chicken

Ingredients
1 tablespoon Lipton onion soup mix
1 cup Coca-Cola
¼ teaspoon Wondra flour
2 6oz. boneless skinless chicken breasts

Servings~ 👤👤
Cooking Time~ Fifteen Minutes
Pan to Use: Divided or Base

Cooking Steps
A. Mix together first three ingredients in a small bowl. Pre-heat and spray lightly with cooking spray. Place one chicken cutlet into each well.
B. Cook 5 minutes. Turn chicken breasts over and top with cola mixture. Cook 10 minutes more until chicken is no longer pink.

Crunchy Coated Chicken

Ingredients
2 5 oz. boneless skinless chicken breasts
1 egg, beaten
1 tablespoon spicy mustard
½ cup finely crushed pecans

Servings~ 👤👤
Cooking Time~ Twelve Minutes
Pan to Use: Divided or Base

Cooking Steps
A. Pre-heat and spray with cooking spray. In small bowl combine egg, mustard and seasonings, beating well. Dip chicken in egg and then roll in crushed pecans until well coated.
B. Place one breast in each well. Close cover; cook 15 minutes, until chicken is done.

Egg Foo Yung

Ingredients
4 eggs, well beaten
1 tablespoon sugar
1 green onion, sliced
1 stalk celery, thinly sliced
1 carrot, finely chopped
½ cup bean sprouts, drained
½ cup cooked shredded chicken
½ teaspoon vegetable oil

Servings~ 👤👤👤👤
Cooking Time~ Eight Minutes
Pan to Use: Divided or Base

Cooking Steps
A. Pre-heat and spray with cooking spray. Put eggs and sugar in shaker, mix well and set aside. Pour ¼ teaspoon of vegetable oil in each well. Mix the chopped veggies together and put about ¼ of mixture in each well and close cover and cook for 2 minutes. Open lid and spread ¼ of cooked chicken over veggies. Top with ¼ of the egg mixture.
B. Close cover and cook for 6 minutes until egg is set. Remove and cook second batch. Serve with Egg Foo Yung sauce below.

Egg Foo Yung Sauce

Ingredients
1 cube chicken bouillon
¾ cup hot water
1 teaspoon sugar
1 tablespoon soy sauce
4 tablespoons cold water
2 teaspoons corn starch

Servings~
Cooking Time~

Cooking Steps
A. Dissolve cube in hot water in a small saucepan. Add sugar and soy sauce. Bring to a boil. Mix cornstarch with cold water, add to broth mixture, stirring until thickened and then serve over Egg Foo Yung.

Crab Stuffed Chicken

Ingredients
2 4-5oz. boneless skinless chicken breasts
½ cup flaked crabmeat
1 tablespoon mayonnaise
2 teaspoons lemon juice, divided
2 tablespoons bread crumbs
1 small shallot, chopped
¼ cup white wine or white grape juice
1 tablespoon butter

Servings~ 👤👤
Cooking Time~ Twelve Minutes
Pan to Use: Divided or Base

Cooking Steps
A. Pre-heat and spray with cooking spray. Cut horizontal slit in chicken to form pocket, mix crab, mayonnaise, lemon juice and bread crumbs. Stuff into pockets.
B. Place chicken in wells and close cover. Cook 12 minutes. Sauté shallots in wine until liquid is reduced by half. Remove from heat; add butter and remaining lemon juice. Stir until butter is melted and serve over chicken.

Chicken Moutarde

Ingredients
1 4oz. boneless skinless chicken breasts
½ cup of cream of asparagus soup
¼ cup half and half or light cream
2 tablespoons Dijon mustard
½ teaspoon dried thyme
½ teaspoon dried rosemary
Salt and pepper to taste

Servings~ 👤👤
Cooking Time~ Ten Minutes
Pan to Use: Divided or Base

Cooking Steps
A. Put chicken breast into a quart sized Ziploc bag and pound to about half its thickness. Remove from bag and cut into cubes. Pre-heat and spray with cooking spray.
B. Divide chicken cubes between wells. Cook chicken 10 minutes until no longer pink. Turn once halfway through cooking for even browning. While chicken is cooking combine remaining ingredients. Divide sauce mixture evenly between wells; cook 3 additional minutes to warm sauce.

Spinach Stuffed Lemon Herb Chicken

Ingredients
2 4-5oz. boneless skinless chicken breasts
¼ cup lemon juice
2 packets splenda
1 tablespoon olive oil
1 teaspoon dried parsley flakes
½ teaspoon dried chives
Fresh spinach leaves

Servings~ 👥
Cooking Time~ Fifteen Minutes
Pan to Use: Divided or Base

Cooking Steps
A. Place all ingredients except chicken and spinach in a plastic bag. Cut a pocket in the thick side of the chicken, place in bag with marinade. Seal bag and squeeze to coat chicken. Marinate for 30 minutes.
B. Pre-heat and spray with cooking spray. Remove chicken from marinade, stuff pocket with spinach leaves and place in wells. Close cover bake 15 minutes or until chicken is done.

Florentine Chicken Pinwheels

Ingredients
1 (8-ounce) boneless skinless chicken breast, butterflied and pounded thin
2 tablespoons garlic and herb flavored cheese spread
1 roasted red pepper, cut into pieces
1 ounce baby spinach, chopped
1 ounce Swiss cheese, thinly sliced

Servings~ 👥
Cooking Time~ Ten Minutes
Pan to Use: Divided or Base

Cooking Steps
A. Pound chicken as thin as possible until it is about 7 inches long. Spoon cheese onto chicken and spread evenly to within 1 inch of edge. Top with peppers, spinach and cheese. Roll tightly and cut in half.
B. Place 1 piece in each well. Cook 10 minutes. Cut each piece into three slices and serve with chicken gravy, if desired.

Blue Cheese Chicken

Ingredients
2 6 ounce boneless skinless chicken breast
Seasoned salt
Poultry seasoning
1/2 cup blue cheese
2 tablespoons water

Servings~ 👥
Cooking Time~ Fifteen Minutes
Pan to Use: Divided or Base

Cooking Steps
A. Pre-heat and spray with cooking spray. Season both sides of chicken breasts with seasoned salt and poultry seasoning.
Place one tablespoon of water into each well. Place one chicken breast into each well and cook 10 minutes. Open cover and pour 1/4 cup blue cheese dressing into each well. Cook five minutes until chicken is no longer pink and chicken is 180°

Asian Honey Chicken Tidbits

Ingredients
2 4oz. chicken cutlets
2 tablespoons honey
2 tablespoons melted butter
2 tablespoons Chinese mustard
1 tablespoon soy sauce
½ teaspoon chopped garlic
1 tablespoon chopped peanuts

Servings~ 👥
Cooking Time~ Twelve Minutes
Pan to Use: Divided or Base

Cooking Steps
A. Pre-heat and spray with cooking spray. Cut chicken into bite sized pieces. Mix together remaining ingredients except peanuts and add chicken.
B. Divide seasoned chicken between wells. Close cover; cook 12 minutes or until done. Sprinkle with chopped peanuts, if desired, and serve.

Low Fat Baked Chicken Chimis

Ingredients
½ small onion chopped
1 clove garlic minced
1 ½ teaspoons vegetable oil
1 cup salsa
1 teaspoon chili powder
¼ teaspoon cumin
¼ teaspoon cinnamon
1 pinch salt
1 cup cooked shredded chicken
4 12 inch flour tortillas
½ cup canned refried beans

Servings~ 👤👤👤👤
Cooking Time~ Six Minutes
Pan to Use: Divided or Base

Cooking Steps
A. Pre-heat and spray with cooking spray. Sauté onion and garlic in oil softened, add salsa, chili powder, cumin, cinnamon and salt. Stir in chicken working with 1 tortilla at a time. Spread 2 tablespoons of beans into tortillas, top with ¼ of chicken mixture. Fold up bottom; fold in sides and roll, ending up with a roll about 5 inches wide. Repeat with all 4 tortillas.
B. Place chimi in well, seam side down, spray with light coating of spray to help crisping. Close cover cook for 6 minutes until browned and filling is hot. Repeat with second two tortillas. Serve with additional salsa and fat free sour cream.

Chicken Yassa (Kwanzaa)

Ingredients
2 tablespoons olive oil
1 tablespoon dried hot chili peppers
½ clove fresh garlic minced
1 teaspoon celery salt
2 4oz. boneless skinless chicken thighs
½ small onion sliced paper thin

Servings~ 👤👤
Cooking Time~ Twelve Minutes
Pan to Use: Divided or Base

Cooking Steps
A. Mix first 4 ingredients in a quart-sized Ziploc bag. Add chicken and marinate in fridge for 30 minutes.
B. Pre-heat and spray with cooking spray. Put equal amounts of sliced onion into cooking wells. Place one chicken thigh on top of onions. Close cover; cook approximately 10 minutes until chicken is no longer pink.

Japanese Chicken Breasts

Ingredients
2 teaspoons ponzo sauce
2 teaspoons soy sauce
2 teaspoons rice wine vinegar
1 teaspoon miso
1 tablespoon water
2 teaspoons prepared wasabi
1 teaspoon minced garlic
1 tablespoon minced fresh ginger
2 green onions (scallions) cut in long thin strips for garnish

Servings~ 👤
Cooking Time~ Five Minutes
Pan to Use: Divided or Base

Cooking Steps
A. In a large Ziploc bag; combine all ingredients except chicken and scallions. Seal bag and shake vigorously until completely blended; add chicken breasts. Reseal; marinate in refrigerator for at least 30 minutes before cooking.
B. Pre-heat and spray with cooking spray. Put one chicken breast into each cooking well. Cook 15 minutes, until chicken is no longer pink. Top with scallions; serve immediately.

Chicken Tetrazzini

Ingredients
4 ounces cook chicken or turkey
1 cup cooked spaghetti
½ cup condensed cream of mushroom soup
¼ cup water
2 tablespoons freshly made breadcrumbs
1 teaspoon melted butter
2 tablespoons grated parmesan cheese

Servings~ 👤👤
Cooking Time~ Ten Minutes
Pan to Use: Divided or Base

Cooking Steps
A. Combine all ingredients except breadcrumbs, butter and cheese. Spray wells lightly with cooking spray. Place half of mixture in each well.
B. Stir butter into breadcrumbs and sprinkle over mixture. Top with cheese.

Easy Chicken Chow Mei Fun

Ingredients
4oz. rice vermicelli noodles
2 tablespoons canned mixed vegetables
2 oz. leftover cooked chicken, cut into thin strips
1 tablespoon canned or fresh been sprouts
1 green onion (scallion) sliced into ¼ inch slices
2 tablespoons canned sliced water chestnuts
1 tablespoon reduced sodium soy sauce
½ teaspoon minced garlic
2 teaspoons water
2 teaspoons oil for frying

Servings~ 👤
Cooking Time~ Five Minutes
Pan to Use: Divided or Base

Cooking Steps
A. Break noodles in half and soak 15 minutes according to package directions. Drain noodles and combine with all remaining ingredients, except oil.
B. Pre-heat and spray with cooking spray. Divide noodle, vegetable, meat mixture evenly between wells. Cook 4-5 minutes, stir for "stir fry": effect.

Mexican Tequila Chicken

Ingredients
1 4oz. boneless skinless chicken breast cubed
1 tablespoon minced fresh cilantro
1 tablespoon minced basil
1 tablespoon minced fresh ginger
1 cup Thai unsweetened coconut milk
1 tablespoon prepared green curry paste
Dash of Thai fish sauce

Servings~ 👤
Cooking Time~ Ten Minutes
Pan to Use: Divided or Base

Cooking Steps
A. Pre-heat and spray with cooking spray. Marinade chicken in tequila and lime juice for 10 minutes; discard marinade. Place 1 tablespoon Guanabana concentrate in each well. Sprinkle both sides of chicken tenders with lime pepper.
B. Place one chicken tender in each well and top with 1 tablespoon remaining Guanabana concentrate. Cook 10 minutes or until chicken is no longer pink, flipping halfway through cooking time; be sure each tender is thoroughly coated with juice. Transfer tenders to serving plate; sprinkle with salt and serve with lime wedges.

Chicken Pot Pie

Ingredients
1 (9 inch) refrigerated prepared pie crust, cut into 4 triangles
6 ounces cooked chicken cut into ½ inch cubes
1 cup frozen mixed vegetables thawed
1 tablespoon chopped onion
½ cup condensed cream of mushroom soup, undiluted
½ teaspoon salt
½ teaspoon garlic salt
¼ teaspoon pepper

Servings~ 👤👤
Cooking Time~ Twenty Minutes
Pan to Use: Divided or Base

Cooking Steps
A. Do not Pre-heat. Place 1 triangle of pie crust in each well, with rounded side of dough in rounded side of well. Allow about 1 inch of dough on rounded side to extend above well. Combine remaining ingredients. Place half of mixture into each pie crust lined well. Top each with remaining crusts. Roll edges to form pies (be sure that all of filling is enclosed).
B. Make 3 small slits in top crust of each pie to allow steam to vent. Cook 20 minutes. Allow to cool 2 minutes before removing from wells.

Squash Stuffed Chicken Breasts

Ingredients
2 4oz. boneless skinless chicken breasts
1 cup frozen pureed squash, prepared as directed
¼ cup large herb flavored croutons
1 tablespoon shredded Swiss or cheddar cheese
1 tablespoon dried cranberries
Dash cinnamon
Dash nutmeg
1 tablespoon apricot preserves
¼ cup orange juice

Servings~ 👤👤
Cooking Time~ Twenty Minutes
Pan to Use: Divided or Base

Cooking Steps
A. Cut a lengthwise slit in sides of chicken breasts without cutting all the way through. Spread chicken breasts open to create pocket. Combine next 6 ingredients in a small bowl until well mixed. Divide mixture in half and spoon into breast pockets.
B. Pre-heat and spray with cooking spray. Mix apricot preserves with orange juice to make glaze and brush top of stuffed chicken breasts. Put chicken into wells of unit. Pour equal amounts of any excess glaze over chicken in wells. Cook for 15-20 minutes until chicken is no longer pink.

Doritos Chicken Fingers

Ingredients
3-6 boneless skinless chicken tenders
½ cup flour for dredging
½ cup crushed Doritos (recommend cool ranch flavor)
1 egg
1 tablespoon water
2 teaspoons butter or margarine for frying

Servings~ 👤
Cooking Time~ Fifteen Minutes
Pan to Use: Divided or Base

Cooking Steps
A. In a small bowl, beat together egg and water thoroughly. Pre-heat. Melt 1 teaspoon of butter or margarine in each cooking well. Dredge chicken strips first in flour, then egg mixture. Coat evenly with crushed Doritos.
B. Divide chicken fingers evenly between wells. Fry 10-15 minutes, depending on thickness of chicken, until meat is cook through and no longer pink. Turn tenders after 6 minutes for even browning.

Chicken Purses

Ingredients
1 3oz package cream cheese
1 tablespoon melted butter
1 cup cooked chicken, diced
2 tablespoons milk
1 tablespoon minced onion
½ teaspoon seasoned salt
Dash of pepper
1 can refrigerated crescent rolls

Servings~ 👤👤👤👤
Cooking Time~ Six Minutes
Pan to Use: Divided or Base

Cooking Steps
A. Pre-heat and spray with cooking spray. Open crescent rolls, unroll and divide into 4 rectangles. Mix together all other ingredients, divide onto each dough square. Bring up the corners and pinch together, making purses.
B. Cook 2 at a time in wells for 6 minutes or until golden brown.

California Chicken Cutlet Sandwiches

Ingredients
2 4-6oz. boneless skinless chicken cutlets
Salt and pepper to taste
2 tablespoons extra virgin olive oil
Juice of 1 fresh lemon, with zest
2 slices Swiss cheese
2 bakery croissants cut in half lengthwise
Toppings: sliced tomatoes, sliced avocado, fresh alfalfa sprouts

Dressing
2 tablespoons plain yogurt or low fat mayonnaise
1 tablespoon minced garlic

Servings~ 👤👤
Cooking Time~ Fifteen Minutes
Pan to Use: Divided or Base

Cooking Steps
A. Season both sides of chicken with salt and pepper. Mix together olive oil and lemon juice; marinate chicken in mixture for at least 1 hour. Pre-heat and spray with cooking spray. Place one cutlet in each cooking well; cook 15 minutes until no longer pink. Turn off unit; top each cutlet with 1 slice of Swiss cheese and croissant to warm.
B. Close cover; let sit 5 minutes more; cheese will melt and croissant will become warm. Remove; put cutlets in croissant. Top with dressing and toppings, if desired.

Healthy Rolled Chicken Scaloppini and Tomatoes

Ingredients
1 4-5oz. chicken cutlet, pounded thin
Salt and pepper to taste
2 tablespoons low fat vegetable cream cheese
2 tablespoons chopped green pimento stuffed olives
2 tablespoons dried Italian seasoning
2 canned whole tomatoes, crushed with your hand or spoon, plus liquid to equal 1 ½ cups
1 tablespoon chicken broth
1 whole garlic clove, peeled and cut into thin slices
Fresh parsley for garnish
2 tablespoons extra virgin olive oil

Servings~ 👤👤
Cooking Time~ Fifteen Minutes
Pan to Use: Divided or Base

Cooking Steps
A. Season chicken cutlet with salt and pepper. Spread one side of cutlet with cream cheese, then top with olives and Italian seasoning. Roll up jelly roll style and cut in half; secure each piece with a toothpick, lengthwise. Pre-heat and heat 1 tablespoon olive oil in each cooking well.
B. Place one scaloppini into each well. Close cover and cook 5 minutes, turning halfway through cooking time to promote even browning. In the meantime, combine tomatoes, chicken broth and garlic; add equal amounts to cooking wells after the first 5 minutes of cooking. Close cover; cook an additional 10 minutes until chicken is tender and no longer pink.

Low-carb Chicken Breast Stuffed with Vegetables Alfredo

Ingredients
2 medium mushrooms, chopped
¼ cup chopped baby spinach leaves
2 tablespoons chopped onion
2 tablespoons chopped red peppers
1 sun-dried tomatoes, chopped
½ teaspoons salt
¼ teaspoons pepper
2 (6-8 ounce) boneless skinless chicken breasts
1 (1.25 ounce) package Alfredo sauce, prepared according to package directions

Servings~ 👥
Cooking Time~ Sixteen Minutes
Pan to Use: Divided or Base

Cooking Steps
A. Pre-heat and spray with cooking spray. Combined all ingredients except chicken and sauce mix. Cut lengthwise slit in each chicken breast to make pocket, being careful not to cut completely through
B. Place half of mixture into each breast, place one stuffed breast into each well. Cook 16 minutes or until well browned and meat thermometer inserted in thickest part of meat reads 180 degrees. Top with prepared Alfredo sauce and serve.

Chicken Cordon Bleu

Ingredients
1 3oz package cream cheese
1 tablespoon melted butter
1 cup cooked chicken, diced
2 tablespoons milk
1 tablespoon minced onion
½ teaspoon seasoned salt
Dash of pepper
1 can refrigerated crescent rolls

Servings~ 👥
Cooking Time~ Twenty Minutes
Pan to Use: Divided or Base

Cooking Steps
A. Pre-heat and spray with cooking spray. Make a pocket in each chicken breast fold a slice of cheese in each slice of ham and place one inside each chicken breast, and coat each with bread crumbs.
B. Carefully fit the stuffed chicken into the wells, cook 20 minutes serve topped with hollandaise béarnaise or your favorite sauce, if desired.
   1. **Cheddar and Broccoli Stuffed Chicken** substitute three tablespoons of chopped broccoli for the ham and cheddar cheese for the Swiss
   2. **Spinach and Feta Stuffed Chicken** substitute 3 tablespoons of chopped spinach, combined with 1 teaspoon pesto and 1 teaspoon chopped sun-dried tomato for the ham and feta for the Swiss cheese

Stuffed Chicken Breasts

Ingredients
1 boneless skinless chicken breasts, cut in half
1 cup instant stuffing mix, divided
1/4 cup hot water
1 tablespoon soft margarine

Servings~ 👥
Cooking Time~ Fifteen Minutes
Pan to Use: Divided or Base

Cooking Steps
A. Pre-heat and spray with cooking spray. Meanwhile, make 1/2 cup stuffing mix, water and margin in a small bowl. Set aside remaining stuffing mix and spread on plate. Slice a pocket inside each piece of chicken, opening butterfly-style lifestyle.
B. Place have of prepared stuffing on each chicken breast fold close. Then roll in crushed stuffing crumbs and place one piece of chicken in each well. Cook 15 minutes or until meat thermometer reaches 180°. Serve with hot chicken gravy if desired.

Aegean Chicken Cutlets

Ingredients
Aegean Topping
2 fresh tomatoes, chopped into bite size pieces
1 large cucumber, peeled and chopped into bite size pieces
1 green pepper, seeded and chopped
1 small red onion, chopped finely
1/2 cup pitted Kalamata olives, chopped
6 ounce crumbled feta cheese

Marinade/Dressing
1 cup olive oil
1 tablespoon lemon juice
1/3 cup red wine vinegar
1 tablespoon chopped garlic
2 tablespoons Dijon mustard
1 teaspoon dried thyme
1 teaspoon dried Rosemary
1 tablespoon fresh finely chopped parsley
1 tablespoon fresh finely chopped chives
Salt and pepper to taste

Servings~ 👤👤
Cooking Time~ Fifteen Minutes
Pan to Use: Divided or Base

Cooking Steps
A. Pre-heat and spray with cooking spray. Prepare marinade/dressing first marinate chicken in two tablespoons dressing in Ziploc bag and refrigerator for at least 30 minutes. Place one marinated chicken cutlet in each well. Cook chicken for 15 minutes or until meat thermometer reads 180°
B. Ok to add one tablespoon of water into each well, if necessary to stop over browning. While chicken is cooking, prepare all topping ingredients and mix with remaining dressing. When chicken is cooled, remove from unit. Top each cutlet with half the Aegean topping and serve.

Turkey Rollatini

Ingredients
½ cup ricotta
1 tablespoon shredded mozzarella
1 tablespoon grated pecorino or Romano cheese
2 tablespoons chopped frozen broccoli, dried
Pinch Italian seasoning blend
2 4 ounce boneless skinless turkey cutlets, flat
½ cup flour
1 egg beaten
½ cup panko breadcrumbs
1 cup prepared Alfredo sauce, heated
Pinch paprika and dried parsley for presentation

Servings~ 👤👤
Cooking Time~ Fifteen Minutes
Pan to Use: Divided or Base

Cooking Steps
A. Pre-heat GT press 101 and spray with cooking spray. Mix first five ingredients together in a small bowl. With a spoon divide ricotta mixture and spread it onto each cutlet, then rollup cutlets. dredge cutlets in flour, dip in egg, coat well with bread crumbs
B. Place one rollatini in each well. Seam side down. Close cover, cook 12 to 15 minutes. Top with heated Alfredo sauce paprika and parsley.

Quicky Chicken Parm

Ingredients
2 leftover cooked breaded chicken cutlets
Favorite jar spaghetti sauce
1/2 teaspoon garlic powder
4 tablespoons parmesan cheese
4 slices fresh mozzarella cheese
Fresh basil garnish for serving

Servings~ 👥
Cooking Time~ Seven Minutes
Pan to Use: Divided or Base

Cooking Steps
A. Pre-heat and spray with cooking spray. Each chicken serving will be two layers, so slice cutlets to fit into each well. When you stack them. Put a thin layer of sauce into each well. Place a piece of chicken cutlet into the well
B. Spread cutlet with another thin layer sauce and top with a piece of mozzarella and a tablespoon of parmesan cheese. Top the final layer of cheese with another dab of sauce. Cook five to seven minutes until heated through.

Buffalo Chicken Wrap

Ingredients
2 tablespoons prepared buffalo wing sauce
2 tablespoons blue cheese salad dressing
2 8 inch corn tortillas
2 small leftover grilled chicken breast (about 3 ounces)
1/2 ribs celery cut into 6, 3inch long. Matchsticks

Servings~ 👥
Cooking Time~ Twenty Minutes
Pan to Use: Divided or Base

Cooking Steps
A. Pre-heat and spray with cooking spray. Mix together buffalo wing sauce and blue cheese dressing. Place one chicken breast on the lower end of one tortilla. Place three celery sticks on top of chicken and cover with half the buffalo sauce/blue cheese mixture
B. Fold in sides of tortilla and roll up. Place in well, tucking tortilla to fit, seam side down. Repeat with second tortilla. Close cover and cook for seven minutes, until filling is heated through.

African Chicken Stew

Ingredients
1 teaspoon creamy peanut butter
4 ounce leftover cooked boneless skinless chicken breasts cut into cubes
1/4 cup canned stew tomatoes
1/4 cup garbanzo beans
1 small or 1/2 large leftover cooked sweet potato, cubed
2 ounce frozen peppers, thawed and chopped
1 teaspoon frozen minced onion, thawed
2 dashes each ground cumin, coriander, garlic powder, kind and, salt and pepper to taste

Servings~ 👥
Cooking Time~ Twenty Minutes
Pan to Use: Divided or Base

Cooking Steps
A. Pre-heat and spray with cooking spray. In a small microwave-safe bowl microwave peanut butter for three to four seconds to soften. Add remaining ingredients to softened peanut butter, mix well
B. Divide stew mixture between cooking wells. Cook five to seven minutes until heated through.

BBQ Chicken Wraps

Ingredients
1 cup of cooked chicken, shredded
1 cup of your favorite barbecue sauce
1 teaspoon honey
1/2 teaspoon soy sauce
1 tablespoon frozen Mexican corn niblets, thawed under cold running water
2 8 inch corn tortilla wraps
Readymade coleslaw

Servings~ 👤👤
Cooking Time~ Three Minutes
Pan to Use: Divided or Base

Cooking Steps
A. Pre-heat and spray with cooking spray. Mix chicken and next 4 ingredients and divide evenly between wells, cook for three minutes.
B. In the meantime, heat tortillas according to package directions. Mound heated BBQ chicken mixture onto warm tortillas, top with a mound of coleslaw. Roll up tortillas and serve with extra barbecue sauce, if desired.

Chicken Vodka Hero Sandwich

Ingredients
1 cup leftover boneless skinless chicken, cubed
1/2 cup canned peas
1 tablespoon fresh basil
1 tablespoon real bacon bits
1/2 cup prepared vodka sauce
Black pepper to taste
1 6-inch Italian roll
Grated Romano cheese, optional

Servings~ 👤
Cooking Time~ Five Minutes
Pan to Use: Divided or Base

Cooking Steps
A. Pre-heat and spray with cooking spray. Combine first six ingredients in a small bowl.
B. Divide chicken mixture between wells. Close cover, cook for five minutes until heated through. Fill roll with cooked chicken mixture and top with grated cheese, if desired.

Salsa Stuffed Chicken Breast

Ingredients
1/4 cup chunky salsa
1/3 cup flavored bread crumbs, divided
2 tablespoons shredded, cheddar cheese
1 skinless boneless chicken breast cut in half

Servings~ 👤👤
Cooking Time~ Fifteen Minutes
Pan to Use: Divided or Base

Cooking Steps
A. Pre-heat and spray with cooking spray. Combine salsa and three tablespoons of bread crumbs with cheese. Make pocket in each chicken breast, spoon half of salsa mixture into each pocket.
B. Spray both sides of chicken with cooking spray. Roll them in bread crumbs and place one piece in each well. Cook 15 minutes or until meat thermometer reaches 180°. Serve with hot salsa.

Pan-Blackened Chicken Caesar Salad

Ingredients
1 skinless, boneless chicken breast cut in half
1 tablespoon Cajun or canned blackening spices
5 large romaine lettuce leaves, torn into pieces
4 tablespoons fat-free or low-fat Caesar salad dressing
1 tablespoon grated parmesan cheese
2 tablespoons fat-free croutons

Servings~ 👫
Cooking Time~ Fifteen Minutes
Pan to Use: Divided or Base

Cooking Steps
A. Pre-heat and spray with cooking spray. Sprinkle spices or rub over chicken and press into surface of meat. Place half of chicken in each well cook 15 minutes
B. Meanwhile, toss lettuce with dressing and sprinkle with cheese divide between two plates. Thinly slice chicken and arrange over lettuce top with croutons.

Chicken Chili

Ingredients
1 cup ground chicken
1/2 small onion, chopped
1/2 cup salsa
1 tablespoon chili seasoning packet
1 tablespoon canned or thawed frozen corn niblets
2 tablespoons canned black beans
Pinch dried red pepper flakes
Shredded cheddar cheese, sour cream and tortilla chips for garnish

Servings~ 👫
Cooking Time~ Fifteen Minutes
Pan to Use: Divided or Base

Cooking Steps
A. Pre-heat and spray with cooking spray. Place 1/2 cup ground chicken in each well and cook five minutes. In small bowl, mix together remaining ingredients except garnishes.
B. Pour equal amounts of salsa mixture over browning chicken and stir. Cook additional 10 minutes until chicken is done.

Chicken Fajitas

Ingredients
2 4 ounce boneless, skinless chicken thighs
1/2 small onion, thinly sliced green and or red pepper slices
1/4 cup bottled fajitas seasoning
2 fajita size flour tortillas

Servings~ 👫
Cooking Time~ Ten Minutes
Pan to Use: Divided or Base

Cooking Steps
A. Pre-heat and spray with cooking spray. Open chicken thighs flat and slice into strips. Place in plastic bag with fajitas seasoning, onion and pepper. Mix and let stand 30 minutes in the refrigerator.
B. Wrap tortillas in foil place half chicken and vegetables in each well. To warm tortillas, place on top of closed unit for last five minutes of cooking.

Chicken & Dumplings

Ingredients
1 tablespoon olive oil
3 chicken tenders
½ cup frozen mixed vegetables
½ teaspoon seasoned salt
2/3 cup baking mix (like Bisquick)
1/3 cup milk
1 tablespoon butter melted
1 jar chicken gravy, heated

Servings~ 👥
Cooking Time~ Fifteen Minutes
Pan to Use: Divided or Base

Cooking Steps
A. In small sauté pan with lid brown chicken in oil. With scissors or sharp knife cut cooked chicken into small pieces. Return to pan, add vegetables. Cover and cook over low heat for 5 minutes. Mix together baking mix, milk and butter in a small bowl. Turn out onto floured board and knead until no longer sticky. Divide dough in half and pat into 2 6 inch circles. Place half of chicken mixture on each round, fold dough in half over filling, pinching edges to seal.
B. Pre-heat and spray with cooking spray. Place one dumpling in each well. Close cover; cook for 10 minutes. While cooking, heat gravy in sauté pan over low heat. To serve, pour gravy in shallow bowls and place dumpling on gravy.

Brochette Chicken

Ingredients
¼ cup flour
1 beaten egg
2 6oz. boneless skinless chicken breasts
2 tablespoons parmesan cheese
2 tablespoons dry Italian bread crumbs
1 tomato, seeded and chopped
1 tablespoon fresh minced basil
1 clove garlic, minced
½ teaspoon olive oil
¼ teaspoon salt
1 teaspoon pepper

Servings~ 👥
Cooking Time~ Twelve Minutes
Pan to Use: Divided or Base

Cooking Steps
A. Pre-heat and spray with cooking spray. Shake breasts in flour; dip in egg, then into cheese and bread crumb mixture, making sure one side is well coated. Place well coated side up in wells. Close cover; cook 10 to 12 minutes until chicken is well browned.
B. Meanwhile, combine remaining ingredients. When chicken is done, remove to a microwave safe plate, spoon tomato mixture over the top of each breast. Cover and microwave for 1 minute to warm tomato topping.

Sweet and Tasty Onion Chicken

Ingredients
2 6oz boneless skinless chicken breasts
¼ cup melted butter or margarine
2 teaspoons Worcestershire sauce
1 small can French fried onion rings

Servings~ 👥
Cooking Time~ Fifteen Minutes
Pan to Use: Divided or Base

Cooking Steps
A. Pre-heat and spray with cooking spray. Cut a slit in the side of each breast and stuff with several onion rings. Crush remaining rings and place in shallow bowl. Mix melted butter or margarine and Worcestershire sauce.
B. Dip chicken in butter, then into crushed onion rings until well coated and place in unit and close cover. Cook for 12-15 minutes until no longer pink in center, turning halfway through if needed for even browning.

Island Spice Sesame Chicken

Ingredients
2 5 ounce boneless skinless chicken breasts
1/3 cup sesame seeds
1/4 teaspoon cinnamon

Servings~ 👤👤
Cooking Time~ Fifteen Minutes
Pan to Use: Divided or Base

Cooking Steps
A. Pre-heat and spray with cooking spray. Combine seeds and ginger and cinnamon on plate. Season chicken with salt and pepper and roll in seed mixture to coat.
B. Pour 1 teaspoon olive oil in each well, place in chicken breast and close lid. Cook for 12 to 15 minutes until done (180°) turning after six minutes if needed to brown top.

Mandarin Chicken Salad

Ingredients
2 4-5 ounce boneless, skinless chicken breasts
4 ounces water chestnuts, drained and sliced
2 green onions, chopped
1 small canned mandarin orange segments, drained
2 tablespoons slivered almonds
1/2 head iceberg lettuce, chopped
1/2 head cabbage, thinly shredded
1/2 cup chow mein noodles
Salt, pepper and garlic to taste

Dressing
1/2 teaspoon dry mustard
1/4 cup salad oil
3 tablespoons rice vinegar
2 tablespoons sugar
2 teaspoons soy sauce

Servings~ 👤👤👤👤
Cooking Time~ Twelve Minutes
Pan to Use: Divided or Base

Cooking Steps
A. Pre-heat and spray with cooking spray. Place one breast in each side of well.
B. Close cover and cook 12 minutes, turning half way through. Allow to cool while assembling salad ingredients. Slice in thin diagonal slices and toss with dressing. Top with slivered almonds and chow mein noodles.

Chicken Lo Mein

Ingredients
1 cup cooked spaghetti
2 teaspoon soy sauce
1/4 teaspoon garlic powder
1/2 cup chopped cooked pork, chicken or beef
1 scallion, chopped

Servings~ 👤👤
Cooking Time~ Eight Minutes
Pan to Use: Divided or Base

Cooking Steps
A. Pre-heat and spray with cooking spray. Combine ingredients and place half of mixture into each well.
B. Cook eight minutes.

Chicken Rolls with Cranberry Filling

Ingredients
2 5 ounce boneless, skinless chicken breast, flattened
3/4 cup complete stuffing mix, like stovetop, crushed, divided
1/3 cup orange juice
1 tablespoon butter or margarine
1/4 cup dried cranberries
1 tablespoon spicy mustard

Servings~ 👤👤
Cooking Time~ Fifteen Minutes
Pan to Use: Divided or Base

Cooking Steps
A. Pre-heat and spray with cooking spray. Put orange juice, butter and cranberries in a small saucepan or microwave dish. He just to boiling, remove from heat and let stand a few minutes to plump cranberries. Flattened chicken breasts with mallet until about 1/4 inch thick and spray each with half of mustard. Combine 1/2 cup stuffing mix with juice and cranberries. Spread 1/2 on each chicken breast and roll.
B. Roll each breast in remaining finely crushed stuffing crumbs. Place chicken in Wells, seam side down, close cover and cook 12 to 15 minutes until done.

Chicken with Corn and Tomato Salsa

Ingredients
2 5 to 6 ounce boneless, skinless chicken breasts
2 tablespoons olive oil
1/2 teaspoon cracked pepper
1 clove garlic, minced
1 sprigs rosemary
2 teaspoon Dijon mustard

Salad ingredients
2 Roma tomatoes, coarsely chopped
1/2 cup corn kernels
1/2 small red onion, finely chopped
2 teaspoons jalapeno chili, seeds removed, finely chopped
2 teaspoons lime juice
2 teaspoons fresh basil, chopped

Servings~ 👤👤
Cooking Time~ Twelve Minutes
Pan to Use: Divided or Base

Cooking Steps
A. Pre-heat and spray with cooking spray. Combine oil, spices and mustard, place in sealable plastic bag with chicken. Marinate 30 minutes. Combine salsa ingredients in a small bowl and refrigerate at least 30 minutes
B. Remove chicken from marinade, place in wells. Close cover 12 minutes until done, turning half way to promote even browning. To serve, place chicken on plate and spoon salsa over chicken.

Polynesian Chicken and Rice

Ingredients
2 4 ounce boneless skinless chicken thighs
1 small can pineapple tidbits, drained, juice reserved
1/4 cup Italian dressing
1/2 cup instant Rice

Servings~ 👤👤
Cooking Time~ Ten Minutes
Pan to Use: Divided or Base

Cooking Steps
A. Pre-heat and spray with cooking spray. Combine Italian dressing with 1/4 cup pineapple juice and chicken in plastic bag. Marinate 30 minutes to overnight.
B. Place 1/2 of rice in each well with two tablespoons pineapple tidbits. Top with chicken thighs, opening for single layer. Spoon two tablespoons marinade into well. Close lid; cook eight to 10 minutes until chicken is done (180°).

Quick Chicken Tostadas

Ingredients
1 8 inch tortilla cut in half
1/2 cup refried beans
1/2 cup shredded, cook chicken
2 tablespoons salsa
1/2 cup shredded Colby Jack cheese
1/2 cup mixed: shredded lettuce, chopped tomato, sliced olives and green onions

Servings~
Cooking Time~ Five Minutes
Pan to Use: Divided or Base

Cooking Steps
A. Pre-heat and spray with cooking spray. Spread half the beans on each tortilla half and drop into well forming bowl.
B. Mix chicken with salsa and divide into bowls, top with cheese. Close cover and cook four to five minutes until cheese is melted.

Bavarian Chicken

Ingredients
2 5 ounce boneless, skinless chicken breasts
1 egg, beaten
1/2 teaspoon seasoned salt
1 tablespoon spicy mustard
1/2 cup finely crushed pretzels

Servings~
Cooking Time~ Fifteen Minutes
Pan to Use: Divided or Base

Cooking Steps
A. Pre-heat and spray with cooking spray. In small bowl combine egg, mustard and seasonings, beat well. Dip chicken in egg and roll in crushed pretzels until coated
B. Place one breast in each well. Close cover and cook 15 minutes, until chicken is done (180°).

Greek Chicken Salad

Ingredients
2 4-5 ounce boneless skinless chicken breasts
2 medium cucumbers, peeled, seeded and chopped
1 cup canned crumbled feta cheese
2/3 cup sliced pitted black olives
1/4 cup fresh minced parsley
1 cup mayonnaise
3 cloves garlic, minced
1 cup plain yogurt
1 tablespoon dried oregano
3 pita bread rounds, halved

Servings~
Cooking Time~ Twelve Minutes
Pan to Use: Divided or Base

Cooking Steps
A. Pre-heat and spray with cooking spray. Place chicken breast in wells close cover and cook 10 to 12 minutes until done. Remove, cool and cut into cubes.
B. Place cucumbers, cheese, olives and parsley in large bowl. Add chicken cubes and toss. Mix remaining ingredients together, toss with chicken mixture, refrigerate for several hours. To serve spoon into pita halves.

Skewerless Satays

Ingredients
1 or 2, 4 ounce boneless skinless chicken cutlets, cut into 1/2 inch strips
3/4 cup plain yogurt
1/2 cup unsweetened coconut milk
1 tablespoon Asian five spice powder
1 teaspoon lemon juice

Servings~ 👤👤
Cooking Time~ Thirteen Minutes
Pan to Use: Divided or Base

Cooking Steps
A. Pre-heat and spray with cooking spray. To make marinade, mix all ingredients except the chicken strips and reserve 1/4 cup for cooking. Marinate chicken in this mixture for at least one hour in the refrigerator, and discard marinade.
Divide chicken between wells and cook for three minutes. Open cover, pour equal amounts of reserved marinade over chicken strips in Wells and stir. Close cover, cook another 7 to 10 minutes or until chicken is no longer pink.

Roasted Red Pepper Turkey Ham & Cheese Wrap

Ingredients
2 8 inch red roasted pepper flavored flour tortillas
½ tablespoon sun dried tomato mayonnaise
2 slices ham
2 slices turkey
12 baby spinach leaves
2 thin slices red onion in rings
2 slices Swiss cheese

Servings~ 👤👤
Cooking Time~ Eight Minutes
Pan to Use: Divided or Base

Cooking Steps
A. Pre-heat and spray with cooking spray. Spread half the mayonnaise on each tortilla. Top each with half the remaining ingredients. Fold in sides and roll.
B. Place wraps into unit and cook for 7-8 minutes until tops are well browned.

Peanut Chicken

Ingredients
2 4 ounce boneless chicken breasts
1/4 cup flour
1 egg
1/4 cup chunky peanut butter
1/4 cup milk
3/4 cup Panko bread crumbs

Servings~ 👤👤
Cooking Time~ Fifteen Minutes
Pan to Use: Divided or Base

Cooking Steps
A. Pre-heat and spray with cooking spray. Mix egg with peanut butter, slowly add milk until blended in (add a little extra milk if mixture is too thick). Dredge chicken in flour dip into peanut butter batter, and coat generously with bread crumbs
B. Place one breast in each well, close cover and cook 15 minutes until chicken is no longer pink (180°)

Almost Thanksgiving Turkey Loaves

Ingredients
1 cup lean ground turkey
1 cup complete stuffing like stovetop
1 cup water
1 tablespoon parsley
1 teaspoon dried minced onion
1 prepared turkey gravy

Servings~ 👤👤
Cooking Time~ Ten Minutes
Pan to Use: Divided or Base

Cooking Steps
A. Pre-heat and spray with cooking spray. Mix all ingredients except gravy together and divide into wells.
B. Close cover, cook eight to 10 minutes or until done through. Serve with heated turkey gravy.

Cream Cheese Turkey Rolls

Ingredients
2 turkey breast cutlets
6 5 inch asparagus spears
2 tablespoons cream cheese
1 small clove garlic minced
1 teaspoon chive or green onion, chopped
1 dash dried tarragon
1 egg, beaten
1/3 cup breadcrumbs made from low-carb bread
2 tablespoons grated parmesan cheese
Dash black pepper

Servings~
Cooking Time~ Twelve Minutes
Pan to Use: Divided or Base

Cooking Steps
A. Pre-heat and spray with cooking spray. Place cutlets between waxed paper and pound flat. Mix cream cheese with seasoning. Spread on cutlets. Place three asparagus spears at one end of the cutlet roll.
B. Dip each cutlet in egg and then roll in breadcrumbs mixed with parmesan cheese and place rolls in wells. close cover and cook 12 minutes or until turkey is no longer pink (180°)

Stuffed Turkey Tenderloin

Ingredients
2 4 ounce turkey tenderloins, pounded thin
1 cup complete stuffing mix, like stovetop, crushed divided
1/3 cup water
1 tablespoon butter or margarine
1 cup prepared turkey gravy, heated

Servings~
Cooking Time~ Twelve Minutes
Pan to Use: Divided or Base

Cooking Steps
A. Pre-heat and spray cooking spray. Combined water and butter in small bowl and heat in microwave till butter is melted and water is hot. add 2/3 cup stuffing mix, stir and place half in center and each tenderloin
B. Roll or fold to encase stuffing, spray with spray and roll in remaining stuffing crumbs and place in wells. Close cover and cook 12 minutes or until turkey is done and browned serve with heated turkey gravy.

Barbecued Turkey Bacon Cheeseburger

Ingredients
8 ounces ground turkey
1 tablespoon BBQ sauce
1 (3/4 ounce) sliced cheese
2 slices fully cooked bacon

Servings~
Cooking Time~ Twelve Minutes
Pan to Use: Divided or Base

Cooking Steps
A. Pre-heat and spray with cooking spray. Combined turkey and barbecue sauce form ¼ of mixture into burger shape, place ½ a piece slice cheese in center, and top with additional ¼ of mixture making sure cheese is fully enclosed.
B. Use remaining meat and cheese to form second burger place one burger in each well. Cook eight minutes. Top with bacon and cook two more minutes.

Grilled Turkey Bacon Ranch Rollup

Ingredients
2 (8 inch) flour tortillas
4 tablespoons ranch dressing
Fresh spinach leaves
4-6 slices deli turkey
4 slices pre-cooked bacon

Servings~ 👤👤
Cooking Time~ Eight Minutes
Pan to Use: Divided or Base

Cooking Steps
A. Pre-heat and spray with cooking spray. Spread half the dressing on each tortilla.
B. Top each with half of spinach, Turkey, bacon and cheese. Fold in sides and roll. Place one in each well, cook for seven to eight minutes.

Elegant Rosemary Turkey

Ingredients
2 4-6 ounce turkey cutlets
1½ cups orange juice
1 tablespoons olive oil
1 tablespoon red wine vinegar
½ to ¾ teaspoon Herbes de Provence
½ teaspoon poultry seasoning
½ teaspoon minced garlic
Pinch of each salt and black pepper
2-3 fresh rosemary sprigs or 1-2 thin orange slices (optional garnish)

Servings~ 👤👤
Cooking Time~ Fifteen Minutes
Pan to Use: Divided or Base

Cooking Steps
A. Pre-heat and spray with cooking spray. For marinade, pour 1 cup of orange juice (reserve other ½ cup for cooking) and the other ingredient to a Ziploc bag, seal and shake bag saturate cutlets. Lay flat in fridge and marinate for one to two hours. Discard marinade. Pour half of reserved orange juice into each well.
B. For additional flavor if desired sprinkle turkey cutlets with about ¼ teaspoon Herbes de Provence. Place one cutlet in each well and cook 12 to 15 minutes until done (make sure you cooked turkey thoroughly). Top with fresh rosemary and orange slices, if desired.

Turkey Chimichangas

Ingredients
¾ cup cooked turkey, shredded
½ cup Pinto beans
2 tablespoons taco sauce
1 tablespoon sour cream
1 teaspoon chopped the pimento olives or jalapenos peppers
2 12 inch flour tortillas
2 tablespoons water
2 tablespoons vegetable oil
2 tablespoons shredded white cheddar or pepper jack cheese
2 tablespoons fresh scallions, sliced into ¼" slices

Servings~ 👤👤
Cooking Time~ Eight Minutes
Pan to Use: Divided or Base

Cooking Steps
A. Pre-heat and spray with cooking spray. Combined first five ingredients and mix well. For each chimichanga, Mound half of turkey mixture onto center of tortilla. Rub inner rim of tortilla with water for a tight seal. Fold tortilla burrito-style: bottom up halfway, sides in top flap over.
B. Brush entire outside of chimichangas with oil. Place one chimichanga in each cooking well (okay, if top cooking surface touches chimichangas). Close cover and fry eight minutes until well browned. Serve browner side up, topped with cheese and scallions, plus additional taco sauce and sour cream, if desired.

Cuban Spiced Turkey

Ingredients
2 4 ounce turkey tenderloins, pounded thin
1 cup complete stuffing mix, like stovetop, crushed divided
1/3 cup water
1 tablespoon butter or margarine
1 cup prepared turkey gravy, heated

Servings~ 👤👤
Cooking Time~ Fifteen Minutes
Pan to Use: Divided or Base

Cooking Steps
A. Pre-heat and spray with cooking spray. Combined all ingredients in list order in a Ziploc bag and marinate in refrigerator for 30 minutes.
B. Place one cutlet in each well, close cover and cook for 15 minutes until turkey is no longer pink.

Turkey Meatballs

Ingredients
1 20 ounce package ground turkey
1 egg beaten or ¼ cup egg substitute
1 cup stuffing mix

Servings~ 👤👤👤
Cooking Time~ Ten Minutes
Pan to Use: Divided, Mini, or Base

Cooking Steps
A. Pre-heat and spray with cooking spray. Mix together the ground turkey, egg and stuffing.
Form Turkey into golf ball size meatballs, place in unit and cook ten minutes.

Swedish Turkey Meatballs

Ingredients
1 cup raisin bran cereal
¼ cup milk
1 pound ground turkey
1 extra large egg
½ cup minced sweet onion
Salt and pepper to taste
1 teaspoon allspice
1½ teaspoons ground cinnamon
1 teaspoon ground nutmeg
Pinch of brown sugar
2 cups prepared beef gravy
¾ cup heavy cream

Servings~ 👤👤
Cooking Time~ Ten Minutes
Pan to Use: Divided or Base

Cooking Steps
A. Pre-heat and spray with cooking spray. Soak raisin bran and milk for five minutes. Mix all remaining ingredients except gravy and heavy cream. form mixture into bite sized meatballs size to fit 3-4 in each well
B. Cook each batch with cover closed about 10 minutes, turning to promote even browning on all sides until cooked thoroughly (no pink). While final batch is cooking, mix together gravy and heavy cream and heat in microwave until warm. Pour sauce over meatballs to serve.

Low Fat Fried Chicken

Ingredients
2 boneless skinless chicken breasts or pieces of choice to fit
¼ cup egg white beaten or egg substitute
1 cup crushed cereal like special K
½ teaspoon seasoned salt

Servings~ 👤
Cooking Time~ Twelve Minutes
Pan to Use: Base

Cooking Steps
A. Pre-heat and spray with cooking spray. Dip chicken in egg white mixed with seasoned salt and then into cereal turning to coat well.
B. Arrange pieces in base and close cover. Cook for 12 minutes or until chicken is cooked through.

Thanksgiving Anytime Turkey Roll

Ingredients
2 3 to 4 ounce turkey cutlets, pounded to ¼ inch thick
Salt and pepper to taste
1 prepared mashed sweet potatoes
1 tablespoon dried cranberries
¾ cup finely crushed pecans, divided
1 egg
1 teaspoon brown sugar

Servings~ 👬
Cooking Time~ Fifteen Minutes
Pan to Use: Divided or Base

Cooking Steps
A. Pre-heat and spray with cooking spray. Season both sides of cutlets liberally with salt and pepper. Mix sweet potatoes, 1 tablespoon of crushed pecans and cranberries. Spread mixture on top of cutlet and roll each cutlet jellyroll style. In a small bowl, beat egg, set aside, in another small shallow bowl mix remaining pecans and brown sugar.
B. Carefully dip each cutlet in beaten egg and roll and pecans until well coated. Place one role in each cooking well cook approximately 15 minutes, until done.

Authentic Turkey Cuban Sandwich

Ingredients
2 Cuban rolls, cut 5 inch long to fit wells
4 thin slices deli boiled or Virginia ham
4 slices deli turkey
4 thin slices white American cheese
Yellow mustard
Mayonnaise
4 dill pickle slices
1 ounce butter

Servings~ 👬
Cooking Time~ Seven Minutes
Pan to Use: Divided or Base

Cooking Steps
A. Pre-heat and spray with cooking spray. Slice rolls lengthwise into separate tops and bottoms. Butter outer top and bottom of roles for browning. spread and her sandwich bottoms with mustard and place in wells
B. Build sandwich as follows: taught muster with two slices American cheese placed evenly to cover bottom of roll, to pickle slices per sandwich, and two slices of turkey and ham folded in half to cover bread evenly. Spread under sign of sandwich top with mayonnaise, cover sandwich, and butter side up. Cook five to seven minutes. Wrapped sandwich half way with parchment paper, foil as a holder to eat on the run.

Mini Turkey Meat Loaves

Ingredients
12 ounces ground turkey
1 egg
1/3 cup flavored bread crumbs
1 envelope dry onion soup mix
2 tablespoons ketchup

Servings~ 👬
Cooking Time~ Twenty Minutes
Pan to Use: Divided or Base

Cooking Steps
A. Pre-heat and spray with cooking spray. Combined all ingredients divide mixture between Wells and cook 20 minutes.

Turkey Corn Dogs

Ingredients
1 7-8.5 ounces corn muffin mix
3 turkey hot dogs whole or cut into pieces

Servings~ 👫
Cooking Time~ Ten Minutes
Pan to Use: Divided or Base

Cooking Steps
A. Pre-heat and spray with cooking spray. Mix corn muffin mix according to package directions. Fill cooking areas half full with muffin batter.
B. Place one hot dog or piece into each area. Add enough muffin mix to fill area. Cook 8-10 minutes or until toothpick inserted into the center comes out clean. Repeat with remaining hot dog and batter.

Chicken Melt

Ingredients
2 slices 100% Whole Wheat Bread
2 tablespoons butter, softened
1/2 cup cooked chopped broccoli
2 ounces cooked chicken breast, diced
1/4 cup diced roasted red peppers
1/2 cup shredded cheddar cheese

Servings~ 👫
Cooking Time~ Twenty Minutes
Pan to Use: Divided or Base

Cooking Steps
A. Pre-heat and spray with cooking spray. Butter one side of each slice of bread. In a bowl combine broccoli, chicken, roasted peppers and cheese.
B. Put one slice of bread in base of unit butter side down and spoon ½ cup of mixture on to the slice in unit. Put other slice of bread on top. Close lid and cook for 4-5 minutes or until golden brown.

Chicken Pot Stickers

Ingredients

Wonton wrappers
2 cups all purpose flour
1 cup water (use chicken stock for more flavor)
1 egg
1 teaspoon salt

Filling
2 chicken breasts, cooked and shredded
1/4 cup +/- soy sauce or your favorite Asian sauce,
3 or 4 green onions, minced
1 teaspoon garlic, minced
1/3-1/2 cup carrots, cooked chopped small
1 teaspoon flour

Servings~ 👫
Cooking Time~ Ten Minutes
Pan to Use: Mini, Divided or Base

Cooking Steps
A. To make the Wonton wrappers, add all wonton ingredients to a bowl and mix until there is a big ball of dough. Then knead for 5 minutes, can use a bread machine on the dough setting. Make 4 equal dough balls out of the one large ball then let rest 30 minutes. Roll out on lightly floured surface, the thinner the better. Cut in to four inch squares, dust with flour and stack. Repeat with remainder of dough. For filling mix all in a bowl until well mixed.
B. Pre-heat and spray with cooking spray. To make the Pot Sticks take a single piece of dough in one hand, place a spoonful of filling mixture in the center. Paint all 4 edges of the square with water, take each corner of wrapper and pull them upward to the center. Pinch to seal the filling inside, repeat till you make what you would like to have. Close lid and cook for 10 minutes or until golden brown.

Marinated Teriyaki Chicken

Ingredients
2 ounces teriyaki marinade or sauce
2 (6-ounce) chicken breasts
2 tablespoons dried plain bread crumbs
Cooking spray

Servings~ 👤👤
Cooking Time~ Fifteen   Minutes
Pan to Use: Divided or Base

Cooking Steps
A. Fill the injector tube with teriyaki marinade. Inject the liquid into the side of the chicken breast in several places. Coat the chicken with the crumbs
B. Spray wells cooking spray. Place one piece in each well. Cook 15 minutes.

Seafood

"Fried" Salmon and Vegetable Rice

Ingredients
1 1-inch thick halibut or salmon fillet cut to fit well
1 tablespoon cornstarch
2 tablespoon water
1/2 tablespoons seasoned salt
1/4 cup instant rice
1/4 cup water
1/4 cup frozen mixed vegetables
Panko crumbs or Japanese breadcrumbs
4 teaspoons olive oil

Servings~ 👥
Cooking Time~ Eleven Minutes
Pan to Use: Divided or Base

Cooking Steps
A. Pre-heat and spray with cooking spray. Mix cornstarch, water and seasoned salt. Dip fillet to coat than roll in Panko crumbs. Heat 1 teaspoon olive oil in the left side well, place fillet in oil, close lid cook five minutes.
B. Place 1 tablespoon olive oil in right side well flip halibut to the right well turning to brown other side. Put rice, water and vegetables into left well close cover, cook six minutes until done.

Honey Mustard Salmon En Croute

Ingredients
2 tablespoons honey mustard BBQ sauce
1 teaspoon lime or lemon juice
1 (6 ounce) piece salmon fillet, skin removed
2 frozen pastry shells thought and rolled into an 8 Inch Circle

Servings~ 👥
Cooking Time~ Fifteen Minutes
Pan to Use: Divided or Base

Cooking Steps
A. Pre-heat and spray with cooking spray. Combined the first two ingredients and spoon into injector tube and inject the liquid into the side of the fish in several places. Place the fish in the center of the pastry, fold two sides over the fish and then fold the other two sides to enclose the fish totally and form a pocket.
B. Place one piece in each well cook 15 minutes.

Corn and Salmon Cakes

Ingredients
1/2 cup dried unflavored breadcrumbs
4 ounces leftover cooked salmon, flaked or 1(6 oz) can
1 tablespoon Dijon mustard
1/4 cup mayonnaise
1 tablespoon lemon juice
1/2 cup grated cheddar or Swiss cheese
1/2 teaspoon each garlic and onion powder
1/2 cup corn chips, finely chopped

Servings~ 👥
Cooking Time~ Eight Minutes
Pan to Use: Divided or Base

Cooking Steps
A. Pre-heat and spray with cooking spray. Combined all ingredients except corn chips. Form mixture in to two ovals and coat with corn chips.
B. Place one oval in each well cook eight minutes or until well browned.

Salmon Puffs

Ingredients
1 can salmon, drained
1½ cup prepared or leftover mashed potatoes
1/2 tablespoons seasoned salt
1/2 teaspoon dill
1 egg, beaten

Servings~ 👤👤
Cooking Time~ Ten Minutes
Pan to Use: Divided or Base

Cooking Steps
A. Pre-heat and spray with cooking spray.
B. Divide mixture into wells. Close cover and cook seven minutes until puffed and golden brown.

Tartar Sauce

Ingredients
1/2 cup mayonnaise
2 tablespoons sweet pickle relish
1 teaspoon dill

Servings~
Cooking Time~

Cooking Steps
A. stir all ingredients together refrigerate until ready to serve

Steamed Clams

Ingredients
1/4 cup white wine
1/4 cup water
1 clove garlic
1 tablespoon freshly chopped parsley
1 tablespoon lemon juice
1 dozen cherrystone clams

Servings~ 👤👤
Cooking Time~ Five Minutes
Pan to Use: Divided or Base

Cooking Steps
A. Pre-heat and spray with cooking spray. Combined all ingredients except clams.
B. Place three clans in each well. Add two tablespoons mixture into each well. Cook five minutes remove from Wells and repeat cooking process with remaining clams spoon liquid from wells over clams.

Mini Salmon Loaves

Ingredients
1 7-ounce can salmon
1 cup soft breadcrumbs
2 tablespoon finely minced onion
2 tablespoons milk
1 egg
1 tablespoon chopped parsley
1 teaspoon lemon juice
1/2 teaspoon seasoned salt
1/4 teaspoon dill weeds
1 dash black pepper

Servings~ 👤👤
Cooking Time~ Eight Minutes
Pan to Use: Divided or Base

Cooking Steps
A. Pre-heat and spray with cooking spray. Drained and flaked salmon, retaining one tablespoon liquid. Combined with remaining ingredients mixing well.
B. Form into to tennis ball sized portions. Place in Wells, close cover and cook eight minutes until lightly browned.

Salmon Omelet

Ingredients
3 eggs, beaten
1 ounce smoked salmon
2 tablespoons sour cream
1 tablespoons fresh build, finely chopped
1 tablespoon chives, chopped
1 tablespoon butter

Servings~ 👥
Cooking Time~ Ten Minutes
Pan to Use: Divided or Base

Cooking Steps
A. Pre-heat and spray with cooking spray. Place half of butter in each well and allowed to melt, place half of salmon in well, close cover and cook for two minutes. Turn salmon pour half of beaten egg into Wells or salmon.
B. Close cover and cook seven minutes until omelet is puffy and set. Stir herbs into sour cream and spoon half over each omelet.

Coconut Crusted Perch

Ingredients
2 (5-6) perch fillets
1 cup crushed butter flavored crackers
1/2 cup coconut, flaked
1 egg
1 tablespoon know
1/4 teaspoon salt
2 teaspoon oil

Servings~ 👥
Cooking Time~ Ten Minutes
Pan to Use: Divided or Base

Cooking Steps
A. Pre-heat and spray with cooking spray. Place 1 teaspoon of oil in each well. In a shallow dish combine cracker and Coconut. In another dish whisk egg, milk and salt. Dip fillet and milk in crumbs to coat.
B. Place one fillet in each well, folding small end over to fit if necessary. Close cover; cook 10 minutes until fish is flaky, turning after six minutes, if needed to promote even browning. Serve with warm sweet and sour sauce.

Caribbean Jerk Seared Tuna

Ingredients
2 sushi quality, fresh tuna steaks (about 4 ounces each)
2 tablespoons olive oil
Dry prepared jerk seasoning
Fresh lime wedges
Jamaican or Caribbean hot sauce (optional)

Servings~ 👥
Cooking Time~ Seven Minute
Pan to Use: Divided or Base

Cooking Steps
A. Pre-heat and spray with cooking spray. Rub tuna thoroughly with all of oil and season all sides with jerk seasoning.
B. Place one tuna steak into each cooking well, close cover and cook three to seven minutes until desired doneness (tuna is best served rare). Serve grilled side up with lime wedges and hot sauce, if desired.

Maple and Mustard Salmon

Ingredients
2 4-5 ounce salmon fillets
2 tablespoons sugar free maple syrup
2 tablespoons lemon juice
2 tablespoons thin sliced green onion tops
1 1/2 teaspoons Dijon mustard
1/4 teaspoon coarse black pepper

Servings~ 👥
Cooking Time~ Ten Minutes
Pan to Use: Divided or Base

Cooking Steps
A. Pre-heat and spray with cooking spray. Place in a resealable bag, mixed marinade ingredients together place in bag with salmon, close mix and let stand 30 minutes. Rinse salmon and pat dry.
B. Place one piece salmon, in each well. Close cover cook 10 to 12 minutes, turning half way through if needed for browning brush on extra marinade during cooking, if desired.

Shrimp Quiche

Ingredients
2 (2 ounce) small frozen cooked shrimp, thawed
1 green sliced onion
1/4 teaspoon dried thyme leaves
2 ounce can sliced mushrooms, drained
1/3 cup gruyere cheese, shredded
1/2 cup milk
1 egg
1/4 cup Bisquick baking mix
2 tablespoons parmesan cheese
1 dash pepper

Servings~ 👥
Cooking Time~ Ten Minutes
Pan to Use: Divided or Base

Cooking Steps
A. Pre-heat and spray with cooking spray. Mix together the shrimp, onion, thyme, and mushrooms. Divide into each well and top each well with half the cheese.
B. In Shaker mix together the egg, milk, baking mix, parmesan cheese and pepper. Pour half into each well over the shrimp and cheese close cover and cook 10 minutes.

Coconut Fish

Ingredients
1 pound flounder or Dover fillets
1 cup finely shredded unsweetened coconut for baking
1/4 cup flour
1 teaspoon salt
1/2 teaspoon paprika
1 egg
1 tablespoon milk
Oil for frying
Lemon wedges for serving

Servings~ 👥
Cooking Time~ Twelve Minutes
Pan to Use: Divided or Base

Cooking Steps
A. Pre-heat and spray with cooking spray. Place 1 teaspoon of oil into each well. Mix coconut, flour, salt and paprika and a shallow bowl. in another bowl beat egg with milk
B. One at a time dip fish pieces into egg, and coat thoroughly with coconut mixture. Fry fish pieces in batches cook 10 to 12 minutes until fish is white and flaky flip for even browning halfway through cooking. Serve with lemon.

Scrambled Eggs and Salmon

Servings~ 👤👤
Cooking Time~ Eight Minutes
Pan to Use: Divided or Base

Ingredients
4 eggs
1 tablespoon heavy cream
1 teaspoon water
Salt and pepper to taste
2 teaspoon butter, plus additional butter for buttering bread
2 slices pumpernickel bread, crusts trimmed, buttered
2 strips smoked salmon
2-3 sprigs fresh dill stripped from stems

Cooking Steps
A. Pre-heat and spray with cooking spray. Beat together eggs, cream, water, salt and pepper. Melt 1 teaspoon butter in each well. divide egg mixture between cooking wells
B. Close cover; cook six minutes (one to two more minutes more if you prefer drier scrambled eggs). Before removing eggs from unit chop with cooking tool. Mound equal amounts of scrambled eggs onto each slice of pumpernickel bread, top with salmon and serve.

Hot Shrimp Big Easy Po' Boy

Servings~ 👤
Cooking Time~ Seven Minutes
Pan to Use: Divided or Base

Ingredients
1 6 ounce can salad shrimp, well drained
1/2 teaspoon old Bay seasoning
1/2 teaspoons cayenne pepper
1/2 teaspoons lemon juice
1/2 tablespoon Worcestershire sauce
1 tablespoon fresh minced parsley
1 heaping tablespoon mayonnaise
2 teaspoons Creole mustard
1 teaspoon fresh minced garlic
1 six-inch Italian roll cut in half lengthwise
Shredded lettuce for topping

Cooking Steps
A. Pre-heat and spray with cooking spray. Combine first six ingredients, set aside. In a separate bowl, mix mayonnaise, mustard and garlic. spread mayonnaise mixture onto inner side of each roll
B. Divide even amounts of seasoned shrimp between Wells. Close cover, cook about five minutes stir and continue cooking two more minutes until brown. Mound shrimp on rolls and top with lettuce to serve.

Simple Thai Curry Basil Shrimp

Servings~ 👤👤
Cooking Time~ Four Minutes
Pan to Use: Divided or Base

Ingredients
6 medium cooked shrimp if using frozen shrimp, thaw under cold water
1/4 teaspoon Thai red curry paste
1/2 can unsweetened coconut milk
1/2 teaspoon lime juice
1/2 teaspoon brown sugar
4 thinly slivered fresh basil leaves, plus a few extra leaves for serving
Chopped unsalted peanuts
Dash fish sauce, if unavailable substitute soy sauce
Lime wedges (optional)

Cooking Steps
A. Pre-heat and spray with cooking spray. Pour a thin layer of coconut milk into each well and reserve rest for cooking. Heat for three minutes. Then stir in a dab of red curry paste. Mix together reserved coconut milk, fish sauce, lime juice and brown sugar.
B. Divide between wells and cook two minutes until sauce thickens. Add shrimp, basil and peanuts and cook another two minutes until shrimp are heated through. Serve over rice and garnish with fresh lime wedges.

Clam Pies

Ingredients
1 cup chopped clams, well drained and squeezed dry with paper towel
1/2 cup chopped leftover potatoes.
1/2 cup condensed cream of mushroom soup.
2 tablespoons heavy cream
1 tablespoon real bacon bits
1/2 teaspoon dried parsley flakes
1 teaspoon dried thyme
1 teaspoon old Bay seasoning
1 egg
1 tablespoon Wondra flour
½ 9 inch refrigerated pie crust, cut into pieces to fit pocket maker

Servings~ 👥
Cooking Time~ Twenty Minutes
Pan to Use: Divided or Base

Cooking Steps
A. Do not Pre-heat spray with cooking spray. Mix together all ingredients except pie crust (if mixture is too watery add additional flour to avoid a soggy pie crust). Set aside. Spoon half of clam mixture into dough and close pocket maker to form pie, crimp edges securely.
B. Pierce top of pies to allow air to escape when cooking and place in well. Repeat for second pie. Spray tops of pies lightly with cooking spray. Cook approximately 20 minutes until pie crust is richly brown allow pies to cool five minutes before removing.

Clam Chowder Soupwich

Ingredients
1 can clam chowder, like Progresso
20 soda crackers, coarsely crushed
1 stalk celery, finely minced

Servings~ 👥
Cooking Time~ Ten Minutes
Pan to Use: Divided or Base

Cooking Steps
A. Pre-heat and spray with cooking spray. Mix soup, crushed crackers and celery and bowl.
B. Put half of soup mixture into each well. Close cover and cook for 10 minutes until brown and slightly crisp. Makes two healthy portions or four small portion.

Cajun Style Swordfish

Ingredients
1 tablespoon minced green pepper
1 tablespoon minced onion
1/2 can condensed tomato soup
2 tablespoons water
1 tablespoons Cajun seasoning blend
2 swordfish steaks (approximately 4 to 6 ounces, 1 inch thick)
Oil for frying
One and wedges, hot sauce for serving (optional)

Servings~ 👥
Cooking Time~ Ten Minutes
Pan to Use: Divided or Base

Cooking Steps
A. Pre-heat and spray with cooking spray. Divide oil evenly between wells. Divide peppers and onions between Wells and fry for two minutes. Mix together soup water and seasoning.
B. Place one swordfish steak into each well. Pour equal amounts of soup mixture over fish in wells. Close cover and cook seven to eight minutes until fish is flaky. Serve with lemon wedges and hot sauce, if desired.

Mussel Fritters

Ingredients
2 4 ounce cans mussels, drained (okay to use fresh cooked mussels removed from Shell)
1 cup stovetop stuffing mix
1 cup water
1 tablespoon chopped fresh parsley
1 tablespoon chopped fresh basil
Freshly ground black pepper to taste
1 tablespoon butter

Servings~ 👥
Cooking Time~ Ten Minutes
Pan to Use: Divided or Base

Cooking Steps
A. Pre-heat and spray with cooking spray. Add equal amounts of butter to each well and let it melt. Gently fold together the rest of the ingredients being careful not to break up the mussels.
B. Divide equal amounts of fritter batter into wells. Close lid and cook eight to 10 minutes until fritters are cooked through.

Crabby Louie Pastry Cups

Ingredients
2 frozen puff pastry trimmed to fit Wells
2 cups crab meat (okay to substitute imitation crab)
1/4 cup mayonnaise
2 tablespoons heavy cream
2 teaspoons ketchup
1 tablespoon lemon juice
1 tablespoon sweet pickle relish
1/2 avocado, peeled and cut into small cubes
Black pepper to taste
2-3, Boston Bibb lettuce leaves for serving

Servings~ 👥
Cooking Time~ Ten Minutes
Pan to Use: Divided or Base

Cooking Steps
A. Pre-heat and spray with cooking spray. Place one frozen pastry shell in each well and cook 10 minutes. While shells cook, combined remaining ingredients except lettuce leaves. If mixture is too thick add a small amount more of heavy cream. When pastry shells are done. Let cool two minutes before carefully removing from wells.
B. Arrange lettuce leaves on plate to make a bed for the pastry cups. Spoon equal amounts of crab mixture into cups, letting excess overflow onto lettuce bed.

Creamed Cod Fish

Ingredients
6 Ounce Fresh Codfish, Cut into Pieces to Fit Wells
Salt and Pepper to Taste
1 Cup Milk
2 tablespoons butter
1 tablespoon Wondra flour
1 cup frozen peas and carrots thawed under cold running water
1 small cooked leftover potato, peeled
1 teaspoon dried parsley

Servings~ 👥
Cooking Time~ Fifteen Minutes
Pan to Use: Divided or Base

Cooking Steps
A. Do not pre-heat but spray with cooking spray. Pour 1/4 cup milk into each well. Season Cod with Salt and Pepper. Divide Codpieces Evenly into Wells and Plug in unit. Cook 10 minutes until fish is well done (should be opaque and very white.).
B. Remove cooked fish to serving plate, leaving leftover cooking liquid. Place one tablespoon butter in each well. Thoroughly mix together remaining milk, flour, salt and pepper to taste. Then mix and potatoes peas, carrots and parsley. Divide equal amounts of vegetables and sauce in wells. Cook five minutes until sauce is thick and vegetables are warm. Stir, spoon over cooked fish and serve.

Crab Quesadillas

Ingredients
2 white corn tortillas
6 ounce crab meat, drained dry
2 teaspoon chopped canned green chilies
1 green onion chopped
1 tablespoon fresh cilantro, chopped
1/2 cup shredded Monterey Jack or mild white cheddar cheese
Oil for frying
Sour cream and salsa for garnish if desired

Servings~ 👥
Cooking Time~ Six Minutes
Pan to Use: Divided or Base

Cooking Steps
A. Pre-heat and brush with oil. Mix crabmeat with chilies, onion, cilantro and cheese and mound the bottom half of each tortilla with the mixture. Fold over tortillas to form a half moon.
B. Place one tortilla in each well, talking in ends to fit. Close cover and cook three minutes. Turn tortillas over for even Browning cook three more minutes until cheese is completely melted. Cut into wedges for serving and garnish with sour cream and salsa.

Fishermen's Wharf Tacos

Ingredients
Leftover fish
Adobo seasoning
Hot sauce to taste
Corn taco shells
Taco slaw
1 cup prepared coleslaw mix
1 tablespoon mayonnaise
1/4 teaspoon Heinz 57 sauce
1/2 teaspoon lime juice
Pinch sugar

Servings~ 👥
Cooking Time~ Three Minutes
Pan to Use: Divided or Base

Cooking Steps
A. To prepare taco slaw, combined all listed ingredients and let this rest for 15 minutes before serving. Cut leftover fish into bite sized cubes and sprinkle with adobo seasoning. spray fish generously with cooking spray
B. Plug in unit. Divide fish evenly into Wells and grill about three minutes until warm. Load fish equally into taco shells, top with slaw and spiked with hot sauce.

Crab Dip

Ingredients
8 ounces imitation crab meat
4 ounces whipped cream cheese, softened
1 tablespoon mayonnaise
1 tablespoon sour cream
1 tablespoon chopped pimentos, well-drained
1 tablespoon chopped green onion
2 tablespoons each parmesan & shredded Swiss cheese
1 teaspoon dry mustard
1 tablespoon old Bay seasoning
Tabasco sauce to taste
Crusty French bread or Melba toast for serving

Servings~ 👥
Cooking Time~ Three Minutes
Pan to Use: Divided or Base

Cooking Steps
A. Pre-heat and spray with cooking spray. Mix together all ingredients except bread/toast.
B. Spoon equal amounts into each well cook three minutes until bubbly. Serve immediately with bread or toast for dipping.

Open Face Tuna Melt

Ingredients
6 Ounce Fresh Codfish, Cut into Pieces to Fit Wells
Salt and Pepper to Taste
1 Cup Milk
2 tablespoons butter
1 tablespoon Wondra flour
1 cup frozen peas and carrots thawed under cold running water
1 small cooked leftover potato, peeled
1 teaspoon dried parsley

Servings~ 👥
Cooking Time~ Five Minutes
Pan to Use: Divided or Base

Cooking Steps
A. Pre-heat and spray with cooking spray. Mix together tuna, mayo, celery, onion and black pepper and salt. Butter one side of each piece of bread and place one piece butter side down in each well. Cook one minute with the lid open.
B. Spoon equal amounts of tuna salad onto bread and spread evenly. Top each of the open face tuna sandwich with one tomato slice and one slice of cheese. Close lid and cook two to four minutes till melted and bubbling.

Fish & Yogurt

Ingredients
4 to 6 ounce fish fillets flounder or soul to fit wells.
1/2 small red onion, sliced thin
2 teaspoons butter
1 single serving container plain younger
1 tablespoon fresh minced garlic
1/2 cucumber, minced
Fresh parsley and fresh lemon slices for garnish

Servings~ 👥
Cooking Time~ Twenty Minutes
Pan to Use: Divided or Base

Cooking Steps
A. Pre-heat and spray with cooking spray. Put 1 teaspoon butter into each well. Add equal amounts of onion into each well. Sauté onion until translucent (3 to 5 minutes).
B. Place one fish fillet into each well and cook 10 to 15 minutes until fish is done. Turn fish once during cooking time, if necessary, to promote even cooking. To make sauce combined yogurt and garlic. To serve, spoon yogurt sauce over cooked fish and top with fresh parsley and lemon slices.

Bacon Wrapped Stuffed Shrimp

Ingredients
2 jumbo shrimp, shelled, deveined and butterflied
3/4 cup crushed saltines or Ritz crackers
1 tablespoon chopped red pimentos
1 egg
Pinch dry mustard
2 pieces bacon

Servings~ 👤
Cooking Time~ Fifteen Minutes
Pan to Use: Divided or Base

Cooking Steps
A. Pre-heat and spray with cooking spray. Lay butterflied shrimp on a clean work surface. mix next five ingredients and divide stuffing in half.
B. For each shrimp place stuffing evenly on length of shrimp. Fold over and wrap with bacon to cover entire shrimp. Place one shrimp into each well and cook 10 to 15 minutes until bacon is very crispy.

Broccoli Fish Burger With Garlic Mayonnaise

Ingredients
Burger ingredients
1 cup leftover cooked fish, flaked
1/2 cup frozen chopped broccoli, thawed and squeeze free of any excess water
1/2 cup cracker crumbs
1 egg
1 heaping tablespoon mayonnaise
1/2 teaspoon baking powder
1/2 teaspoon dry mustard
1/2 teaspoon lemon pepper
Salt pepper to taste
Garlic Mayo ingredients
1/2 cup mayonnaise
1 tablespoon minced garlic

Servings~ 👥
Cooking Time~ Eight Minutes
Pan to Use: Divided or Base

Cooking Steps
A. Pre-heat and spray with cooking spray. Mix together all burger ingredients and form mixture into to oval patties to fit wells.
B. Cook one burger in each well for eight minutes until well browned. While burgers are cooking, mix together mayo and garlic. Serve burgers on rolls, topped with garlic mayonnaise.

Tuna Burgers

Ingredients
1/2 pound deli prepared tuna salad
1 egg
1 tablespoon pickle relish
1/2 cup soft bread crumbs
Dijonaise
Sweet pickle chips

Servings~ 👥
Cooking Time~ Twenty Minutes
Pan to Use: Divided or Base

Cooking Steps
A. Pre-heat and spray with cooking spray. Combine first three ingredients. Form tuna mixture into to oval patties to fit wells. Press gently in to bread crumbs to coat on both sides.
B. Place tuna patties in to each well and cook for 20 minutes turn if necessary for even browning. Serve with a dollop Dijonaise and pickle chips.

Poached Fish with Pineapple Salsa

Ingredients
1/2 cup crushed pineapple drained
2 tablespoons chopped red pepper
1 small jalapeno pepper, seeded and diced
1 teaspoon apple cider vinegar
1 pinch sugar
1/2 cup orange juice
Adobo seasoning to taste
2 4-ounce fish fillets (recommended halibut or scrod)

Servings~ 👥
Cooking Time~ Fifteen Minutes
Pan to Use: Divided or Base

Cooking Steps
A. Pre-heat and spray with cooking spray. Mix together first five ingredients and set aside. Pour 1/4 cup orange juice into each well. Season both sides of fish fillets with adobo seasoning.
B. Place one fillet into each well. Close lid and cook 15 minutes until fish is white and flaky. Remove cooked fish from wells and top with pineapple salsa to serve.

Scallops Puttanesca

Ingredients
4 sea scallops
1 cup diced tomatoes with juice
2 anchovy fillets, chopped
1 tablespoon sliced black olives
1 tablespoon capers
1 tablespoon minced parsley
Pinch dried red pepper flakes to taste

Servings~
Cooking Time~ Nine Minutes
Pan to Use: Divided or Base

Cooking Steps
A. Pre-heat and spray with cooking spray. Place two scallops in each well and sear for one minute flip with spatula and sear on other side for one minute. Combine next six ingredients and pour over scallops and wells.
B. Cook five minutes more until done. Serve over Angel hair, spaghetti, parmesan cheese sprinkled on top.

Warm Fish and Spinach Salad

Ingredients
1 4-6oz flounder fillet, cut to fit well
Fresh red pepper, carrots and sweet onion, sliced paper thin
1/4 cup chicken broth or water

Salad
2 cups baby spinach, washed thoroughly
1 small avocado, peeled and cut into wedges
2 tablespoons lemon juice
1 tablespoon sesame seeds garnish

Dressing/marinade
3/4 cup vegetable oil
1/4 cup rice wine vinegar
1½ tablespoons low-salt soy sauce or tamari
2½ teaspoon sesame seeds
1/4 teaspoon minced garlic
1 pinch dried cilantro
1 pinch crushed red pepper flakes

Servings~
Cooking Time~ Twenty Minutes
Pan to Use: Divided or Base

Cooking Steps
A. In a shallow bowl or zip lock bag, marinate flounder 1/4 cup dressing for at least 30 minutes (reserve remainder of dressing for serving). Place the spinach on a large dinner plate and arrange the avocado wedges over the spinach and a star like fashion, creating a "bed" for the cooked fish. Divide chicken broth between wells.
B. Pre-heat and spray with cooking spray. Remove flounder from Ziploc bags and discard remainder. place flounder in one well and the sliced veggies in another well close lid and cook for 7 to 10 minutes, depending on thickness of flounder. Flounder should be white and flaky vegetables al dente.
C. Place cooked fish and veggies over bed of spinach topped with reserved dressing and sprinkle with some sesame seeds.

Codfish Cakes

Ingredients
3/4 cup leftover cooked codfish, flaked
1/2 cup prepared mashed potatoes
1/4 flavored bread crumbs
1 tablespoon grated parmesan cheese
1 egg
1/2 cup tomato sauce
Salt & pepper to taste

Servings~
Cooking Time~ Fifteen Minutes
Pan to Use: Divided or Base

Cooking Steps
A. Pre-heat and spray with cooking spray. Mix together all ingredients except tomato sauce (mixture is too sticky at a little milk). form two oval patties to fit wells
B. Cook one cake in each well for 12 to 15 minutes. Top with warm tomato sauce and served.

Pan-Blackened Swordfish W/ Sun-Dried Tomato Mayonnaise

Ingredients
2 (4 ounce) pieces swordfish, 1 inch thick
1 tablespoon Cajun blackening spices
<u>Sun Dried Tomato Mayonnaise</u>
2 tablespoons mayonnaise
1 tablespoon chopped sun-dried tomatoes
1/8 each garlic powder, salt and pepper

Servings~ 👨👨
Cooking Time~ Ten Minutes
Pan to Use: Divided or Base

Cooking Steps
A. Pre-heat and spray with cooking spray. Press spices into both sides of fish.
B. Place one piece of fish in each well. Cook seven to 10 minutes or until fish is flaky. Meanwhile, combine sun-dried tomato mayonnaise and serve with fish.

Low Carb Tuna Melts

Ingredients
2, 4 1/2inch thick slices from ripe tomatoes
1 cup prepared tuna salad
4 slices Swiss cheese

Servings~ 👨👨
Cooking Time~ Seven Minutes
Pan to Use: Divided or Base

Cooking Steps
A. Pre-heat and spray with cooking spray. Place one or two tomato slices and each cooking well.
B. Put equal amounts of tuna salad on tomato slices and top with two slices of cheese. Cook five to seven minutes until cheese is melted.

Orange Scallops

Ingredients
1/2 cup mandarin oranges with liquid
1 tablespoon white wine
1/2 teaspoon minced garlic
1 teaspoon soy sauce
4 6 sea scallops to fit wells
1 pinch dried red pepper flakes
1 teaspoon sesame seeds for garnish
2 dashes, sesame oil

Servings~ 👨👨
Cooking Time~ Eight Minutes
Pan to Use: Divided or Base

Cooking Steps
A. Pre-heat and spray with cooking spray. Mix together first four ingredients in small bowl.
B. Place equal amounts of scallops into each well and pour equal amounts of orange marinade covers scallops. Close cover heat five to eight minutes until scallops are done to your likeness. Top with sesame seeds and oil before serving.

Tuna Puffs

Ingredients
1 ½ cups mashed potatoes
1 egg
½ teaspoon seasoned salt
1 can tuna drained

Servings~ 👨👨
Cooking Time~ Seven Minutes
Pan to Use: Divided or Mini

Cooking Steps
A. Pre-heat and spray with cooking spray. mix all ingredients together in a bowl
B. Divide equal amounts of tuna mixture between wells. Close cover; cook seven minutes until golden brown.

Open-Face Crab Melt

Ingredients
4-5oz. canned crab meat, well drained
2 tablespoons mayonnaise
1 tablespoon finely chopped celery
1 teaspoon sweet pickle relish
1 teaspoon chopped pimento
2 slices ripe avocado
2 slices Muenster or white American cheese
1 croissant sliced in half sideways

Servings~ 👤👤
Cooking Time~ Seven Minutes
Pan to Use: Divided or Base

Cooking Steps
A. Pre-heat and spray with cooking spray. Mix together first five ingredients in small bowl. Spray outside of each croissant half with cooking spray. Place one half into each cooking well. Put even amounts of crab salad mixture onto each croissant half.
B. Top each half with one slice of avocado and one slice of cheese. Close cover, heat five to seven minutes or until cheese is melted.

Seafood Stuffed Salmon

Ingredients
2 skinless salmon fillets
2/3 cup cooked shrimp or crabmeat or mixture of both, finely chopped

Servings~ 👤👤
Cooking Time~ Eight Minutes
Pan to Use: Divided or Base

Cooking Steps
A. Pre-heat and spray with cooking spray. Slice salmon fillets vertically without going all the way across to form pockets for stuffing.
B. Stuff each with half the chopped seafood, place one half in each well cook six to eight minutes.
   1. **Seafood Stuffed Sole-** substitute 2 large fillets of soul for salmon spread filling on one half of each fillet and fold in half.

Sherried Mussels

Ingredients
1/2 cup cooking sherry
2 tablespoons
2 chopped green onions
1 teaspoon dried thyme
Black pepper to taste
12 fresh mussels
2 tablespoons heavy cream
2 pats butter

Servings~ 👤
Cooking Time~ Eight Minutes
Pan to Use: Divided or Base

Cooking Steps
A. Pre-heat and spray with cooking spray. Mix together first five ingredients.
B. Place six mussels in each well. Pour Sherry mixture over mussels. Close cover and cook three minutes. Add one tablespoon cream to each well and top with one Pat butter. Cook another five minutes until mussels open.

Grilled Shrimp and Asparagus Pizza

Ingredients
1 6 inch pita pocket
1/4 cup prepared Alfredo Sauce
1 4 ounce can baby shrimp, drained and patted dry
2 spears asparagus, cut into bite size pieces
1/4 cup shredded mozzarella
2 tablespoons grated parmesan cheese
1/2 tablespoons dried sage

Servings~
Cooking Time~ Ten Minutes
Pan to Use: Divided or Base

Cooking Steps
A. Pre-heat and spray with cooking spray. Cut pita in half so you have two semicircle pieces. Spread top of each pita half with equal amounts of Alfredo sauce. top each have 2 ounces of shrimp and equal amounts of asparagus
B. Top each half with mozzarella, parmesan and sage. Place one pizza half in each cooking well. Cook eight to 10 minutes (cheese should be melted completely and crust crunchy brown.

Flounder Stuffed with Broccoli and Cheese

Ingredients
1/3 cup chopped broccoli
1/4 cup shredded cheddar cheese
4 teaspoons mayonnaise
1 teaspoon prepared mustard
2 (4-6oz.) flounder fillets
2 tablespoons seasoned bread crumbs

Servings~
Cooking Time~ Ten Minutes
Pan to Use: Divided or Base

Cooking Steps
A. Pre-heat and spray with cooking spray. Combined broccoli, cheese, mayonnaise and mustard place half of mixture and center in each fillet and rollup jellyroll style. Spray fish with cooking spray and coat with bread crumbs.
B. Place one roll in each well cook 10 minutes or until crumbs are lightly browned and fish flakes easily with fork. Serve with lemon wedges and horseradish mayonnaise, if desired.

Swordfish with Marinated Tomatoes

Ingredients
4 ounce great cherry tomatoes, chopped
1 tablespoon olive oil
1 small clove garlic, crushed
1 teaspoon balsamic vinegar
1/4 teaspoon each salt ever
2 4-6 ounce swordfish steaks, 1 inch thick

Servings~
Cooking Time~ Seven Minutes
Pan to Use: Divided or Base

Cooking Steps
A. Pre-heat and spray with cooking spray. Combined tomatoes, oil, garlic, vinegar, salt and pepper allow to marinate at room temperature for at least 30 minutes before cooking fish.
B. Place one piece of fish in each well, cook seven minutes or until fish flakes easily with fork. Remove from well and spoon marinated tomatoes overfished before serving.

Crab Stuffed Mushrooms

Ingredients
6 medium-size mushrooms, stems removed
1/2 cup crab meat
1 tablespoon mayonnaise
1 teaspoon mustard
1/4 teaspoon garlic powder
1/4 teaspoon onion powder

Servings~ 👥
Cooking Time~ Seven Minutes
Pan to Use: Divided or Base

Cooking Steps
A. Pre-heat and spray with cooking spray. Combined, the crabmeat, mayonnaise, mustard, garlic powder and onion powder. spoon the mixture into mushroom caps
B. Place 3 stuffed mushroom caps in each well. Cook seven minutes.

Teriyaki Salmon with Wasabi Mayonnaise

Ingredients
2 teaspoons teriyaki sauce
1/2 teaspoons prepared mustard
1/2 teaspoons ground ginger
1/8 teaspoon garlic powder
1/8 teaspoon freshly ground pepper
2 (8 ounce) salmon steaks, 1.5 inches thick
1/4 cup wasabi mayonnaise

Servings~ 👥
Cooking Time~ Fifteen Minutes
Pan to Use: Divided or Base

Cooking Steps
A. Pre-heat and spray with cooking spray. Combine teriyaki sauce, mustard, ginger, garlic powder and pepper and brush on both sides of fish steaks.
B. Place one stake in each well cook 15 minutes or until fish flakes easily with fork. Serve with wasabi mayonnaise and lemon wedges.

Crab Cakes

Ingredients
8 ounces crabmeat
1 egg
1 teaspoon Worcestershire sauce
2 tablespoons mayonnaise
1 teaspoon lemon juice
1 tablespoon honey mustard
1/4 teaspoon dill
1/2 teaspoon garlic powder
1/8 teaspoon ground black pepper
1/2 cup freshly made soft breadcrumbs

Servings~ 👥
Cooking Time~ Twenty Minutes
Pan to Use: Divided or Base

Cooking Steps
A. Pre-heat and spray with cooking spray. Combined ingredients except bread crumbs, put bread crumbs on a flat plate.
B. Shaped crab mixture into to ovals press bread crumbs into both sides of crab cakes place one oval in each well. Cook 20 minutes or until well browned. Serve with tartar sauce or horseradish mayonnaise and lemon wedges.

Shrimp Stuffed Salmon Paddies

Ingredients
1/2 cup cooked baby shrimp
1/2 teaspoon garlic salt
1 teaspoon minced parsley
1 7 ounce package pink salmon
1 egg
1/2 cup breadcrumbs
1 celery stalk, finely chopped
2 green onions, finely sliced
1 teaspoon dill
1 teaspoon seasoned salt
1/4 cup mayonnaise

Servings~ 👤👤
Cooking Time~ Ten Minutes
Pan to Use: Divided or Base

Cooking Steps
A. Pre-heat and spray with cooking spray. Mix shrimp, garlic salt and parsley in a small bowl. In another bowl, mix salmon and breadcrumbs, celery, onion, dill, salt and mayonnaise until well blended.
B. Place about one half cup of salmon mixture into each well pressed down with the lifting tool to form a layer in the bottom. Spread half the shrimp mixture across the center of each well and top with remaining salmon mixture. Cook 8 to 10 minutes until paddies are browned.

Open Face Tuna Crostini Sandwiches

Ingredients
2 3 ounce fresh tuna fillets
2 tablespoons bottled Italian salad dressing
2 slices day old Baguette or sliced white Italian bread
Olive oil
Garlic Lemon Mayonnaise
2 tablespoons fresh minced garlic
2 tablespoons mayonnaise
Dash lemon juice

Servings~ 👤👤
Cooking Time~ Ten Minutes
Pan to Use: Divided or Base

Cooking Steps
A. Pre-heat and spray with cooking spray. Marinate tuna in Italian dressing in refrigerator for at least 30 minutes. Mix together Mayo ingredients and refrigerate until use. To make crostini, just before cooking toast bread and brush one side with olive oil. Place crostini, oil site out, on serving dish.
B. Cook each tuna fillet for eight to 10 minutes or until desired tenderness, turn once for even browning. Place one piece of cook tuna on top of each Crostini. Top each with a dollop of flavored mayonnaise and served.

Elegant Salmon and Zucchini Bake

Ingredients
1 small zucchini, sliced paper thin, preferably on mandolin
1 tablespoon sesame oil
2 teaspoon lime juice
1 teaspoon soy sauce
1/2 teaspoon minced garlic
1 teaspoon water
2 teaspoon mayonnaise
1/2 teaspoon Asian hot chili sauce
2 4 ounce salmon fillets, skin removed
1/2 and onion, sliced a person (garnish)
1 tablespoon black sesame seeds (garnish)

Servings~ 👤👤
Cooking Time~ Twelve Minutes
Pan to Use: Divided or Base

Cooking Steps
A. Do not Pre-heat, but spray with cooking spray. Mix zucchini with next five ingredients. Divide even amounts of zucchini between cooking wells, mix together mayonnaise and chili sauce. Place one salmon fillet into each cooking well and top each with half the chili mayonnaise.
B. Plug-in and cook 10 to 12 minutes or until salmon reaches desired doneness and mayonnaise is lightly browned. Serve topped with slivered onion and sprinkled with black sesame seeds.

Low-Carb Mussels Marinara

Ingredients
2/3 cup prepared roasted garlic tomato sauce
2 tablespoons red wine
2 tablespoons chopped onions
2 dozen small muscles

Servings~ 👫
Cooking Time~ Five Minutes
Pan to Use: Divided or Base

Cooking Steps
A. Pre-heat and spray with cooking spray. combined all ingredients except mussels place six mussels in each well, add 1/4 cup sauce mixture into each well.
B. Cook five minutes remove from wells and repeat cooking process with remaining muscles and sauce.

Fiji Island Sea Bass

Ingredients
2 5-6 oz, sea bass fillets (okay to substitute any whitefish)
Old Bay seasoning
Juice and zest of one small orange
1 tablespoon sesame oil
1/4 cup crushed pineapple with juice
2 tablespoons Cran-orange fruit sauce
1 green onion, cut into 1/4 inch slices
1 tablespoon minced fresh sweet onion
1/4 cup crushed macadamia nuts

Servings~ 👫
Cooking Time~ Ten Minutes
Pan to Use: Divided or Base

Cooking Steps
A. Pre-heat and spray with cooking spray. Season fish liberally with old Bay seasoning. Combined orange juice and sesame oil in Ziploc bag add fish and marinade in refrigerator for 30 minutes. In a small bowl, mix remaining ingredients except macadamia nuts and orange zest, set aside.
B. Cook fish six minutes, then open lid and top each fillet with half the fruit sauce mixture. Close cover and continue cooking until desired doneness cooking time will vary based on thickness of a fillet. To serve, garnish with macadamia nuts and orange zest.

Oriental Sea Bass

Ingredients
8 ounce sea bass fillet, cut into chunks
2 tablespoons sweet and sour stir-fry sauce
1 tablespoon peanut or canola oil
1 7 ounce box frozen green giant healthy weight vegetables (okay to substitute any Asian vegetable medley with sauce if unavailable in your area)
1 bag microwave brown rice, prepared as directed

Servings~ 👫
Cooking Time~ Six Minutes
Pan to Use: Divided or Base

Cooking Steps
A. Pre-heat and spray with cooking spray. Marinate fish in sweet and sour sauce and oil in Ziploc bag for 30 minutes, keep refrigerated. Prepare vegetables and microwave as directed.
B. Place equal amounts of fish into each cooking well. Cook approximately 3 minutes on each side until done. Assemble each plate, restaurant style, by topping rice with half the vegetable medley and half the fish.

Poached Dill and Cucumber Salmon

Ingredients
1 medium sized cucumber
1 tablespoon white vinegar
2 tablespoons water
1 tablespoons white sugar or Splenda
1 pinch salt
2 tablespoons fresh dill, stems removed, chopped
1 tablespoon fresh parsley, minced
1 heaping tablespoon sour cream
1 heaping tablespoon mayonnaise
2 teaspoon lemon pepper
2 4 ounce salmon Fillets cut to fit cooking Wells
1/2 cups low-salt chicken broth
Lemon pepper to taste
Garlic powder to taste
Fresh lemon slices for garnish

Servings~ 👤👤
Cooking Time~ Twelve Minutes
Pan to Use: Divided or Base

Cooking Steps
A. Pre-heat and spray with cooking spray. Cut cucumber in half lengthwise, seed in sliced thinly. In a separate bowl, mix next six ingredients. Pour over cucumbers, mix well, refrigerate. In a small bowl, mix sour cream mayo and lemon pepper, and refrigerate until ready to serve.

B. Put 1/4 cup broth into each cooking well. Season both sides a salmon fillets with lemon pepper and garlic butter place one fillet in broth in each well. Cook about 10 minutes, until flaky and done. Let fillets cool to room temperature. To serve top each fillet with equal amounts of cucumber salad and a dollop of sour cream mixture, then garnish with lemon slices.

Filet of Sole Veronique

Ingredients
1/3 cup green or red seedless grapes
4 ounce filet of sole or flounder
1 teaspoon thyme
1/2 teaspoon seasoned salt

Sauce
2 tablespoons butter
2 tablespoons flour
1½ cups white grape juice
Salt and pepper to taste

Servings~ 👤👤
Cooking Time~ Eight Minutes
Pan to Use: Divided or Base

Cooking Steps
A. Pre-heat and spray with cooking spray. To make sauce, melt butter in small saucepan. In a small bowl, add grape juice to flour and stir vigorously until flour is dissolved. Pour liquid into melted butter and pan, stirring. Continuously with whisk until butter and flour mixture is dissolved together. Cook about five minutes until sauce thickens. Add salt and pepper to taste if desired.

B. Slice grapes in half. Season fish in thyme and seasoned salt. Spoon enough sauce to cover bottom of each well. Divide fish evenly between wells. Top with equal amounts of grapes. Just enough sauce to cover. Cook six to eight minutes until flaking cooking time will depend on thickness of fish. Warm any leftover sauce for serving.

Almond Tilapia

Ingredients
1 5 ounce tilapia fillet
1 egg white beaten
¼ cup crushed almonds
Salt, pepper, and parsley

Servings~ 👤👤
Cocking Time~ Seven Minutes
Pan to Use: Divided or Mini

Cooking Steps
A. Pre-heat and spray with cooking spray. Dip fillet in egg white to coat both sides. Lay on bed of almonds and turn to coat well.

B. Season with salt, pepper, and dried parsley. Place fillet into unit and cook 5-6 minutes until fish flakes with fork.

Steamed Oyster Dim Sum

Ingredients
1/2 cup cooked baby shrimp
1/2 teaspoon garlic salt
1 teaspoon minced parsley
1 7 ounce package pink salmon
1 egg
1/2 cup breadcrumbs
1 celery stalk, finely chopped
2 green onions, finely sliced
1 teaspoon dill
1 teaspoon seasoned salt
1/4 cup mayonnaise

Servings~ 👥
Cooking Time~ Eight Minutes
Pan to Use: Divided or Base

Cooking Steps
A. Pre-heat and spray with cooking spray. Mix soy sauce and garlic in small bowl. This will be used as a dipping sauce for serving. In a separate bowl add hot water to stuffing mix until moist. Add bamboo shoots, sesame oil and red pepper flakes to stuffing and mix well. Gently fold in oysters (if mixture is too thick, add a little more hot water). Place equal amounts of moisture mixture into each wonton wrapper. Gather at the edges to form a cup, no need to seal edges just overlap.
B. Pour 1/4 cup broth into each well. Cook eight minutes until cooked through. Serve with a soy dipping sauce and scallion strips.

Clams Casino

Ingredients
1 can chopped clans approximately 6 ounces
1/2 cup breadcrumbs
2 tablespoons real bacon bits
2 tablespoons grated parmesan cheese
1 tablespoon chopped red pimentos with juice
2 tablespoons melted butter
1 teaspoon Italian seasoning
1 dash white wine vinegar

Servings~ 👥👥
Cooking Time~ Ten Minutes
Pan to Use: Divided or Base

Cooking Steps
A. Pre-heat and spray with cooking spray. mix all ingredients together
B. Divide equal amounts of clam mixture between wells. Close cover; cook eight to 10 minutes until heated through.

Mexican Catfish

Ingredients
2 Catfish Fillets
1 cup Picante Sauce
3 oz Monterey Jack Cheese Grated

Servings~ 👥
Cooking Time~ Six Minutes
Pan to Use: Divided or Base

Cooking Steps
A. Pre-heat and spray with cooking spray. Place catfish in well and top with Picante sauce and cheese.
B. Cook for 5-6 minutes or till fish is just flakey and cheese is melted.

Vegetables and Side Dishes

Spinach and Potato Croquettes

Ingredients
1 cup mashed potatoes
¼ cup grated cheddar or parmesan cheese
½ cup cooked chopped spinach
2 Tablespoons condensed cream soup
¼ each garlic and onion powder
¼ cup dried flavored bread crumbs
Cooking spray

Servings~ 👤👤
Cooking Time~ Eight Minutes
Pan to Use: Divided or Base

Cooking Steps
A. Combined all ingredients except bread crumb. Form mixture in to ovals and coat with bread crumbs.
B. Spray wells lightly with cooking spray. Place one oval in each well.

Veggie Pockets

Ingredients
4 Unbaked refrigerated biscuits
½ cup chopped cooked spinach, dried
¼ cup chopped cooked carrots
¼ cup chopped green beans
2 teaspoons Ranch dressing
2 Tablespoons grated cheddar, Swiss or mozzarella cheese
Salt and pepper

Servings~ 👤👤
Cooking Time~ Eight Minutes
Pan to Use: Divided or Base

Cooking Steps
A. Spray wells lightly with cooking spray. Place 2 biscuits, side by side, on to lightly floured board and sprinkle the top of the dough lightly with flour. Roll the biscuits together to form one dough round. Repeat with remaining 2 biscuits. Combine all the remaining ingredients. Place a dough circle on to the open pocket maker. Spoon about ½ cup of mixture into the bottom section of the dough circle.
B. Close the lid and press firmly to crimp the edges of the sandwich. Repeat process with remaining dough and ingredients.

Couscous for One

Ingredients
1/3 cup water
¼ cup couscous
1 teaspoon butter or olive oil
Salt, pepper, and seasoning to taste

Servings~ 👤
Cooking Time~ Four Minutes
Pan to Use: Divided or Base

Cooking Steps
A. Spray wells with cooking spray
B. Place all ingredients in to one well. Close lid cook for four minutes.

Stuffed Peppers

Ingredients
1 Large pepper tall and thin (red, yellow, or green)
½ cup cooked ground beef
½ teaspoon seasoned salt
½ cup instant rice, divided
½ cup V8 Juice divided
2 tablespoons frozen corn kernels
1 tablespoon water
3 Tablespoon finely grated cheese

Servings~ 👤👤
Cooking Time~ Ten Minutes
Pan to Use: Divided or Base

Cooking Steps
A. Slice pepper in half from top to bottom and remove seeds. Place halves in saucepan of boiling water. Cook 5 minutes or until tender. Remove from pan and drain on paper towel. Spray each well with cooking spray. Place 1 tablespoon each of rice, corn, water, and V8 in to wells. Place ground beef, salt, remaining rice and V8 in to a saucepan. Bring to a boil. Cover and remove from heat.
B. Let stand 5 minutes. Stuff each pepper half with half of the meat mixture, place on top of rice and corn in well. Close cover and plug in. When serving, sprinkle the cheese on top.

Hot & Spicy Olives

Ingredients
1 ½ cup mixed olives with pits
1 tablespoon dried Rosemary
1 Teaspoon dries red pepper flakes
1 tablespoon chopped garlic
1 tablespoon orange juice
½ tablespoon orange zest
¼ cup extra virgin olive oil
1 tablespoon balsamic vinegar

Servings~ 👤
Cooking Time~ Twelve Minutes
Pan to Use: Divided or Base

Cooking Steps
A. Mix all ingredients except olives. Add olives and toss to coat. Pre heat.
B. Add equal amounts of olive mixture to each well. Close cover and cook 8-10 minutes serve warm.

Arroz con Gandules (Rice and Pigeon peas)

Ingredients
¾ cup pigeon peas
1 table spoon sofrito
2 tablespoons tomato sauce
¼ cup water
2 teaspoons vegetable oil
2 tablespoons cooked chorizo or ham, cubed small
½ teaspoon Savon seasoning with achiote
½ cup instant rice

Servings~ 👤👤
Cooking Time~ Six Minutes
Pan to Use: Divided or Base

Cooking Steps
A. Mix pigeon peas, sofiro, tomato sauce, and water. Set aside. Place one teaspoon of oil into each cooking well. Pre heat GT Express 101.
B. Season meat with Savon and divide into each well. Fry 2 minutes until brown. Top meat with even amounts rice mixture and peas. Close cover, cook 6 minutes or until rice is done to desired tenderness.

Warm German Potato Salad

Ingredients
½ tablespoon white vinegar
1 tablespoon vegetable oil
1 tablespoon water
1 packet splenda
4-5 Chive sprigs, minced
Pinch onion powder
1 can sliced white potatoes, rinsed and drained
¼ cup bacon bits

Servings~ 👬
Cooking Time~ Two Minutes
Pan to Use: Divided or Base

Cooking Steps
A. Combine first six ingredients in medium mixing bowl and beat with fork. Add bacon bits and potatoes; toss to coat
B. Pre heat and spray with cooking spray. Divide potatoes between the 2 wells evenly. Cover and heat for 2 minutes.

Spanish Rice

Ingredients
3 Tablespoons long grain rice (not instant)
1/3 cup tomato sauce
1/3 cup water
2 Tablespoons each red & green peppers, chopped
½ teaspoon each salt & garlic powder
¼ cup shredded cheddar cheese

Servings~ 👬
Cooking Time~ Fifteen Minutes
Pan to Use: Divided or Base

Cooking Steps
A. Do not pre heat, combined all ingredients except cheese. Coat wells with cooking spray. Combined all ingredients except cheese.
B. Spoon half of mixture into each well. Sprinkle cheese right before serving.

Beet and Goat cheese Tapas

Ingredients
½ cup canned beet slices
2 tablespoons wet walnuts (ice cream topping)
4 1/2inch slices herbed goat cheese
4 egg roll wraps

Servings~ 👬
Cooking Time~ Eight Minutes
Pan to Use: Divided or Base

Cooking Steps
A. Place equal amounts of beet slices and walnuts onto each wrapper and top with goat cheese slice. Fold in half, point to point to make a triangle, and then fold over other 2 sides. Pre-heat and spray wells with cooking spray.
B. Place on piece in each well and cook 7-8 minutes turning half way to promote even browning.

Tuscan Stromboli

Ingredients
½ lb. prepared pizza dough
½ cup canned small white or cannellini beans
4 sundried tomatoes packed in oil, chopped
1 ½ teaspoon prepared pesto
1 tablespoon chopped, pitted olives
¼ cup chopped mozzarella
Salt and red pepper flakes to taste
Warm marinara sauce for dipping (optional)

Servings~ 👥
Cooking Time~ Fifteen Minutes
Pan to Use: Divided or Base

Cooking Steps
A. Divide pizza dough in half and role in do 7 inch circles. Mix all remaining ingredients together in a small bowl. Place half the mixture onto each dough circle. Tuck sides in and roll "burrito style" so Stromboli will fit well.
B. Pre-heat and spray with cooking spray. Place one Stromboli into each cooking well. Close cover cook 15 minutes until golden brown.

Samosa

Ingredients
1 can refrigerated crescent rolls
1 cup prepared mashed potatoes
2 tablespoons chickpeas
1 tablespoon thawed frozen peas
1 teaspoon India five spice powder
Black pepper
Chutney and plain yogurt

Servings~ 👥
Cooking Time~ Six Minutes
Pan to Use: Divided or Base

Cooking Steps
A. Unroll and divide crescent dough into four rectangles. Mix together mashed potatoes, chickpeas, peas and seasonings, and spoon even amounts into dough. For each Samosa, fold over dough and pinch together to make an envelope (no need for perforation).
B. Prick each Samosa with a fork to allow steam to escape while cooking. Pre-heat and spray with non-stick cooking spray. Place one Samosa in each well and cook for 6 minutes, cook in 2 batches. Serve with yogurt and chutney.

Loaded Mashed Potato Cakes

Ingredients
¼ cup flour for dredging
½ teaspoon salt
Pinch black pepper
¾ cup leftover mashed potatoes
2 tablespoons canned corn niblets, drain
¼ cup shredded Monterey jack cheese
2 tablespoons milk

Servings~ 👥
Cooking Time~ Ten Minutes
Pan to Use: Divided or Base

Cooking Steps
A. Pre-heat and spray with cooking spray. Mix together first three ingredients in set aside. In a separate bowl, combine remaining ingredients. Divide potatoes mixture in half in shape in equal size ball. Dredge balls in flour mix.
B. Place one potato ball in each well in close lid to "smash" potato mixture down. Cook 8 to 10 minutes until deep brown and crispy on the outside.

Mac & Cheese Boats

Ingredients
1 red or green pepper, cut in half lengthwise to fit
¾ cup heat and serve macaroni and cheese
¼ cup diced ham cubes
1 tablespoon grated parmesan cheese
Dash Worcestershire sauce
1/4 cup canned potato sticks

Servings~ 👥
Cooking Time~ Ten Minutes
Pan to Use: Divided or Base

Cooking Steps
A. Precook pepper pieces in boiling water or microwave too soften. Combine next two ingredients and mound into pepper halves. top pepper with potato sticks
B. Pre-heat and spray with cooking spray. The 10 minutes until bubbly.

Italian Pepper and Egg Sandwich

Ingredients
2 tablespoons jar fried peppers
2 eggs
2 tablespoons milk
2 slices provolone cheese
2, pepper, oregano or Italian seasonings to taste

Servings~ 👥
Cooking Time~ Seven Minutes
Pan to Use: Divided or Base

Cooking Steps
A. Pre-heat and spray lightly with non-stick cooking spray. place one spoon of fried peppers in each well and let Fry while beating the eggs with milk. Pour half the egg mixture in each well over fried peppers.
B. Close cover and cook for 7 minutes. split roll down the side without totally cutting through put cheese slice in roll. Break up fried eggs with the spatula and spoon onto roll. Sprinkle with seasoning.

Stilton & Bacon Bits

Ingredients
4 mini potato bread dinner rolls
½ cup stilton blue cheese, crumbled
½ cup real bacon bits
1 tablespoons minced scallions
Butter

Servings~ 👥
Cooking Time~ Five Minutes
Pan to Use: Divided or Base

Cooking Steps
A. Spread butter on outside top and bottom of dinner rolls. For filling, mixed Aitkin bits crumbled Stilton and scallions. Divide mixture evenly onto roll bottoms and cover with tops.
B. Pre-heat and spray with cooking spray. Put one filled roll into each well at a time and grill 3 to 5 minutes, repeat with remaining rolls.

Warm Zucchini Salad

Ingredients
1 small zucchini
½ cup water
½ tablespoon light olive oil
1 tablespoon red wine vinegar
1 tablespoon balsamic vinegar
1 tablespoon Splenda or sugar
Salt and pepper to taste

Servings~ 👥
Cooking Time~ Five Minutes
Pan to Use: Divided or Base

Cooking Steps
A. Pre-heat and spray with cooking spray. Add ¼ cup water to each well. Cut ends off the zucchini and discard; slice zucchini induced in sticks. Sprinkle with salt and pepper.
B. Divide zucchini evenly between walls and cook 3 to 5 minutes until tender. For dressing mix together remaining ingredients. Toss cooked zucchini with dressing and serve immediately.

Fiddlehead Ferns & Linguine

Ingredients
1 serving linguine, cooked according to package directions
1 cup fiddlehead firms, washed and patted dry
2 tablespoons extra virgin olive oil
1 tablespoon butter
2 tablespoons lemon juice
1 green onion (scallions), chopped
Dash garlic powder
Salt and pepper to taste
Grated parmesan for serving

Servings~ 👤👤
Cooking Time~ Seven Minutes
Pan to Use: Divided or Base

Cooking Steps
A. Pre-heat and spray with cooking spray. Divide all of oil and butter between wells in a melt 2 minutes. Toss fiddlehead salt, green onion, garlic powder, lemon juice, salt and pepper.
B. Sites seasoned fiddleheads between wells, cook 5-7 minute until tender. Serve immediately or linguine, talk to parmesan (see if desired; add additional olive oil or butter).

Baby Spinach Frittata

Ingredients
2 eggs
½ teaspoon seasoning blend
1 tablespoon minced fresh parsley.
½ teaspoon dried crushed red pepper flakes.
Salt to taste
¾ cups baby spinach, chopped finely.
½ cup Bisquick baking mix
2 tablespoons oil
2 tablespoons grated Asiago cheese

Servings~ 👤👤
Cooking Time~ Ten Minutes
Pan to Use: Divided or Base

Cooking Steps
A. Pre-heat and spray with cooking spray. The eggs and seasoning in small bowl with fork or wire whisk. Add remaining ingredients.
B. Divide mixture evenly between wells. Cook 8 to 10 minutes until golden brown.

Grilled Summer Vegetable Pita

Ingredients
1 ½ cups fresh vegetables of your choice, cut into bite sizes
3 tablespoons extra virgin olive oil
1 teaspoon fresh lemon juice
1 teaspoon orange juice
Pinch of dried crushed red pepper flakes
1 Pita, sliced in half

Servings~ 👤
Cooking Time~ Fifteen Minutes
Pan to Use: Divided or Base

Cooking Steps
A. Pre-heat and spray lightly with cooking spray. Mix together remaining ingredients and toss with cutup vegetables.
B. Divide vegetables between wells. "Grill" vegetables 12 to 15 minutes until desired tenderness. Spoon mixture into pita halves and serve immediately.

Peas with Bacon and Dill

Ingredients
1 tablespoon butter
1 cup fresh baby peas shelled (can substitute for thawed frozen baby peas)
½ teaspoon Italian seasoning blend
2 tablespoons minced onion
½ teaspoon red pepper flakes
1 tablespoon finely chopped fresh dill
Salt and pepper to taste
2 tablespoons real bacon bits

Servings~ 🚻
Cooking Time~ Ten Minutes
Pan to Use: Divided or Base

Cooking Steps
A. Pre-heat and spray with cooking spray. Melt ½ tablespoon butter in each well (approximately 2 minutes). Mix together remaining ingredients accept the Bacon bits.
B. Divide mixture evenly between wells and cook 3 minutes. Add one tablespoon bacon bits to each well and stir. Cook 3 more minutes.

Cauliflower "Fritters"

Ingredients
½ cup baking mix
1 cup cooked chopped cauliflower
2 tablespoons grated parmesan cheese
½ teaspoons each garlic and onion powder
1/3 cup milk
1 egg, slightly beaten

Servings~ 🚻
Cooking Time~ Ten Minutes
Pan to Use: Divided or Base

Cooking Steps
A. Pre-heat and spray Wells with cooking spray. Combined all ingredients.
B. Pour half of batter into each well. Cook 10 minutes or until well brown and toothpick inserted in center comes out clean.

Mushroom Pockets

Ingredients
½ package refrigerator pizza dough, cut in half
1 cup crumbled breakfast sausage
1 teaspoon butter
1 teaspoon of oil
1 8 ounce package mushrooms, sliced
1 teaspoon Worcestershire sauce
½ teaspoon nutmeg
Black pepper to taste
1 cup white cheddar or mozzarella cheese
¼ cup sour cream

Servings~ 🚻
Cooking Time~ Twelve Minutes
Pan to Use: Divided or Base

Cooking Steps
A. Pre-heat and spray with cooking spray. Melt butter in frying pan on stovetop. Sauté sausage and mushrooms on medium heat for about 10 minutes or until sausage is no longer pink and mushrooms are soft. Add remaining ingredients and mix to incorporate; set aside. On a floured surface, knead dough according to package instructions and stretch into 2, 6 inch circles.
B. Mount half of mushroom mixture into the center of each circle. Brush outer edges of circle with water. Fold over each circle into a half moon shape in a pinch to seal so filling will not leak out while cooking. Heat pockets about 12 minutes until golden brown.

Potato Wedges

Ingredients
2 medium new potatoes, washed and cut into 8 wedges
1 tablespoon olive oil
1 tablespoon bacon bits
1 tablespoon parmesan cheese
Salt, parsley

Servings~ 👤👤
Cooking Time~ Ten Minutes
Pan to Use: Divided or Base

Cooking Steps
A. Pre-heat and spray lightly with cooking spray. put potatoes, oil and seasoning into bowl, toss to coat
B. Arrange half of potato wedges in each side. Close lid and cook eight to 10 minutes until browned, and tender.

Cheesy Bacon Potato Skins

Ingredients
1 medium russet potato, baked and microwave
¼ cup grated cheddar cheese
2 tablespoons real bacon bits
1 green onion, chopped
Sour cream for garnish

Servings~ 👤👤
Cooking Time~ Five Minutes
Pan to Use: Divided or Base

Cooking Steps
A. Pre-heat and lightly spray with cooking spray. Scrubbed and bake potato in microwave (about 5 minutes). Cut in half; scoop out inside and reserved for later use (great in an omelet).
B. Fill each half with cheese, bacon and green onion. Place a potato in each well, close cover and cook 5 minutes until cheese is melted. Garnish with sour cream and serve.

Garlic Green Beans

Ingredients
2 Handfuls fresh baby green beans
1 tablespoon olive oil
1 tablespoon real bacon bits
1 clove garlic, minced
1 pinch kosher salt and cracked pepper

Servings~ 👤👤
Cooking Time~ Ten Minutes
Pan to Use: Divided or Base

Cooking Steps
A. Pre-heat and lightly spray with cooking spray. Pinch off ends up being.
B. Toss in bowl with all other ingredients. Place half of beans in each well, close cover and cook 10 minutes.

Stuffing Rice

Ingredients
2 tablespoon onion, finely chopped.
2 tablespoon celery, finely diced
2 tablespoons butter
2/3 cup instant rice
2/3 cup chicken broth mixed while
2 teaspoons parsley
½ teaspoon sage

Servings~ 👤👤
Cooking Time~ Two Minutes
Pan to Use: Divided or Base

Cooking Steps
A. Do not pre-heat but spray Wells with cooking spray. Place half of butter and one tablespoon onion and celery in each well, plug in unit and sauté for two minutes, lid closed.
B. Add half of rice to each well and half of broth, mixed with seasoning over rice. Cook two minutes. Unplug and let stand 5 minutes before serving.

Paprika Potatoes

Ingredients
2 medium russet potatoes, cut into 1 inch pieces
1 tablespoon oil
2 green onions, chopped
1 clove garlic, minced
½ teaspoon paprika
½ teaspoon salt
½ teaspoon pepper

Servings~ 👤👤
Cooking Time~ Ten Minutes
Pan to Use: Divided or Base

Cooking Steps
A. Pre-heat and spray lightly with cooking spray. Wash and chopped potatoes, place in bowl or in a bag with all other ingredients. Mix well to coat.
B. Arrange half of potatoes in each well close lid and cook 10 minutes or until tender.

"Grilled" Veggies

Ingredients
½ cup frozen mixed vegetables, like carrots, broccoli and cauliflower
2 tablespoons water
1 teaspoon butter or margarine
Salt and pepper

Servings~ 👤
Cooking Time~ Ten Minutes
Pan to Use: Divided or Base

Cooking Steps
A. Pre-heat and lightly spray with cooking spray. Place all ingredients in to Wells.
B. Close cover and cook for 10 minutes or until water has evaporated.

EZ Spanish Rice

Ingredients
1 cans Campbell Select Mexican Chicken Tortilla Soup
½ cup instant rice

Servings~ 👤👤
Cooking Time~ Five Minutes
Pan to Use: Divided or Base

Cooking Steps
A. Pre-heat and spray with cooking spray. Place remaining drained soup solids into a small bowl. Drain liquid off soup into measuring cup. Add an equal amount of instant rice (E.G. if there is ½ cup liquid add ½ cup rice) to the drained soup solids and stir.
B. Place ¼ of rice mixture into each well and cover with ¼ of drained soup broth. Close cover and cook 5 minutes. Unplug and let stand with lid closed for five minutes. Refrigerate remainder for use another time or repeat for two additional servings.

Portabella Mushroom Burgers

Ingredients
2 tablespoons Italian dressing
2 (3-4 inch) Portabella mushroom caps
4 ounces roasted red peppers cut into strips
2 (1/2-ounce) slices Muenster cheese

Servings~ 👤👤
Cooking Time~ Five Minutes
Pan to Use: Divided or Base

Cooking Steps
A. Marinate mushrooms in dressing for about ½ hour. Pre-heat and spray with cooking spray.
B. Place one mushroom in each well cook 3 minutes. Place half of peppers and cheese on each mushroom cook two minutes longer.

Spinach Pickups

Ingredients
5 ounces frozen spinach (about half a package)
1 egg, beaten
½ cup sour cream
2 tablespoons minced onion
¼ cup grated parmesan cheese
1½ tablespoons flour
1 ½ teaspoons butter
¼ teaspoon salt
¼ teaspoon pepper

Servings~ 👥
Cooking Time~ Ten Minutes
Pan to Use: Divided or Base

Cooking Steps
A. Pre-heat and spray with cooking spray. Cook spinach, according to package directions and drain well squeezing out excess moisture. Combined all ingredients in a bowl and mix well.
B. Divide spinach mixture in to Wells. Close cover and cook 10 minutes or until firm. Can be served hot as a side dish or cooled and cut into small wedges and served as an appetizer.

Rice and Veggie Cakes

Ingredients
1 cup cooked brown rice
¼ cup leftover mashed potatoes
¾ cup leftover cooked vegetables, mashed
2 tablespoons milk
¼ teaspoon garlic powder
Pepper to taste
¾ cup parmesan cheese, divided
2 teaspoons butter
Oil for cooking

Servings~ 👥
Cooking Time~ Twenty Minutes
Pan to Use: Divided or Base

Cooking Steps
A. Pre-heat and spray with cooking spray. Mix together first six ingredients, plus ¼ cup of parmesan cheese. Divide rice mixture between cooking wells.
B. Top with equal amounts of reserved, and dot with butter. Close cover; 20 minutes until tops are brown and crunchy.

Eggplant Cheese Bake

Ingredients
Two small (4 to 5 ounce) baby eggplants, peeled and cut into half lengthwise
2 tablespoons egg substitute or ½ egg, beaten
1/8 teaspoon each salt, garlic powder and
Onion powder
½ cup roasted garlic flavored tomato sauce
½ cup grated parmesan cheese

Servings~ 👥
Cooking Time~ Six Minutes
Pan to Use: Divided or Base

Cooking Steps
A. Pre-heat and spray with cooking spray. Combined egg and seasonings in a bowl. Coat both sides of eggplant halves with egg mixture.
B. Place one eggplant half in each well. Cook six minutes, turn eggplant topped with sauce and cheeses cook for six more minutes. Remove and repeat for second eggplant.

Cheese- Onion Potato Casserole

Ingredients
1 ½ cups instant mashed potatoes, prepared according to package
1 oz. cream cheese, cut into small cubes
1 tablespoon sour cream
2 tablespoons shredded cheddar cheese
1 teaspoon butter
1 3.5-oz. jar cocktail onions, drained
1/8 teaspoon garlic powder
Fresh chives for garnished (optional)

Servings~ 🕴
Cooking Time~ Ten Minutes
Pan to Use: Divided or Base

Cooking Steps
A. Pre-heat and spray with cooking spray. Mix together all ingredients except chives.
B. Divide potatoes mixture between cooking wells. Cook 10 minutes until cheese is entirely melted. Serve topped with fresh chives for garnish, if desired.

Cheesy "Mashed Potato" Bake

Ingredients
1 ½ cup leftover cooked cauliflower
1 tablespoon half-and-half
2 tablespoons grated parmesan cheese
2 tablespoons shredded white cheddar cheese
1 tablespoon butter
Salt and pepper to taste

Servings~ 🕴
Cooking Time~ Seven Minutes
Pan to Use: Divided or Base

Cooking Steps
A. Pre-heat and spray with cooking spray. Mashed cauliflower with fork. Mix in half-and-half and cheddar cheese and seasoning.
B. Divide cauliflower mixture evenly between wells and top each side with parmesan cheese and butter. Cook 5 to 7 minutes until hot and cheeses is melted.

Bacon & Swiss Stuffed Baby Bella Mushrooms

Ingredients
2 slices cooked bacon, finely chopped
½ ounce Swiss cheese, finely chopped
1 scallion finely chopped
1 tablespoon ranch dressing
1/8 teaspoon pepper
6 small baby Bella mushrooms

Servings~ 🕴🕴
Cooking Time~ Five Minutes
Pan to Use: Divided or Base

Cooking Steps
A. Combined bacon, cheese, scallion, dressing, pepper, and chop stems. fill caps with mixture
B. Place three mushrooms in each well. Cook five minutes or until hot.

Potato Rice Pancakes

Ingredients
½ cup mashed potatoes (any flavor you choose)
½ cup cooked rice
1 egg
½ teaspoon garlic powder
¼ Italian flavored bread crumbs

Servings~ 👥
Cooking Time~ Fifteen Minutes
Pan to Use: Divided or Base

Cooking Steps
A. Pre-heat and spray with cooking spray. Combined all ingredients except bread crumbs. Form mixture into to ovals and coat with bread crumbs.
B. Place one oval in each well. Cook 15 minutes or until well browned.

Fried Rice

Ingredients
1 cup cooked rice
¼ cup soy sauce
1 teaspoon oil
½ cup chopped cooked pork, chicken or beef
2 tablespoons chopped bamboo shoots
2 tablespoons frozen or cooked peas

Servings~ 👥
Cooking Time~ Eight Minutes
Pan to Use: Divided or Base

Cooking Steps
A. Pre-heat and spray with cooking spray. Combined all ingredients.
B. Spoon half of mixture into each well. Cook for 8 minutes.

Tofu Hash

Ingredients
2 tablespoons minced onion
½ of a green or red pepper, chopped
¼ teaspoon garlic powder
¼ teaspoon paprika
¼ teaspoon onion powder
1 tablespoon "Liquid Smoke"
Salt and pepper to taste
1 small tofu cake, diced into small cubes

Servings~ 👥
Cooking Time~ Ten Minutes
Pan to Use: Divided or Base

Cooking Steps
A. Pre-heat and spray with cooking spray. Combined all ingredients except tofu in a Ziploc bag; close and shake vigorously to combine. Add tofu cubes, many in refrigerator 15 minutes.
B. Divide mixture evenly between cooking wells. Close cover cook 10 minutes turn for even browning.

Ranch Veggie French Bread Pizza

Ingredients
4 ounces whipped cream cheese
2 tablespoons bottled ranch dressing
1 4 inch piece Italian roll sliced in half lengthwise to make pizza crusts
Chopped broccoli, red peppers, onions (any leftover veggies will do)
2 tablespoons shredded mozzarella cheese
1 tablespoon parmesan choose
1 pinch Italian seasoning blend

Servings~ 👥
Cooking Time~ Five Minutes
Pan to Use: Divided or Base

Cooking Steps
A. Pre-heat and spray with cooking spray. Mix together cream cheese and ranch dressing. Spread mixture on tops of "pizza crusts". top each pizza with equal amounts of veggies, mozzarella, parmesan, and seasoning;
B. Place one pizza in each well. Close cover; he 5 minutes.

Carrot Dumplings

Ingredients
1 cup mashed cooked carrots
2 scallions, chopped
2 cloves garlic, minced
2 tablespoons soy sauce
1 tablespoon brown sugar
2 tablespoons unsalted sunflower seeds
8 eggroll wraps
2/3 cup apple juice

Servings~ 🚹🚹🚹🚹
Cooking Time~ Eight Minutes
Pan to Use: Divided or Base

Cooking Steps
A. Do not Pre-heat. Mix together first six ingredients. Place approximately 2 tablespoons of carrot mixture on the center of each wonton wrapper and wet edges with water. Gather up edges of wonton wrapper to form a little sack; pinch in twister close. Spray wells with cooking spray.
B. Put one tablespoon of juice and two dumplings into each well. Plug in unit. Close cover, cook 8 minutes. Repeat with remaining dumplings. Serve with duck sauce, if desired.

Rutabaga Casserole

Ingredients
1 fork tender cooked rutabaga, mashed
½ cup dried cranberries
1 tablespoon chopped pecans or walnuts
3 tablespoons melted butter
2 teaspoons light cream or milk
Pinch nutmeg
Salt and pepper to taste
1 4-section large sugared graham cracker crashed

Servings~ 🚹
Cooking Time~ Seven Minutes
Pan to Use: Divided or Base

Cooking Steps
A. Pre-heat and spray with cooking spray. Mix together all ingredients except graham cracker crumbs and one tablespoon melted butter. If mixture is too stiff add more light cream or milk.
B. Divide equal amounts of rutabaga mixture into cooking wells. Top rutabagas with equal amounts of graham cracker topping. Close cover; cook 7 minutes.

Spanish Rice Omelet

Ingredients
1 cup Spanish rice
2 tablespoons shredded Monterey jack cheese
2 eggs

Servings~ 🚹🚹
Cooking Time~ Sixteen Minutes
Pan to Use: Divided or Base

Cooking Steps
A. Pre-heat and spray with cooking spray. Combined all ingredients.
B. Place half of mixture in each well. Cook 16 minutes or until omelet as well brown and puffy and toothpick inserted in center comes out clean.

Greek Pitawich

Ingredients
1 (6 inch), pita bread, sliced in half vertically forming to pockets
¼ cup artichoke hearts, chopped
2 tablespoons Greek olives, chopped
1 small tomato, chopped
¼ cup crumbled feta cheese

Servings~ 🚹🚹
Cooking Time~ Three Minutes
Pan to Use: Divided or Base

Cooking Steps
A. Pre-heat and spray with cooking spray. Mix artichoke hearts, olives, tomato and feta cheese together in a small bowl. Divide mixture in half and stuff into each pocket.
B. Place one half in each well, cook 2 to 3 minutes or until cheese is melted.

Hominy Bake

Ingredients
2 teaspoons vegetable oil
5 Cherry tomatoes, halved
1 tablespoon minced red onion
Salt to taste
¾ cup canned Hominy, rinsed and drained
1 teaspoon white vinegar
½ teaspoon chili powder
½ teaspoon cayenne pepper
1 teaspoon raw sugar

Servings~ 👤👤
Cooking Time~ Six Minutes
Pan to Use: Divided or Base

Cooking Steps
A. Pre-heat input 1 teaspoon oil into each cooking well. Place 5 Cherry tomato halves and ½ tablespoon onion into each cooking well; sprinkle with salt.
B. Close cover; cook three minutes to soften. Mix together remaining ingredients in divide evenly between wells. Close cover; cook three minutes.

White Asparagus & Tomato Pie

Ingredients
1/3 cup Bisquick baking mix
2 tablespoons low-cholesterol liquid egg substitute
1 tablespoon water
¼ cup shredded mozzarella cheese
1 tablespoons ricotta cheese
2 cooked asparagus spears, chopped
3 cherry or grape tomatoes, diced
¼ cup parmesan cheese
Pinch red pepper flakes
Pinch garlic salt

Servings~ 👤👤
Cooking Time~ Ten Minutes
Pan to Use: Divided or Base

Cooking Steps
A. Pre-heat and spray with cooking spray. Combined first three ingredients in Shaker. Divide batter evenly between wells; smooth with Xpress 101 spatula to cover bottom of Wells.
B. Close cover; cook 2 minutes. In a small bowl, mix ricotta, parmesan, asparagus, tomatoes and seasonings. Divide mixture in half and spread on pies. close cover; cook 5 minutes
C. Open cover and sprinkle pies with mozzarella. Brush inner top of lid with olive oil, close lid and cook an additional 1 to 2 minutes until mozzarella completely melted.

Meatless Meatloaf

Ingredients
1 cup mashed cooked carrots
2 scallions, chopped
2 cloves garlic, minced
2 tablespoons soy sauce
1 tablespoon brown sugar
2 tablespoons unsalted sunflower seeds
8 eggroll wraps
2/3 cup apple juice

Servings~ 👤👤
Cooking Time~ Twenty Minutes
Pan to Use: Divided or Base

Cooking Steps
A. Pre-heat and spray with cooking spray. Mix together all ingredients, reserving two tablespoons of the barbecue sauce. Mixture should be fairly moist it to dry add additional water.
B. Divide mixture evenly between wells. Close cover; cook 10 minutes. Brush each loaf with reserved barbecue sauce. Close cover and continue cooking 5 to 10 minutes until heated through and barbecue sauces browns.

Savory Chickpea Patties

Ingredients
¾ cup chickpeas (garbanzo beans)
¼ cup frozen thawed or canned green peas
½ teaspoon grant masala Italian seasoning
2 tablespoons plain yogurt
1 pinch salt
½ cup Cathy's "Pie Batter"
Major Gray's chutney for dipping

Servings~ 👤👤
Cooking Time~ Ten Minutes
Pan to Use: Divided or Base

Cooking Steps
A. Pre-heat and spray with cooking spray. Mix together first five ingredients.
B. Divide even amounts of chickpea mixture between cooking wells. Pour pie batter over chickpea mixture, filling to the top of each well. Close cover; cook 10 minutes. Serve with Major Gray's Chutney.

Polenta with Creamy Tomato Sauce and Cheese

Ingredients
2 ½-inch thick slices prepared Polenta
¾ cup creamy tomato sauce
2 tablespoons crumbled Gorgonzola cheese
1 tablespoon grated Asiago cheese
2 teaspoons Italian seasoning
2 teaspoons olive oil (for cooking surface)
Fresh basil for garnish

Servings~ 👤👤
Cooking Time~ Ten Minutes
Pan to Use: Divided or Base

Cooking Steps
A. Pre-heat and brush cooking surface with olive oil. Carefully place one polenta piece into each well. Combine remaining ingredients except garnish.
B. Top polenta slices with equal amounts of creamy tomato sauce. Close cover; cook 8 to 10 minutes until bubbly. Top with fresh basil before serving.

Twice-Baked Cheesy Potatoes

Ingredients
1 (8-ounce) Idaho baking potato, 5 inches long, unpeeled, cut in half lengthwise
1 tablespoon sour cream
2 tablespoons grated cheddar cheese
1 teaspoon butter or margarine
¼ teaspoon each onion and garlic powder
½ teaspoon salt

Servings~ 👤👤
Cooking Time~ Twelve Minutes
Pan to Use: Divided or Base

Cooking Steps
A. Pre-heat and spray with cooking spray. Place half of potato into each well. Cook 12 minutes or until potato is soft enough to be removed from skin. Remove and scoop potato out of this skin, leaving the skin intact.
B. Combined potato with remaining ingredients match with fork until smooth. Spoon back scans and return to wells. Cook 5 more minutes.

Veggie Filled Puff Pastry Bundles

Servings~ 👤👤
Cooking Time~ Ten Minutes
Pan to Use: Divided or Base

Ingredients
½ cup finely chopped zucchini
½ cup finely chopped eggplant
2 tablespoons finely chopped green peppers
2 mushrooms, finely chopped
2 tablespoons finely chopped onion
1 clove garlic, crushed
½ teaspoon each salt, dried basil, parsley, and oregano
1/8 teaspoon pepper
2 teaspoon olive oil
2 teaspoons tomato paste
¼ cup water
2 tablespoons grated parmesan cheese
4 frozen puff pastry shells, thawed

Cooking Steps
A. Pre-heat and spray with cooking spray. Sauté vegetables in oil. Stir in tomato paste and water; cook for 5 minutes. Stir in grated cheese. Rolled puff pastry out into 6x5 inch rectangles. Spoon 3 tablespoons of filling into center of each rectangle.
B. Fold two sides into each other and then fold other two sides over to form a pocket. Place to pockets into each well; cook 10 minutes or until nicely browned.

Sun Dried Tomato Goat Cheese Roasted Pepper Roll

Servings~ 👤
Cooking Time~ Five Minutes
Pan to Use: Divided or Base

Ingredients
1 croissant sliced in half lengthwise
4 oz sun-dried tomato flavored goat cheese
2 sun-dried tomatoes, chopped
1 roasted pepper (jar is fine, but drain well)
Drizzle of olive oil
Italian seasonings blend to taste
1 teaspoon garlic powder
Crushed red pepper (optional)

Cooking Steps
A. Pre-heat and spray with cooking spray. To assemble, sprinkle cheese onto sandwich bottom. Top with remaining ingredients and cover with croissant top.
B. Cut sandwich in half and place one half in each well. Close cover; heat 5 minutes until croissant is brown and warm.

Veggie Pitawich

Servings~ 👤👤
Cooking Time~ Three Minutes
Pan to Use: Divided or Base

Ingredients
½ cup vegetables (mushrooms, onions, peppers, olives), chopped or thin sliced
1 (6 inch), pita bread, cut in half vertically forming to pockets
¼ cup shredded mozzarella cheese
2 tablespoons pizza sauce

Cooking Steps
A. Pre-heat and spray with cooking spray. Add vegetable to Wells and cook two minutes stirring once if necessary until lightly browned. Stir together cheese and sauce. add cooked vegetables to cheese and sauce mixture
B. Divide mixture in half and stuff in each pocket. Place one half in each well 2 to 3 minutes until cheese is melted.

Melted Cheese and Tomato Sandwiches

Ingredients
4 slices Italian bread
4 slices cheese
4 thin slices of tomato
2 teaspoons pesto, mayonnaise or your favorite sandwich spread

Servings~ 👤👤
Cooking Time~ Five Minutes
Pan to Use: Divided or Base

Cooking Steps
A. Pre-heat and spray with cooking spray. Spread each slice of bread with chosen condiment. Place cheese and tomatoes on bread, top with second slice.
B. Fit the sandwiches into the wells. Cook four to five minutes or until bread is toasted allow sandwich too cool for a few minutes before serving as filling will be very hot.

Hot Tomato Stacked Sandwiches

Ingredients
4 ½ inch thick slices of firm, ripe beefsteak tomatoes
Extra virgin olive oil
Salt and pepper to taste
14 slices Rosemary ham (recommended Citterio brand)
2 ½ inch thick slices of fresh mozzarella
½ teaspoon dried Italian seasoning
Handful fresh arugula
Fresh basil leaves for garnish

Servings~ 👤👤
Cooking Time~ Twelve Minutes
Pan to Use: Divided or Base

Cooking Steps
A. Pre-heat and spray with cooking spray. Brush both sides, tomato slices with oil and season with salt and pepper. Place one tomato slice into each cooking well. To assemble, start each tomato slice with half of ham & a slice of mozzarella and fresh arugula and sprinkle with Italian seasoning and top with another tomato slice.
B. Close cover; grill 10 to 12 minutes until cheese is melted and tomatoes are soft, gently flip for even cooking halfway through. Carefully remove stacks from Wells and serve with fresh basil.

Crispy Baked Potatoes

Ingredients
2 medium potatoes, washed and sliced in half lengthwise

Servings~ 👤👤
Cooking Time~ Fifteen Minutes
Pan to Use: Divided or Base

Cooking Steps
A. Pre-heat and spray with cooking spray. Lay one half skin side down in each cooking well, lay the second half, skin side up over the but offset so the unit closes.
B. Cook 15 minutes serve with butter or sour cream.

Xpress Rice

Ingredients
1 cup instant rice
1 cup water or chicken broth
½ cup finely chopped vegetables (broccoli, carrots, onions, and green or red peppers)

Servings~ 👤👤
Cooking Time~ Five Minutes
Pan to Use: Divided or Base

Cooking Steps
A. Pre-heat and spray with cooking spray. divide rice between the two wells
B. Carefully add half of water to each well. Top with chopped vegetables. Cook 4 to 5 minutes or until rice is fluffy.

Spinach Salad with Hot Bacon Dressing

Ingredients
1 6 ounce bag prewashed Baby spinach
1 small red onion, peeled and sliced into rings
6 fresh, clean mushrooms cut into slices
2 hard-boiled eggs, peeled and cut into slices
½ cup croutons
4 slices bacon, chopped
½ cup balsamic vinegar
¼ cup sugar
1 teaspoon Dijon mustard
¼ cup water

Servings~ 👥
Cooking Time~ Twelve Minutes
Pan to Use: Divided or Base

Cooking Steps
A. Pre-heat and spray with cooking spray. To assemble salad, put spinach into large bowl and top with onion, mushrooms and hard-boiled egg slices. Put equal amounts of chopped bacon into each cooking well.
B. Close cover and cook six minutes. In the meantime mixed together remaining ingredients to make dressing. After bacon is cooked, pour equal amounts of dressing over bacon in Wells and heat another two minutes until hot. Do not over fill wells; any excess dressing can be poured on the salad. Spoon hot bacon dressing over salad to serve.

Sweet Carrot Sandwich

Ingredients
2 slices of banana nut bread
Butter
Chunky peanut butter
2/3 cup prepared carrot salad (available at the deli)
1 tablespoon honey

Servings~ 👥
Cooking Time~ Ten Minutes
Pan to Use: Divided or Base

Cooking Steps
A. Pre-heat and spray with cooking spray. Lightly butter one side of each slice of bread. Spread non- butter side of one slice of bread with peanut butter, honey, and carrot salad. top with other slice of bread, butter side up
B. Cut sandwich in half and place one half into each well, buttered side down. Grill for 7 to 10 minutes, turning after four minutes to promote even browning.

Broccoli Dream Pocket

Ingredients
1 package prepared pizza dough (15 ounce)
1 cup thawed frozen chopped broccoli
½ cup shredded mozzarella
2 tablespoons blue cheese salad dressing
½ tablespoon minced garlic

Servings~ 👥
Cooking Time~ Twelve Minutes
Pan to Use: Divided or Base

Cooking Steps
A. Pre-heat and spray with cooking spray. Roll out dough on a lightly floured surface. With a small bowl, cookie or pastry cutter, cut to 6 inch circles (four thin crust pockets, reserved a quarter of the dough for another meal). Mix together remaining ingredients. Place filling on one half of each circle. Fold dough over into a half moon shaped and pinch edges to seal.
B. Place one pocket in each well. Bake for 10 to 12 minutes turning half way through to promote even Browning.

Exotic Succotash Boat's

Ingredients
¾ cup thawed shuttled edamame
½ cup thawed frozen or canned yellow or white corn niblets
2 tablespoons sliced green onion
1 tablespoon rice wine vinegar
2 tablespoons sesame oil
1 teaspoon honey
½ teaspoon ground or minced fresh ginger
Dash soy sauce
1 avocado, peeled, pitted and halved

Servings~ 👤👤
Cooking Time~ Five Minutes
Pan to Use: Divided or Base

Cooking Steps
A. Do not Pre-heat spray with cooking spray. In a small bowl, mix together all ingredients except avocado. Divide even amounts of succotash between cooking wells.
B. Plug in, unit and cook 5 minutes or until warmed through. Serve mounted on top avocado halves, with additional soy sauce, if desired.

Eggplant Vegetable Boats

Ingredients
1 white or purple eggplant (5" long) cut in half lengthwise
½ cup canned diced tomatoes with herbs or roasted garlic
1 tablespoon grated parmesan cheese
¼ teaspoon each salt, pepper, garlic and onion powder
¼ cup Italian flavored bread crumbs

Servings~ 👤👤
Cooking Time~ Eight Minutes
Pan to Use: Divided or Base

Cooking Steps
A. Pre-heat and spray with cooking spray. Scoop out the center of the eggplant and chopped into small pieces. Combine the chopped eggplant with the tomatoes cheese and seasonings. Fill the eggplant shells with the mixture and sprinkle half the bread crumbs on each boat.
B. Carefully placed the boats in wells. Cook 8 minutes.
   1. **Yellow squash vegetable Boats**-substitute a small yellow squash about 8 ounces for the eggplant. Trim off the narrow and if necessary to fit in wells

Zucchini Boats

Ingredients
1 large cucumber size zucchini
2 tablespoons sour cream
1 tablespoon butter or margarine
¼ cup cottage cheese
¼ cup parmesan cheese
2 tablespoons season breadcrumbs
Salt and pepper to taste

Servings~ 👤👤
Cooking Time~ Ten Minutes
Pan to Use: Divided or Base

Cooking Steps
A. Scrub zucchini, cook in large pan of boiling water for 15 minutes or until almost tender. Drain and cool. Slice off top 1/3 and discard. Scoop out pulp, place in strainer, drain and press dry. Combine pulp with sour cream, butter, cottage cheese, salt and pepper in bowl. Mix well and spoon into zucchini.
B. Pre-heat and lightly spray with cooking spray. Cut zucchini in half and place in wells. Sprinkle with parmesan cheese and breadcrumbs. Close cover and cook for 7 to 10 minutes until filling is heated through and topping is golden brown.

Broccoli and Cheddar Tarts

Ingredients
1 egg
1/3 cup half and half
1 tablespoon chopped green onions
1/3 cup shredded cheese
½ cup chopped broccoli florets
½ cup individual or quiche crust

Servings~ 👤👤
Cooking Time~ Twelve Minutes
Pan to Use: Divided or Base

Cooking Steps
A. Spray unit with cooking spray. Follow directions for individual pie or quiche crust to form a crust in each well. Plug in unit and bake crust for 2 minutes. Mix together all ingredients and pour into shells after the 2 minute cook time.
B. Close cover and bake for 8-10 minutes until knife inserted in center comes out clean.

Twice Baked Potato

Ingredients
1 medium Russet potato scrubbed and baked in microwave
1 tablespoon butter or margarine
½ cup cottage cheese
1 tablespoon real bacon bits
Salt and pepper to taste
Finely grated cheese and chives if desired for garnish

Servings~ 👤👤
Cooking Time~ Five Minutes
Pan to Use: Divided, Mini or Base

Cooking Steps
A. Pierce potato with fork and place in microwave until done, about 5 minutes. Cut in half lengthwise and scoop out potato, leaving shell intact about ¼ inches thick. Place potato pulp on plate, add butter, cottage cheese, bacon bits, salt and pepper and mix with fork, mashing until smooth. Scoop half of mixture into each potato shell.
B. Pre-heat and spray with cooking spray. Place a potato half in each well, close cover and cook for about 5 minutes until filling is heated and top is lightly brown. To serve, open a slit in top and fill with grated cheese and chives.

Sweet Potato Puffs

Ingredients
1 cup mashed sweet potato
1 ripe banana mashed
½ teaspoon curry powder
2 tablespoons sour cream
Dash of salt
1 egg

Servings~ 👤👤
Cooking Time~ Seven Minutes
Pan to Use: Divided or Base

Cooking Steps
A. Pre-heat and spray with cooking spray. Mix all ingredients together and divide into wells.
B. Close cover and cook for 7 minutes until puffed and brown.

"Fried" Rice with Vegetables

Ingredients
1 small zucchini thinly sliced
2 medium mushrooms thinly sliced
2 tablespoons frozen mixed vegetables
3 tablespoons (leftover) cooked rice
2 tablespoons water
2 teaspoons soy sauce

Servings~ 👤👤
Cooking Time~ Eight Minutes
Pan to Use: Divided or Base

Cooking Steps
A. Pre-heat and spray with cooking spray. Stir vegetables and rice together and divide into wells.
B. Drizzle water into wells around edge and shake soy sauce over the top of veggie mixture. Close cover and cook for 8 minutes.

Bean and Veggie Wraps

Ingredients
2 fat-free flower tortillas
1/2 cup sliced mushrooms
1/2 small onion, sliced thin
1/2 can black beans, drained and rinsed
1 cup fresh spinach leaves
1/4 cup reduced fat cheese, shredded

Servings~ 👤👤
Cooking Time~ Four Minutes
Pan to Use: Divided or Base

Cooking Steps
A. Pre-heat and spray with cooking spray. Sauté onions and mushrooms until onions are transparent. Add black beans, cooking, just until heated. Lay tortillas flat, cover with a layer of spinach leaves, top with the black bean mixture and sprinkle cheese.
B. Fold the end, fold in sides and roll into a 5 inch wide roll to fit wells. Place seam side down close cover and cook four minutes, until lightly browned.

Spicy Orange Broccoli

Ingredients
4 cooked fresh or thawed frozen broccoli spears
3/4 cup lime juice
2 tablespoons orange marmalade
1 tablespoon chopped jalapeno peppers
1 clove garlic, minced
1 teaspoon Louisiana hot sauce
1 tablespoon cilantro
Salt and pepper to taste

Servings~ 👤
Cooking Time~ Five Minutes
Pan to Use: Divided or Base

Cooking Steps
A. Pre-heat and spray with cooking spray. Slice broccoli spears in half lengthwise to fit wells if necessary. Mix together and main ingredients in medium bowl, add broccoli and toss to coat with marinade.
B. Divide broccoli and all the marinade equally between the two wells. Cook five minutes until heated through. Serve with crusty French bread, if desired.

Thyme Lime Potato Wedges

Ingredients
1 medium potato baked in microwave
1/4 cup melted butter (substitute liquid margarine, if desired)
1 tablespoon lime juice (preferably fresh)
1 teaspoon lime zest
1 teaspoon dried thyme or two sprigs fresh thyme
1/4 cup grated parmesan cheese
Pinch seasoned salt
Pinch paprika
Fresh lime wedges, if desired

Servings~ 👤👤
Cooking Time~ Five Minutes
Pan to Use: Divided or Base

Cooking Steps
A. Pre-heat and spray with cooking spray. In a medium-size bowl, mix butter, lime juice, zest and thyme, cut potatoes into eight wedges. Add potato wedges to butter mixture and gently toss to coat. combine parmesan, salt, paprika in a small bowl
B. Divide potato edges between Wells and sprinkle with parmesan mixture. Heat five minutes until cheese is melted. Serve with fresh lime wedges.

Greek Spanakopita

Ingredients
1/2 cup frozen chopped spinach
1 sheet thawed frozen phyllo dough (9" x 14")
2 tablespoons melted butter
1 teaspoon prepared pesto
1/2 teaspoon dried dill
1 tablespoon chopped, pitted Kalamata olives
2 tablespoons crumbled feta cheese

Servings~ 👤👤
Cooking Time~ Eight Minutes
Pan to Use: Divided or Base

Cooking Steps
A. Pre-heat and spray with cooking spray. Squeeze thawed spinach on a clean paper towel until no access water remains (moisture will cause recipe to be soggy). Lay phyllo sheet on a flat surface and brush the top with melted butter. Mix together spinach, pesto, dill, olives and feta. Mound spinach mixture in a strip on middle of phyllo, leaving a 1 inch border around the side. Fold up phyllo sheet as if you were folding a piece of paper into fours, brushing the top of each fold with melted butter.
B. When finished, cut the folded piece in half (at this point all surfaces of stuffed phyllo should have been brush with butter). Place one spanakopita into each well, cutting off 1 inch unstuffed in order to fit if necessary. Cook five to eight minutes until phyllo is brown and crunchy. Peek half way through cooking to avoid overcooking cook time varies based on phyllo brand used.

Spinach Soufflé

Ingredients
1/2 (10 ounce) package, creamed spinach
1 egg
1/4 cup milk
2 tablespoon chopped onion
2 tablespoons grated parmesan cheese
1/4 teaspoon pepper
1/2 cup low-carb baking mix

Servings~ 👤👤
Cooking Time~ Ten Minutes
Pan to Use: Divided or Base

Cooking Steps
A. Pre-heat and spray with cooking spray.
B. Combined all ingredients place half of mixture into each well cook 10 minutes.

Curscous Vegetable Medley

Ingredients
1 cup (1/2 of 5.8 ounce package) couscous mix
1 tablespoon spice mix
1 teaspoon olive oil
1 tablespoon chopped onion
1 tablespoon each chopped red and green pepper
3/4 cup chicken broth

Servings~ 👤👤
Cooking Time~ Five Minutes
Pan to Use: Divided or Base

Cooking Steps
A. Do not Pre-heat but spray with cooking spray. Combined all ingredients place half of mixture into each well.
B. Plug-in and cook five minutes. Top with margarine and grated cheese, if desired.

Take-Out Dim Sum

Ingredients
4 egg roll wrappers
1 cup leftover Chinese food (drain excess sauce)
4 tablespoons chicken bouillon or water

Servings~ 👤👤
Cooking Time~ Eight Minutes
Pan to Use: Divided or Base

Cooking Steps
A. Pre-heat and spray with cooking spray. Divide Chinese food into four equal portions. Place one portion onto center of each egg roll wrapper. In the corners of wrapper, rub with water and pinch to close.
B. Put two tablespoons of broth in each well and cook 2 dim sum in each well for eight minutes.

Fresh Tomato Tart

Ingredients
1 pita pocket, cut in half to fit wells
1 small tomato, thinly sliced
1/2 cup shredded cheddar cheese
1 tablespoon grated parmesan cheese
1 heaping tablespoon mayonnaise
1 tablespoon chives
Salt and pepper to taste

Servings~ 👤
Cooking Time~ Ten Minutes
Pan to Use: Divided or Base

Cooking Steps
A. Pre-heat and spray with cooking spray. Combined cheeses, mayonnaise, chives, salt and pepper. Spread mixture on top of pita halves.
B. Top with tomato slices. Place each half in each well, close cover and cook for 10 minutes.

Vegetarian Spring Rolls

Ingredients
8 ounce frozen oriental medley vegetables
1 tablespoons cornstarch
1 tablespoon water
1 tablespoon minced fresh garlic
2 tablespoons soy sauce
2 dashes sesame seed oil
2 spring roll wrappers

Servings~ 👤👤
Cooking Time~ Eight Minutes
Pan to Use: Divided or Base

Cooking Steps
A. Pre-heat and spray with cooking spray. Thaw oriental vegetables under cold running water and squeeze out excess water. Combine cornstarch and water in shallow bowl. Mix vegetables with remaining ingredients except wrappers. Place each spring roll wrapper on a flat surface one point down so diamond shaped is facing you.
B. Using fingers wet edges of wrappers with water & cornstarch mixture. Divide vegetable mixture evenly between wrappers. Roll each wrapper over once, tuck in sides and continue to roll. Place one spring roll in each well, cook five minutes turn and cook five more minutes.

Irish Bubble and Squeak Loaves

Servings~ 👥
Cooking Time~ Seven Minutes
Pan to Use: Divided or Base

Ingredients
3/4 cup prepared mashed potatoes
1/2 cup cooked shredded cabbage
2 tablespoons real bacon bits
1/2 teaspoon onion powder
Salt and pepper to taste
1 egg, beaten with fork
2 teaspoons butter

Cooking Steps
A. Pre-heat and spray with cooking spray. Combined all ingredients except butter, mix until well blended. form mixture into 2 equal sized balls
B. 1 teaspoon butter in each well and cook until melted. Place one potato ball into each cooking well, push down on potato balls with cover. Cook six minutes; flip as needed to promote even browning.

Broccoli Nut Wraps

Servings~ 👥
Cooking Time~ Five Minutes
Pan to Use: Divided or Base

Ingredients
3/4 cup broccoli florets, finely chopped
1/4 cup cashews, chopped
1 green onion
2 tablespoons red pepper, finely minced
1/4 cup mayonnaise
2 tablespoon parmesan cheese
2 tortillas (sun-dried tomato, spinach or whole wheat)

Cooking Steps
A. Pre-heat and spray with cooking spray. Bring small saucepan of water to boil add broccoli and cook three minutes. Place in bowl with remaining ingredients except for tortillas and mix well.
B. Spread half of mixture on each tortilla and wrap by folding up ends and tucking in sides to fit wells. Place one wrap in each well, close cover and cook for five minutes until filling his warm and outside is lightly browned.

Grilled Hot Chili Sandwiches

Servings~ 👥
Cooking Time~ Seven Minutes
Pan to Use: Divided or Base

Ingredients
2 slices of white bread
3 caned whole green chilies, drained while
4 slices Monterey Jack cheese
2 tablespoons pimento stuffed green olives, chopped
2 tablespoons butter or margarine for grilling

Cooking Steps
A. Pre-heat and spray with cooking spray. Slice chilies, assemble sandwich by layering two slices cheese, chilies, olives, additional two slices of cheese and top with second slice of bread.
B. Butter outside of sandwich cut in half to fit well. Place one half of sandwich in each well. Close lid and grill for five to seven minutes until bread is golden brown and cheese is melted. Flip halfway through cooking to promote even Browning.

Spanish Rice

Ingredients
1 cup instant rice
1 cup water
1 cup V8 juice
½ cup finely chopped vegetables of your choice

Servings~ 👤👤
Cooking Time~ Five Minutes
Pan to Use: Divided or Base

Cooking Steps
A. Pre-heat and spray with cooking spray. Divide the rice between cooking areas. Carefully add half the water to each area. Top with chopped vegetables.
B. Cook 4 to 5 minutes until rice is fluffy.

Leftover Tater Cakes

Ingredients
1 medium potato, baked, peeled and grated
2 Tbsp. chopped green onion
1 large egg, beaten
2 tsp. butter, melted
1 Tbsp. all-purpose flour
1/4 tsp. baking powder
1/4 tsp. salt
1 bacon slice, cooked crisp and crumbled

Servings~ 👤👤
Cooking Time~ Seven Minutes
Pan to Use: Divided or Base

Cooking Steps
A. Pre-heat and spray with cooking spray. Combined all ingredients in a bowl. Scope ¼ cup of mixture in to well.
B. Cook 6-7 minutes or until golden brown.

Broccoli Fritters

Ingredients
1/2 cup baking mix
1 cup cooked chopped broccoli
4 Tablespoons shredded cheddar cheese
1/2 teaspoon each garlic and onion powder
1/3 cup milk
1 egg, slightly beaten

Servings~ 👤👤
Cooking Time~ Five Minutes
Pan to Use: Divided

Cooking Steps
A. Pre-heat and spray with cooking spray. Combined all ingredients. Pour half of batter in the wells.
B. Cook 10 minutes or until golden brown and a tooth pick stuck in the center comes out clean.

Made in the USA
Lexington, KY
29 December 2011